CHARTERS,
VOUCHERS,
and PUBLIC
EDUCATION

CHARTERS, VOUCHERS, *and* PUBLIC EDUCATION

PAUL E. PETERSON
DAVID E. CAMPBELL
Editors

BROOKINGS INSTITUTION PRESS
Washington, D.C.

ABOUT BROOKINGS

The Brookings Institution is a private nonprofit organization devoted to research, education, and publication on important issues of domestic and foreign policy. Its principal purpose is to bring knowledge to bear on current and emerging policy problems. The Institution maintains a position of neutrality on issues of public policy. Interpretations or conclusions in Brookings publications should be understood to be solely those of the authors.

Copyright © 2001
THE BROOKINGS INSTITUTION
1775 Massachusetts Avenue, N.W., Washington, D.C. 20036
www.brookings.edu

Library of Congress Cataloging-in-Publication data

Charters, vouchers, and public education / Paul E. Peterson and
David E. Campbell, editors
      p.   cm.
Includes bibliographical references and index.
   ISBN 0-8157-7026-X (cloth : alk. paper)—ISBN 0-8157-7027-8 (pbk. :
alk. paper)
   1. Charter schools—United States. 2. Educational vouchers—United
States. I. Peterson, Paul E. II. Campbell, David E., 1971–
   LB2806.36 .C55   2001
   371.01—dc21   2001004201

9 8 7 6 5 4 3 2 1

The paper used in this publication meets minimum requirements of the
American National Standard for Information Sciences—Permanence of Paper
for Printed Library Materials: ANSI Z39.48-1992.

Typeset in Adobe Garamond

Composition by
Betsy Kulamer
Washington, D.C.

Printed by
R. R. Donnelley and Sons
Harrisonburg, Virginia

Contents

1

Introduction: A New Direction in Public Education?

PAUL E. PETERSON AND
DAVID E. CAMPBELL

The twenty-first century mark may define when American education veered off in a new direction. For more than a hundred years, the education trail seemed to lead irreversibly toward a standardized, centralized system controlled by larger and more powerful entities. But just as dot.coms may be enhancing the power of small entrepreneurs and savvy consumers, so may similar forces be gaining new life in education. If charter schools or school vouchers should become prevalent, public education would change dramatically, becoming more varied, decentralized, and locally controlled.

Because the potential for change is large, the public debate is intense. Policy experts, interest groups, and political leaders alike have formed strong opinions on one side or another. For those who favor charters and vouchers, the new direction holds great promise. In their view, teachers will be more effective, parents more engaged, students increasingly challenged, and minority learning problems better addressed. Opponents are no less certain. If they are right, schools will become more stratified, and students will be placed in old-fashioned educational straitjackets. Teachers will suffer salary cuts and a loss of control over their professional lives, and the common educational culture will fragment—all in violation of constitutional principles and with no positive benefits for students.

This book contains the essays first presented at a Program on Education Policy and Governance conference held at Harvard University in March 2000. The reader will discover that both the wildest hopes and darkest fears of the political protagonists are seriously overstated. Yet the initiatives do carry the potential for reversing the direction in which public education in America has long been heading.

Trends in Public Education

Throughout the twentieth century, the design of the American school system became increasingly comprehensive, uniform, centralized, and professionally directed. Raw statistics reveal how powerfully all these forces have played out. In 1900, 72 percent of all children ages five to seventeen were enrolled in public school; by 2000, the percentage had increased to 92 percent. More telling, perhaps, the average number of days attended by those enrolled nearly doubled from 86 days in 1900 to 161 days in 1980. The number of students graduating from high school increased from 62,000 students in 1900 to 2,341,000 students in 1997.[1]

Financial commitments to education increased more dramatically, even when the numbers are adjusted for inflation. Between 1920 and 1996, expenditures per pupil climbed from $535 to $6,400. Teacher salaries rose from less than $7,300 to more than $40,500. Over the seventy-year period, the number of teachers increased at nearly twice the rate as the number of pupils in average daily attendance. Between 1955 and 1998, the pupil-teacher ratio tumbled from 27:1 to 17:1.

The trend toward professional control over the educational system has been no less impressive. In the 1920s, the mother of one of this book's editors taught public school in rural Minnesota, even though she had received only one year of "normal school" beyond her high school diploma. In that time and place, her training was more or less the norm. Subsequently, lengthy training programs sprouted in most state colleges and universities, and today virtually all teachers have a bachelor's degree, with 48 percent in possession of a master's or other advanced degree. Nor is professional training limited to classroom teachers. Curriculum specialists, guidance counselors, psychologists, school librarians, special educators, and a host of other specialties have come into being. Principals are now expected to have advanced training in management and leadership. And professionally trained superintendents, doctoral degree in hand, have assumed the helm in most school districts of any size.

Centralizing trends are no less pronounced. Americans moved from small towns to metropolitan areas served by school districts that steadily grew in size and importance. Small, rural school districts gave way to consolidated ones. Nearly 120,000 school districts served the nation's schoolchildren in 1937; by 1998, the number was less than 15,000. The trend to larger districts continued through the 1990s. In 1989, 650 school districts had a pupil enrollment in excess of 10,000 students; a decade later, the number of such districts exceeded 800. School finance was also being centralized. State and federal dollars augmented local ones such that the local share dropped from 82 percent in 1920 to just 45 percent in 1997.

Larger, better-funded, more centralized school systems were more easily organized by school employees, and, beginning in the 1960s, teacher organizations gained the right to bargain collectively with local school boards. The American Federation of Teachers (AFT), affiliated with the larger labor union movement, shut down numerous big-city schools until they secured collective bargaining rights. As AFT membership rolls quickly expanded, the National Education Association (NEA), for years dominated by administrators, dropped their anti-strike, anti-union philosophy and became a strong force for teacher rights and prerogatives. In the end, most of the larger school districts signed collective bargaining agreements with one or another of the two organizations. By the end of the twentieth century, the two organizations had grown so similar that they merged some of their functions, and leaders proposed an outright merger of the two organizations. Curiously, union success has had only limited impact on teacher compensation, which has just kept pace with pay in other sectors of the economy. The more important achievements have been a standardized pay scale, grievance procedures that protect worker prerogatives, and contracts that limit board and administrative discretion.

Other regulations handed down by both legislators and courts have further limited local boards. Many new requirements have had the salutary objective of increasing educational opportunity for disadvantaged groups. The 1954 *Brown* v. *Board of Education* decision outlawed de jure segregation, and for the next several decades schools purchased buses and struggled in other ways to comply with the law. Beginning in the 1970s, many state courts also asked legislatures to ensure that per pupil funding among school districts be more or less equal. In 1974 a new federal law reinforced court orders demanding that school doors be opened to the disabled. Shortly thereafter, a combination of legislative and court action created new programs for those who spoke little English.

Not all the new regulations focused on equal opportunity questions, however. State legislatures gave schools new tasks, asking them to teach students to drive, guard their health, practice safe sex, and learn how to provide public service. Courts said schools could not ask students to salute the flag, pray in school, or be subject to a dress code that infringed on their beliefs. All in all, schools in America were fundamentally altered in the twentieth century.

Countercurrents

Only a few initially voiced objections to these trends. Some school board members complained that they were being frozen out of the decisionmaking process by a combination of state legislation, court rules, union contracts, and professional jargon. Farmers lamented the loss of the little red schoolhouse. Segregationists worried about the consequences of racial mixing. Back-to-basics educators decried the new curricula. Others objected to uniform instruction of heterogeneous populations. Religious denominations desperately tried to find ways to keep their schools financially viable. Conservatives objected to increasing federal regulation of local schools. Free-market economists said competition was as much needed in education as anywhere else.

Until the 1980s, these groups operated mainly on the fringe—odd clusters of intellectuals and malcontents who counted for little more to the dominant forces in education than hobbits to the "Lord of the Rings." But as the century drew to a close, these whispers of opposition found a clearer voice. For all the centralization, standardization, and professionalization that had occurred, schools seemed no more adequate to the task before them. Despite rising expenditures and falling class sizes, student performance, as measured by the National Assessment of Educational Progress, failed to improve. American students fell further behind their peers in other countries with each passing year. In fourth grade, American students ranked at the very top in math and science, but by eighth grade, they were only in the middle of the pack, and by the twelfth grade, they ranked near the bottom. A federal task force was moved in 1982 to declare that American schools were suffering from a "rising tide of mediocrity."

Nor were schools becoming more egalitarian. Despite the disruption caused by school busing and other integration strategies, schools remained as segregated at the close of the century as they had been in 1972. Despite bilingual instruction, Hispanic scores remained well below those achieved by Anglos. The percentages of students said to be in special education programs increased from 8.3 percent of all those under the age of twenty-one in 1976 to 12.8 percent in 1997. Though the black-white test-score gap closed during the 1970s and 1980s, it began opening up again in the 1990s.

By the beginning of the twenty-first century, most Americans seemed to agree that something needed to be done to improve America's schools. In a poll taken just before the 2000 presidential election, for example, more people named education than any other issue as the most important factor influencing their vote. However, it is less clear whether a consensus can be reached on how education reform should be brought about. The public split on the alternatives offered by candidates Al Gore and George W. Bush. When read descriptions of the contrasting proposals, 45 percent of registered voters supported the Gore plan, and 43 percent the Bush plan (statistically, a tie).

The range of suggestions for improving American education is highly diverse. Some have called for smaller classes, higher teacher salaries, and more expenditure. Others have called for tighter governmental control, focusing especially on testing devices that hold schools more strictly accountable for student performance. But others have called for more flexibility, competition, and parental choice.

This last idea is to be explored in this volume. Charter schools and school vouchers are of particular interest in that they carry the potential for reversing long-standing trends in American education. But they raise many questions. What promise do they hold? What problems do they pose? What can be learned from the few experiments already in place? Who takes advantage of choice when the opportunity is offered? Does a choice benefit students? What impact does choice have on traditional public schools? What are the impacts on civic education? Are charters and vouchers just another of the numerous reform movements in American education that will have their fifteen minutes but in the end leave no lasting impact? Or will charters and vouchers reshape American education in the twenty-first century as decisively as centralization and professionalization defined its shape in the twentieth? If charters and vouchers continue to spread, are these new phenomena to be welcomed or resisted? Or are the consequences of school choice so complex that the outcomes will defy the simplistic assessments that so far have marked political debates over this issue?

To these and other questions, this volume provides some preliminary answers.

Charter Schools

Charter schools evolved out of the magnet school idea, originally developed in the 1960s as a way of increasing racial integration of urban schools. Magnet schools were expected to entice families from all racial groups to choose voluntarily integrated schools by offering in them distinctive, improved education programs. When the federal government established the magnet schools assistance program in 1984, the idea began to have a national impact.

"Between 1984 and 1994, 138 districts nationwide received a total of $955 million" in federal funds to implement this form of school choice.[2] As a consequence, the number of schools with magnet programs doubled between 1982 and 1991, while the number of students tripled.[3] Nationwide, in the early 1990s, more than 1.2 million students attend 2,400 magnet schools in more than 200 school districts.[4]

The goals to be achieved by choice soon broadened out beyond racial integration. School choice experiments as part of broader school reform first began to appear in East Harlem, Massachusetts, Minnesota, and Wisconsin. When test-score gains were reported for East Harlem, the potential for improving low-income inner-city education became apparent.[5]

The charter school idea was initially tried out in Minnesota in 1992. Just eight years later, some thirty-four states and the District of Columbia had enacted charter school legislation, and more than 2,000 charter schools were educating over some half million students.[6] Although the percentage of students in charter schools nationwide is still a small fraction of all students, in some states charter schools are providing the school of choice for a significant fraction of the student population. For example, in 1997, 4.4 percent of the students in Arizona were attending charter schools.[7]

Charter schools are those schools granted a charter by a state agency giving them the right to receive state funds in exchange for commitments contained in the charter. They may have their charter withdrawn if they fail to meet their obligations under the charter. The schools admit students regardless of their residence, a rule that distinguishes them from traditional public schools, which are governed by boards that have the responsibility for the education of students living within a particular school district. Also, charter schools are either nonprofit or profit-making corporations, not governmental entities in the manner of a school board. However, charter schools usually receive most of their operating revenue from state and local governments.

The legal framework within which charter schools operate varies from state to state. Some states allow charter schools only if the local school board grants its permission; others can contract freely with a university or some other state agency. Some states place heavy restrictions on admission policies; others are permissive. Some states have developed oversight mechanisms expected to hold charter schools accountable; other states allow charter schools wide latitude, with parents and students deciding whether or not the school is offering a quality education. Some states allow only one school per charter; others permit many. Most states provide charter schools the same amount of money per pupil that traditional public schools in the jurisdiction receive, and some provide additional monies to cover start-up costs. Other

states are less generous. Many charter schools compete with traditional public schools for their students, but some charters take only those students who
have dropped out or have been counseled out of public schools. Although a
goodly number of charter schools serve a higher-income clientele, many serve
disadvantaged and special needs populations.

When questioned by pollsters, Americans say they support the idea of
charter schools. In a nationwide survey, 70 percent of respondents said that
they favored a charter school program that "frees some public schools from
certain state regulations and lets them work independently from the local
school district."[8] As a further indication that charter schools are broadly supported, both major party presidential candidates endorsed them during the
2000 campaign. Perhaps because public support seems broad, the constitutionality of charters has not been seriously challenged in court litigation.
Despite these indications of general support, the charter school concept is
only slowly being translated into practice. Most states have hedged their
charter initiatives so as to limit both the numbers and the autonomy of charter schools. And in Washington State, a charter initiative failed to win voter
acceptance in the 2000 election, though the proposal did muster 48 percent
of the votes cast.

School Vouchers

School vouchers offer a more dramatic departure from the status quo in that
they give families government dollars to be used to attend any school the
family chooses, whether public, charter, religious, or private. Unlike charter
school schemes, schools in a voucher system need not be chartered by the
government—though some voucher programs require that the school be recognized as such by the state. Under most voucher plans currently in existence, most families choose private schools.

School vouchers first gained notice when University of Chicago economist Milton Friedman, writing in 1955, proposed an arrangement in which
the government finances the education but families choose the school.[9] The
idea gained considerable public currency in the 1970s, when the Office of
Economic Opportunity helped fund a school choice experiment in the Alum
Rock school district in California. When this experiment encountered strong
opposition from teacher organizations and failed to be implemented effectively, enthusiasm for school choice waned for about a decade, except for sporadic use of the magnet school concept as a tool for school desegregation.[10]

Then, in the 1980s and early 1990s, a number of events helped give the
school choice movement new impetus. First, a major study by a research

team headed by James S. Coleman reported that students in Catholic schools outperformed their public school peers. Coleman interpreted his findings as showing that students learn more when surrounded by an adult community where strong ties were established among parents, teachers, and religious leaders. His findings were subsequently replicated by a second major study by the Brookings Institution that in addition explained the original results by showing that private schools had more autonomy and, as a result, were organized more effectively than public schools.[11] The authors, John E. Chubb and Terry M. Moe, proposed school vouchers as the solution.

The first voucher plan was established in Milwaukee, Wisconsin, in 1990. The program originally allowed students to attend only those schools that had no religious affiliation, and only a few hundred students participated in the program in its first years. In the 1998–99 school year, the program, after overcoming constitutional objections, was expanded to include religious schools, and the number of participating students in 2000 increased to approximately 10,000. Since then, school voucher programs have, with public and private funds, established themselves in many cities and states. In just ten years, the number of students involved has climbed from zero to more than 60,000. During the 1999–2000 school year, nearly 50,000 students were participating in sixty-eight privately funded voucher programs, and another 12,000 or more in three publicly funded ones.[12]

In addition to Milwaukee, publicly funded voucher programs are to be found in Cleveland, Ohio, and the state of Florida. In Cleveland, students began matriculation in private schools in the fall of 1996, and in the fall of 1999 the number of participating students was nearly 4,000. A fairly small number of students became eligible for participation in the Florida program for the first time in the fall of 1999, when the legislature said that students attending "failing" schools could apply for vouchers. Initially, only five schools met the legislative definition of failing, but many more were expected to fall within this category in subsequent years. But no additional students became eligible in 2000, because the concept of failing was redefined and the performances on statewide tests of students attending potentially failing schools improved. Nationwide, the size and extent of voucher programs could increase substantially, if a proposal offered by the Bush administration in the spring of 2001 were enacted into law. The plan would give families federal subsidy to be used for their child's education, if that child were attending a failing school that had not improved over a three-year period of time.

Privately funded voucher programs are operating in many cities, including Charlotte, North Carolina; Chicago; Dayton, Ohio; Los Angeles; New York

City; San Antonio, Texas; San Francisco; and Washington, D.C. In 1999, the Children's Scholarship Fund greatly expanded the size and range of these programs by providing 40,000 vouchers to students from low-income families nationwide. Several of these privately funded voucher programs are being evaluated by independent investigators, who will provide valuable information about the way in which voucher programs operate in practice.

Public support for vouchers, as determined by pollsters, varies with the wording of the question citizens are asked. In the fall of 2000, a Pew Research Center Survey found that 53 percent of Americans favored "federal funding for vouchers to help low and middle income parents send their children to private and parochial schools." Similarly, a Gallup Poll found that 56 percent of Americans would vote for "a system giving parents government funded school vouchers to pay for tuition at the public, private, or religious school of their choice." But a Phi Delta Kappan poll found that when asked to make a choice between "improving and strengthening the existing public schools" and "providing vouchers for parents to use in selecting and paying for private and/or church-related schools," only 22 percent of Americans chose the latter response.

Even though responses to pollsters vary, in practice vouchers have yet to gather the necessary political support to win widespread enactment. When asked to vote on voucher proposals in statewide initiatives, voters have regularly rejected them, most recently in Michigan and California in the 2000 election. Perhaps because public opinion can be mobilized against vouchers, neither presidential candidate was willing to give the concept explicit support during the 2000 presidential campaign. Gore opposed vouchers outright, while Bush steadfastly refused to use the word *voucher* to describe his proposal to give low-income families money for educational alternatives if their children were attending failing public schools.

The constitutionality of all three publicly funded school voucher programs has been challenged by those who regard them as a violation of the First Amendment requirement that there be no "establishment of a religion." In Wisconsin, the state supreme court said that the program did not establish a religion because parents were free to choose among schools, whether they were secular or religious and regardless of their religious affiliation. The U.S. Supreme Court chose not to accept an appeal of the state court decision. Similarly, the Ohio and Florida state supreme courts found their states' voucher programs to be consistent with federal constitutional requirements. However, a three-judge panel of a federal appeals court found the Cleveland, Ohio, program in violation of the constitution, and that decision, together with the Florida decision, is currently being appealed to the U.S. Supreme

Court. Until the Supreme Court rules definitively on the issue, the constitutionality of school vouchers will remain in question.

Vouchers and Charters: Complements or Competitors?

Discussions of vouchers and charters have typically been conducted on parallel tracks. By juxtaposing the discussion of vouchers and charters in one volume, the similarities and differences between the two interventions can be compared. Both seek to improve education by giving families greater school choice. Both are shaped by the theory that students will do better within a more varied, more competitive educational system. Both are defended as mechanisms that can create voluntary communities in which parents, schools, and students work together.

But if justified by similar theories of educational improvement, charters and vouchers differ in important respects. One way to think of the difference between the two is in terms of supply and demand. Vouchers increase demand for competitors to traditional public schools by providing individual students with the means to attend alternative, usually private, schools. Charter schools operate on the *Field of Dreams* theory: "If you build it, they will come." They increase the supply of competition to traditional public schools by creating new schools.

The two interventions differ in other ways as well. Most significant, perhaps, school vouchers have the potential for enhancing the role of religious institutions in American education, whereas charter schools do not. Charter schools must be secular institutions, because they are established by the government and cannot adopt a religious affiliation without violating the First Amendment. School vouchers may be used by families to attend any school they wish, secular or religious. If vouchers survive constitutional scrutiny, it will be because government assistance is given to parents, not directly to schools.

School vouchers provide a framework for the broadest possible competition among educational providers. At least in theory, any organization, public or private, secular or religious, nonprofit or for-profit, could establish a school and accept payment by school voucher. Charter schools come into being only upon being granted a charter by the state. A state can limit competition at any time by restricting the establishment of new charter schools.

In practice, charter schools are more heavily funded by governments than vouchers are. Charter schools typically receive the same per pupil funding as the average school in a district or state—around $6,000, if the district or state is at the national average. But the largest voucher program (in Milwaukee) gives families only $5,000 per student. And most other voucher programs provide much less. Charters also serve a more wide-ranging set of students from a wider range of social backgrounds than vouchers do. The latter are focused on serving low-income, inner-city families.

There is nothing inherent in these differential financial and constituency arrangements for charters and vouchers. They are instead products of their differential political support. With a broader base of political backing, charters are better positioned than vouchers to obtain adequate funding under state law. And vouchers have been limited to serving low-income groups, because for this group a more compelling political case for educational alternatives can be made. The danger of this development to those who wish to extend school vouchers to a broader population is that their concept, in practice, is becoming identified with welfare programs that serve a targeted population.

Still, the contrasts between vouchers and charters can be exaggerated. If a state should devise a school voucher program that fully funded all students without regard to family income and subjected the participating schools to state accountability and other state standards, it would not appear much different from a charter school law that placed no limit on the number of charter schools that might be established.

Are charters and vouchers complementary or competitive? Some think the two movements complement one another, if only because the political demand for vouchers has created a climate that has facilitated enactment of charter legislation. Others think the less controversial charters have taken the sting out of the voucher movement. Some think that charters, which do not ask parents to pay tuition, are attracting as many families from private as public schools, thereby undermining a private sector that is otherwise an essential part of any school voucher plan. Some groups fear that private schools will give up their religious affiliation to win charter status, with all its financial advantages, only to become subject to many of the rules currently applied to traditional public schools.

The Essays

The essays that follow contain a rich body of information and analysis designed to help the reader sort through many of the issues raised by these new educational institutions. They do not promise to resolve all the reader's questions, however. The authors give different perspectives on the issues at hand, and they do not always agree in their assessment of the trends they observe. Charters and vouchers are too new for research to yield definitive answers. Yet enough is known already to indicate that the reality is more complex than the public debate. The reader is invited to learn more about this complexity.

Part 1, devoted to charter schools, begins with Chester E. Finn Jr., Bruno V. Manno, and Gregg Vanourek's survey of the charter landscape, synthesizing an array of research from across the country. They conclude that many of the hypothetical concerns about charter schools have so far not been borne out by experience. However, on some questions (particularly whether charter schools lead to improved academic performance) the verdict is not yet in. Next, Michael Mintrom and David N. Plank examine in more detail the way in which school choice has been implemented in Michigan. The state has both an interdistrict school choice plan and sizable numbers of charter schools, thereby providing an opportunity to see how choice works in a specific institutional context. On a similar note, Edward B. Fiske and Helen F. Ladd draw lessons for charter schools in the United States from New Zealand's experience with self-governing schools that in some ways resemble American charter schools. In particular, they laud the role of an independent "inspectorate" in evaluating New Zealand's schools and call for a similar office to be created in the United States to hold charter schools accountable to the public.

In Part 2, school vouchers are discussed. In an overview of the research literature, Jay P. Greene makes the case that a consensus has emerged that awarding of vouchers to offset private school tuition offers real benefits to disadvantaged children. While he pays closest attention to test scores, he finds numerous other positive effects of voucher programs—from classroom discipline to racial integration. Although his findings come from small-scale interventions, not full-blown voucher programs, the early returns indicate striking benefits to recipients. Terry M. Moe then draws on results from a detailed national survey that gathered information designed to answer two key questions: Who supports vouchers? And who would be likely to use them if they were made generally available? He concludes that when vouchers are explained to parents in detail, they draw widespread support. But not all parents would move their children from public to private schools, were a voucher system to be introduced. The demand for vouchers is the greatest among minorities, he says, and if private schools were open to all and money were not an obstacle to attending private schools, the overall effect of a national voucher plan would be to create a greater socioeconomic and ethnic balance between the public and private school sectors.

Joseph P. Viteritti looks at the constitutional issues involved in the debate over vouchers. Although he acknowledges that the Supreme Court has yet to resolve this question in a definitive way, he argues that vouchers should be able to survive a constitutional test. Because families will have a choice of secular and religious schools, and because no religion is preferred over any other, the money given to families does not seem to constitute the establishment of a religion.

Even if the public supports vouchers and would use them, and the courts would allow them, the question remains of what effect vouchers would have on the students who use them. What happens to their academic performance? Do vouchers help (or harm) some students more than others? Three existing private voucher programs have been designed to allow for randomized field trials of vouchers' effects, modeled on how medical research is conducted. In analyzing the data from these three programs, our own research (with William G. Howell and Patrick J. Wolf) offers conclusions that will probably not satisfy either advocates or opponents of school vouchers. We find that, for reasons that we do not yet understand, vouchers lead to an increase in African Americans' test scores, while having no measurable impact on the academic performance of other ethnic groups. This finding suggests that voucher programs have the potential to shrink the long-observed test-score gap between blacks and whites. However, more research is needed first to confirm these results, and then to offer an explanation for them.

Part 3 examines how school choice is affecting conventional public schools. Market theory suggests that the competition school choice evokes should provide incentives to public schools to improve. But only limited empirical information is available to determine whether or not the theory translates well into practice. The best evidence comes from Milwaukee, the site of the nation's largest and longest-running public voucher program. In a provocative analysis, Frederick M. Hess has found, in an enlightening metaphor, that competition created by the voucher program reveals "hints of a pickaxe" chipping away at the bureaucratic hurdles to change in one of America's most troubled urban school systems.

Paul Teske, Mark Schneider, Jack Buckley, and Sara Clark look at the response of traditional public schools to charter schools in six communities. They show that the attitudes of public school administrators are an important factor determining the public school response. Unless they feel significantly threatened by the competition, traditional public school administrators do not implement changes to meet the challenge posed by charter schools. Similarly, Frederick M. Hess, Robert Maranto, and Scott Milliman find that in Arizona, the state with the greatest number of charter schools, conventional public schools generally demonstrate little reaction to competition. The exception is in those schools that previously had what these authors describe as a "cooperative culture," a school environment facilitating teacher autonomy.

In Part 4, a neglected, but still extremely important, topic—the potential impact of school choice on the civic education of young people—is examined. Would a choice-based system undermine the creation of a common citizenry? Are private schools capable of preparing students to live and work in a democratic society? David E. Campbell provides evidence that, with a few exceptions, private (especially Catholic) schools do a better job than public schools in offering instruction in civics—whether measured by participation in community service, political knowledge, civic skills, or political tolerance. Likewise, Patrick J. Wolf, Jay P. Greene, Brett Kleitz, and Kristina Thalhammer find that beginning college students coming from private secondary schools are more politically tolerant than their peers from public schools.

Part 5 contains two chapters that reflect on the evidence previously presented. Echoing a number of authors in the book, Paul Hill stresses the continuing need to study the impact of choice on traditional public schools, recommends the implementation of better accountability systems when choice is introduced, and calls for a careful evaluation of why student outcomes vary among voucher programs. While Diane Ravitch also advocates more research, she makes the critical point that "you cannot study what does not exist." She thus provocatively proposes a five-year moratorium on all legal challenges to school voucher programs to allow for an examination of their effects.

Ravitch's point is persuasive. The evidence to date offers no reason to think that students are harmed when choice—whether in the form of charter schools or vouchers—is introduced. On that basis alone, larger-scale voucher and charter school experiments are justified, if only to determine their effects with greater certainty. Virtually everyone seems to agree that America needs to improve its schools, particularly in urban centers. The time has come to begin a full-fledged effort aimed at determining whether vouchers and charter schools can lead to the necessary improvement. As the editors of the *Washington Post* have pointed out, even if it is not certain whether vouchers will lead to a net educational gain, "we do know the status quo. To the many children losing out in the current system, some state-by-state experimentation might offer relief."[13] Efforts can begin with a large-scale, publicly funded voucher program in Washington, D.C. The research evidence from the District of Columbia indicates that vouchers have a particularly large payoff in this city, and the popularity among parents of D.C.'s existing private voucher program demonstrates that the demand for increased choice in this, one of the worst urban school districts in the country, is palpable. What better place to put such an important policy innovation to the test than in the nation's capital, where policymakers can observe the effects firsthand?

Expanded opportunities should be made for charter schools across the country. Too many states put too many restrictions on charter schools, and sixteen states do not allow them at all. With the implementation of accountability mechanisms discussed in this volume, no reason exists to fear further experimentation with charter schools. Most important, legislators need to design charter school legislation so that their effects on individual students' academic performance, and other relevant aspects of their educational experience, can be gauged. Because many charter schools already use a randomized lottery to determine who is admitted, randomized field trials could be conducted, as has been done with voucher programs.

This volume will not be the final word on either charter schools or vouchers. Both forms of school choice are relatively new, and much remains to be learned about them. As school choice has moved from theory to practice, the results clearly are messier in the real world than those predicted by theoretical models. But without further experimentation with choice, there is no way to know which findings are idiosyncratic and which are systematic. Without knowing that, public policy cannot be fashioned to accomplish the end everyone agrees on: providing all of America's youth the best education possible.

Notes

1. The facts in the next few paragraphs are taken from U.S. Department of Education, Office of Educational Research and Improvement, National Center for Education Statistics, *Digest of Education Statistics* (Washington, D.C.: Government Printing Office, 2000), tables 39, 53, 65, 69, 90.

2. Bruce Fuller and others, *School Choice* (University of California, Berkeley, Policy Analysis for California Education and Stanford University, 1999), p. 26.

3. Lauri Steel and Roger Levine, *Educational Innovation in Multicultural Contexts: The Growth of Magnet Schools in American Education* (Palo Alto, Calif.: American Institutes for Research, 1996).

4. Dennis P. Doyle and Marsha Levine, "Magnet Schools: Choice and Quality in Public Education," *Phi Delta Kappa,* vol. 66, no. 4 (1984), pp. 265–70; Rolf K. Blank, Roger E. Levine, and Lauri Steel, "After 15 Years: Magnet Schools in Urban Education," in Bruce Fuller, Richard Elmore, and Gary Orfield, eds., *Who Chooses? Who Loses?: Culture, Institutions and the Unequal Effects of School Choice* (New York: Teachers College Press, 1996), pp. 154–72.

5. Joseph P. Viteritti, *Choosing Equality: School Choice, the Constitution, and Civil Society* (Brookings, 1999), pp. 60–62; and Fuller and others, *School Choice.*

6. "It's School by the Rules in a Bronx Experiment," *New York Times,* October 31, 2000, p. A29; and Bryan C. Hassel, *The Charter School Challenge* (Brookings, 1999), p. 1.

7. Robert Maranto, Scott Milliman, Frederick Hess, and April Gresham, "Real World School Choice: Arizona Charter Schools," in Robert Maranto, Scott Milliman, Frederick Hess, and April Gresham, eds., *School Choice in the Real World: Lessons from Arizona Charter Schools* (Boulder, Colo.: Westview, 1999), p. 7.

8. *Washington Post,* Henry J. Kaiser Family Foundation, and Harvard University Education Survey, June 29, 2000.

9. Milton Friedman, "The Role of Government in Education," in Robert Solo, ed., *Economics and the Public Interest* (Rutgers University Press, 1955), p. 127.

10. See note 4, above.

11. John Chubb and Terry Moe, *Politics, Markets, and America's Schools* (Brookings, 1990).

12. Children First America, "68 Private Programs and Counting," *School Reform News,* October 1999, insert, p. B.

13. "Voucher Wars," *Washington Post,* November 1, 2000, p. A32.

PART 1

Charter
Schools

2

Charter Schools: Taking Stock

CHESTER E. FINN JR.,
BRUNO V. MANNO, AND
GREGG VANOUREK

W hen the first charter schools burst on the scene in 1992, nobody knew that they would be viewed at the beginning of the twenty-first century as the most vibrant force in American education. Connecticut Democratic senator Joseph I. Lieberman writes: "Competition from charter schools is the best way to motivate the ossified bureaucracies governing too many public schools. This grass-roots revolution seeks to reconnect public education with our most basic values: ingenuity, responsibility, and accountability."[1] The Ford Foundation and the Harvard University John F. Kennedy School of Government think highly enough of the charter idea to have awarded one of their "innovations in American government" awards—the Oscars of public service—to Minnesota's pioneering charter law.

In a short time, these independent public schools of choice, freed from rules yet accountable for results, have spread like wildfire across much of the land, providing schooling alternatives for hundreds of thousands of families and challenging some basic assumptions about public education. In this paper, we discuss the present status of the charter movement, what is known about it, and what is not yet known.[2]

Figure 2-1. *Number of States with Charter Schools, 1992–93 to 2000–01*

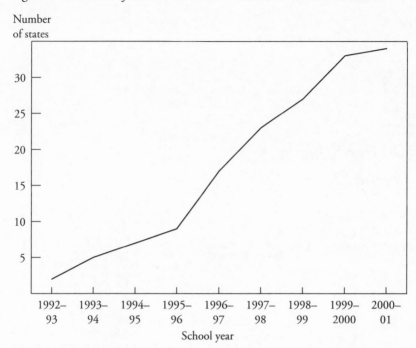

Number
of states

The Situation Today

As of mid-2001, there were over 2,100 charter schools, located in thirty-four
states and the District of Columbia (see figures 2-1 and 2-2), with federal
officials predicting that there would be 3,000 schools by 2002. About
518,000 youngsters are enrolled in charter schools. Thirty-seven states and
the District of Columbia have enabling legislation for charter schools and
several more are considering it.

Future growth in the number of charter schools depends in considerable
part on state legislation, especially whether limits on charters remain in
effect. There is a heated debate now under way in several states over raising
these caps, while other states have already loosened them because of demand-
side pressures. Clearly, the fuel for charter growth will have to come either
from amending state laws to lift those caps or from states without real limits
(such as Arizona and Texas) or with high limits (such as California and New
Jersey).

Figure 2-2. *Charter School Growth, 1992–93 to 2000–01*

Number of
charter schools

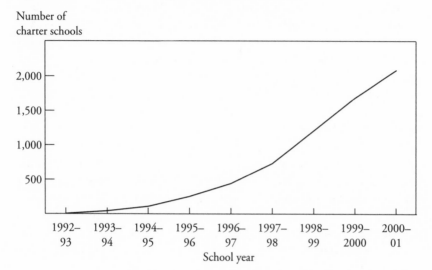

School year

Largely as a result of these statutory constraints—not lack of interest or demand—charter schools are distributed unevenly. Eleven states account for over 80 percent of them.[3] Arizona alone had 416 in 2000–01; there were 302 in California, 185 in Michigan, 165 in Texas, and 149 in Florida.[4] A large proportion of charters is concentrated in the three states of Arizona, California, and Michigan, but that percentage decreased from 79 percent in 1995–96 to 45 percent in 1999–2000.

Charter schools are found in all types of communities: cities, suburbs, and rural areas; industrial towns, deserts, and Indian reservations; ethnic neighborhoods, commuter towns, and even in cyberspace. A tour of the charter landscape does not stop at the U.S. border. Similar developments can be found in Argentina, Australia, Brazil, Canada, Chile, New Zealand, Pakistan, and the United Kingdom.

Numerous cities across the United States have been profoundly affected by charter schools, and a few are beginning to reveal a glimpse of what a system of public education based on the charter principle might look like. In Washington, D.C., nearly 15 percent of public school students are now enrolled in charter schools; in Kansas City, Missouri, the total is almost 18 percent; and in Arizona, 4 percent of all youngsters are in charter schools—which comprise one-fifth of all the state's public schools.[5]

Still, when compared with the vastness of American K–12 education, charters are a flea on the elephant's back, representing 2 percent of all public schools and slightly more than 1 percent of total enrollments. There are about twelve times as many private schools as charter schools. But thus far, the number of charter schools exceeds voucher schools. As of spring 2000, there were only about 150 publicly funded voucher schools compared with about 2,100 charter schools.[6]

Charter schools are much studied and intensively scrutinized, so a great deal is known about them. According to the major federal study, 72 percent of them are new schools, 18 percent are preexisting district public schools that converted to charter status, and the remaining 10 percent are preexisting private schools that have converted. Furthermore, the percentage of newly created schools is increasing over time. Eighty-five percent of charters opening in 1998–99 were newly created, compared with just over half of the schools that opened in 1994–95 and earlier.[7] Moreover, most charter schools are relatively young; the average charter school at the end of 1999–2000 was less than three years old.

One can obtain ample information on charter enrollments, demographics, laws, curricula, founders, sponsors, staff, missions, funding, and facilities. According to the Center for Education Reform, over half of all charter schools are in urban districts, one-quarter have a back-to-basics curriculum, 40 percent serve dropouts or students at risk of dropping out, and one-quarter are geared to gifted and talented youth. About 10 percent of charter schools are managed by for-profit organizations, such as Edison Schools, Advantage Schools, and Charter Schools USA.[8]

Most charter schools are small. The federal study estimates their median enrollment at 137 students, compared with the 475-pupil public school average in twenty-seven charter states. Almost two-thirds (65.2 percent) of charters enroll fewer than 200 students. (Just 17 percent of regular public schools are that small.)[9] With small scale comes intimacy and familiarity that are often missing from the larger and more anonymous institutions of public education.

Unfortunately, some schools called "charter schools" are in fact Potemkin charters, displaying the façade but not the reality. So-called weak charter laws place constraints on schools' educational, financial, and operational autonomy—for example, teacher certification requirements, uniform salary schedules, and collective bargaining agreements. And many charter schools receive less than full per pupil funding, with no allowance for facilities and other capital expenses. The upshot is that some charter schools are pale shadows of what they are meant to be.

According to researcher Bryan Hassel, many legislatures "have departed substantially from the 'charter school idea' in the charter laws they have adopted."[10] Hassel calculates that

> fifteen of the first 35 charter laws allow local school boards to veto applications. Fifteen make charter schools part of their local school districts, denying them legal independence. Only 17 of the laws permit full per-pupil operating funding to follow the child from a district to a charter school; fewer than five allow capital funding to follow the child. And many laws restrict the number of charter schools that can open, the types of people and organizations that can propose charter schools, or both.[11]

What Is Known

Five conclusions can be drawn from the information presently available on the charter movement.

Charter Schools Are Passing the Market Test—They Are in Demand and Are Generally Satisfying Their Primary Constituents

The demand for charter schools has been explosive, taking several forms. First, more would-be operators are seeking charters than can be awarded due to the numerical limits that states have placed on their numbers. For example, Central Michigan University has been inundated with requests for charter licenses. Second, many teachers are actively seeking out these innovative schools of choice. For example, City on a Hill Charter School in Boston received 350 applications for 3 staff positions, and Massachusetts charter schools received 9,588 applications for 399 teaching slots between 1995 and mid-1998.[12] Third, more people want to attend charter schools than they can accommodate. The federal study found that 70 percent of charter schools had waiting lists, concluding that "if success is judged by parents and students voting with their feet, charter schools are in demand."[13] The marketplace appears to be signaling that the charter movement has strong appeal—and is poised to grow faster where permitted.

Much is known about what students, parents, and teachers think of their charter schools, though such evidence is inevitably vulnerable to what economists call "revealed preferences" and the biases of self-selection. A 1997 national survey of nearly 5,000 charter pupils revealed impressive satisfaction levels.[14] Students were asked what they like and dislike about their charter school. The most frequently cited "likes" were "good teachers" (59 percent), "they teach it until I learn it" (51 percent), and "they don't let me fall behind"

(39 percent). The next cluster of answers—"computers and technology" (36 percent), "nice people running the school" (35 percent), "teacher's attention" (34 percent), "class size" (34 percent), and "curriculum" (33 percent)—mostly had to do with educational practices as well.

By contrast, three of the four most common student "dislikes" concerned nonacademic matters and the fourth involved a classic pupil gripe: "poor sports program" (29 percent), "not enough other activities" (29 percent), "food" (29 percent), and "too much homework" (29 percent). Three-fifths of charter students also report that their teachers are better than those in their previous schools—just 5 percent say their new instructors are worse—while half report being more interested in their school work, compared with 8 percent who are less interested.

As for parents who have suddenly become empowered education consumers, survey data show that they are pleased with their children's charter schools. At least two-thirds from the 1997 study say the charter school is better than their child's previous school with respect to class size, school size, teacher attention, quality of instruction, and curriculum—compared with just 2–3 percent who believe the new school is worse. Over three-fifths of parents say their charter school is better with respect to parental involvement, extra help for students, academic standards, accessibility, and discipline.

According to the 1997 survey data, over 90 percent of charter teachers are "very" or "somewhat" satisfied with their school's educational philosophy, size, fellow teachers, and students; more than three-quarters are content with their school's administrators, level of teacher decisionmaking, and the challenge of starting a new school. Fewer than 3 percent say they hope to be elsewhere next year. The National Education Association (NEA) reports that 72 percent of the charter teachers whom it surveyed, if they had to do it over again, would still teach in a charter school. (Just 10 percent said they would not; 18 percent were undecided.)[15]

One of the secrets of charter schools is their success in tapping vast reservoirs of parent involvement. Some of this dynamic can be traced to the fact that these schools are chosen by families—that is, engagement begins with seeking out the school and registering one's child. And the schools themselves are creating mechanisms to ensure family involvement and interaction. For example, it is common for charter schools to have parents sign "learning contracts" for their children and to require that they volunteer a certain number of hours per week.[16] Some also offer special adult classes. And the federal report estimates that 72 percent of charters offer before- and after-school care and 82 percent offer social and health services.[17] In Massachusetts, charter parents report twice as many meetings with their child's teacher as do district school parents, more phone conversations, and almost twice as many written communications from school.[18] Many charters also include parents in institutional governance. A California study found that 88 percent of that state's charter schools included parents on their governing bodies. Twenty-one percent of teachers surveyed by the NEA say their charter schools were initiated and developed mainly by parents—and 24 percent point to a "collaborative of teachers and parents."

Charter Schools Are Seedbeds of Innovation and Educational Diversity, Particularly in the Context of Their Own Communities

Many charters are fonts of educational originality and organizational creativity. According to the federal study, "realiz[ing] an alternative vision for schooling" was most often cited by charter founders as the primary reason for starting their schools (cited by 59 percent of respondents).[19] A California study found that 78 percent of that state's charters were experimenting with new instructional practices, compared with 3 percent of comparison public schools; 72 percent of charters were implementing site-based governance, compared with 16 percent of conventional schools; and two-thirds of charters had adopted increased parent participation practices, compared with 14 percent.[20] A Massachusetts study found that Bay State charters were engaged in innovative practices while also implementing "good old-fashioned education practices," which the researchers termed "retrovations."[21] The charters' "innovation" sometimes lies in their rejection of fads and their embrace of the tried-and-true. It also suggested that the true charter innovation is primarily institutional—that is, making each school a self-governing, independent entity—not necessarily pedagogical.

Much that is found in charter schools is also visible in some conventional schools, but often not in the same community. The fact that many charter schools simply offer a curriculum, program, or philosophy that differs from the norm in their particular locale should not be discounted. The job of charter schools is to satisfy their customers, not to demonstrate to outside analysts that they have devised something never before observed in this galaxy.

In addition to this contextual variance, the charter mechanism invites remarkable diversity of learning designs and educational opportunities. Charter schools sometimes offer unconventional grade configurations, organizational structures, and governance arrangements. Their pedagogy ranges from ultra-traditional to super-progressive. Their founders can be parents, teachers, civic organizations, universities, and even municipalities. They can be affiliated with nonprofit or for-profit organizations, or they can be unaffiliated. There are even a few "virtual" charter schools that exist primarily in cyberspace.[22]

Charters Are Having Effects Beyond the Schoolhouse Door

While many parents view charter schools as havens for their own children and many teachers seek a similar refuge for themselves, many watchers of education reform see charters as catalysts for systemic change in stodgy school districts. There now exists a growing array of visible "spillover," "multiplier," and "pioneer" effects by charters on neighboring school systems.[23]

The four stages in the public school establishment's typical reaction to charter schools are (1) stop them cold, (2) keep them few and weak, (3) fight back and out-do them, and (4) embrace the concept. A gauntlet of efforts to restrain competition and keep the school market closed (stage 1) or restrict access to it (stage 2) awaits the would-be charter starter, including lobbying campaigns to block enabling legislation, judicial strategies to overturn legislation, re-regulation of charters so that they have scant autonomy, ensuring that charters do not get their full per pupil revenues, and so forth. Most U.S. communities are stuck in these first two stages.

Some communities affected by charters, however, have reached stage 3. They are responding to the competition by trying to out-do charters and thereby win back their students. An Arizona analysis suggests that such competition is making a positive difference for district schools in the state with America's liveliest charter program. The study sorts district responses into the low-cost kind (for example, using flyers and other marketing tools) and costlier moves that change the available educational services (such as starting a full-day kindergarten program). While the mere whisper of charters may trigger the former, the authors contend that only "direct competition from charter schools pushes districts to adopt high cost school reforms. Further, positive achievement results are most apparent in the sub performing districts. This is in sharp contrast to the fears of many school choice opponents, who believe that competition will harm poorly performing students."[24]

Stage 4 districts—still few in number—seek to achieve their own purposes with the help of charter schools, creating schools not possible under the usual ground rules and using them as labs to test innovations or employing them as part of a broader reform strategy. Mesa, Arizona's, new Montessori school would have been difficult to staff due to state certification requirements, but the charter law enabled the district to disregard that red tape. Houston's school board and then-superintendent Dr. Rod Paige joined forces to use the charter strategy to create six different types of charter schools, from charter programs within district schools to fully autonomous charters, including a charter cluster of schools. There are now "charter districts" in California, Florida, and Georgia.

Eric Rofes has documented district responses in twenty-five communities, cataloguing the following initial impacts: student (and money) transfers to

Table 2-1. *Charters' Impact on District Operations*[a]

Areas of change in district operations	Percentage of districts
Central office operations	93.9
Accountability and autonomy	77.6
Facilities	61.2
Public relations and parent involvement	61.2
School-level staffing	28.6

a. $N = 49$.

charter schools; loss of particular kinds of students to "niche" charter schools; departure of disgruntled parents; changes in the district's staff morale and attitudes; and central office planning and management problems.[25] Nine of the twenty-five districts Rofes examined claimed that charter schools had induced no effects; five experienced "strong" effects (significant loss of students and money and at least two other effects); seven felt "moderate" effects (some loss of students and money and at least two other effects); and four acknowledged "mild" effects (little loss of students or money and up to two other effects). In response, districts mounted various efforts of their own. These included opening new schools organized around a specific philosophy or theme, creating "add-on" programs (for example, after-school programs, all-day programs), offering more diverse activities or curricular resources, and outsourcing services through contracts with private vendors.

According to a federal study of forty-nine districts with charter schools, "every district . . . made changes in district education and/or operations that they attributed to charter schools."[26] (See table 2-1.) Additional effects were seen on district educational programs, with 61 percent of the districts making changes by forming new specialty schools, implementing new educational programs, or changing educational structures in existing schools.[27]

How do the forty-nine districts in the federal study view charter schools? They are nearly evenly divided, with 49 percent seeing charters as a "challenge" and 51 percent seeing them as an "opportunity." The researchers' conclusion was that "every district in our sample reported that charter schools affected their district in some way. Indeed, this report provides some evidence to substantiate the claims of charter advocates that charter schools may be producing ripple effects beyond the schoolhouse doors."[28]

The Charter Movement Is Advancing the School Accountability Effort

Though freed from much input-driven accountability (rules and regulations), charter schools are accountable to two major constituencies when it comes to their outcomes. First, they are accountable to the marketplace of parents who choose whether or not to send their children to the school and to the teachers who choose to teach there. Each of these key groups is free to vote with its feet. Second, they are accountable to the charter sponsor, which scrutinizes them during the application phase, monitors them during the term of their charter, and evaluates them when the time for renewal arrives.

Beyond their clients and authorizers, charter schools are also ultimately accountable to the state in which they operate. States presently tackle the charter accountability challenge in different ways. Some have adopted a centralized, state-run approach, others a market-based strategy, and still others a district-managed framework that relies on local accountability augmented by statewide tests. In 1998–99, charter schools reported external monitoring in the following areas: school finances (94 percent of the schools), compliance with state or federal regulations (88 percent), student achievement (87 percent), student attendance (81 percent), instructional practices (63 percent), school governance (56 percent), school completion (47 percent), and student behavior (44 percent).[29]

Charter schools use various types of assessment methods to report on student achievement, with 96 percent using standardized tests, though more use norm-referenced (86 percent) than criterion-referenced (62 percent) assessments. Many also use student demonstrations of their work (89 percent), pupil portfolios (81 percent), and performance assessments (74 percent) to augment test scores.[30]

How are these varied accountability systems working? Looking across the present landscape, we make two related observations. First, charter closures are demonstrating a rare and important point in education: that public schools need not be immortal and accountability can have teeth. According to the Center for Education Reform, about 80 charter schools had closed by the end of 2000—a closure rate of about 4 percent. Although hardship usually results when a school shuts down, school closures can generally be construed as achievements for the charter movement. The charter movement buries its dead, while the regular public school system tends to keep them on life-support long after all brain function has ceased.

Second, a lack of viable alternatives exists to outright closure when schools are showing signs of trouble. If the charter movement is to succeed in the long run, it needs to develop more gradations of accountability to distinguish between schools that can and cannot be salvaged. Clearly, some schools would benefit from intervention, technical assistance, monitoring, perhaps even a penalty, but they do not deserve the electric chair. The death sentence might be imposed less often if states and communities, and especially charter authorizers, were better supplied with rehabilitation options.

Thus charter schools are advancing the theory and practice of school accountability, but there is still room for improvement—particularly if they are to help regular public schools develop an effective, efficient, and transparent accountability system.

Most of the Allegations against Charter Schools Turn Out to Be False; Others Are Exaggerated

When charter schools are proposed in a state or district, a chorus of protests nearly always follows.[31] The most common allegations are that charters threaten districts with bankruptcy because they rob funds and students from districts, that they "cream" the most fortunate children and leave the neediest kids behind, and that they do not adequately serve disabled children. Some have even claimed that the charter movement will balkanize American society. Others assert that charter schools are too risky and unproven. Still others complain that charter schools are not that different from district public schools. Some critics allege that charters invite profiteering by allowing for-profit firms to operate in a dangerously deregulated environment. Lastly, many fear that charter schools are the Trojan horse that will enable vouchers to slip in through the gates of public education.

Most of these allegations are false. Charter schools have not bankrupted school districts. Some have faced financial pressures due to the competition from charters, but the astute ones have responded by improving their educational offerings.

In the aggregate, charter schools are populated by a more diverse population of American schoolchildren than regular public schools (though these demographics vary by state and district). Over half (51.8 percent) of charter pupils belong to minority groups (compared with 41 percent in conventional schools). Nearly two-fifths (38.7 percent) come from low-income families, slightly above the poverty rate among regular public school pupils (37.3 percent). About one-tenth (9.9 percent) have limited English proficiency (compared with 9.8 percent in regular public schools), and 8.4 percent are special education students (compared with 11.3 percent in regular public schools). (See figure 2-3.)

According to the U.S. Department of Education, one in five charter founders cited their desire to serve a special population of students as the most important reason for creating the school.[32] And that is exactly what many charters are doing. Some states encourage—or even compel—charter schools to serve at-risk children. In the end, the federal study of charter schools found "no evidence that charter schools disproportionately serve white and economically advantaged students. . . . Charter schools generally mirror the state's racial composition" of students in all public schools.[33]

Figure 2-3. *Demographics of Charter Schools and Regular Public Schools,*
1994–95 to 1998–99 [a]

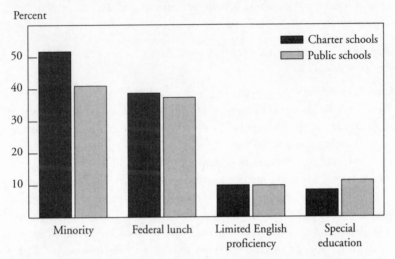

Source: RPP International, *The State of Charter Schools 2000: Fourth-Year Report* (U.S. Department of Education, January 2000) pp. 30–38.
    a. The data straddle different years.

Far from balkanizing communities, charters bring together in common cause new communities of parents, educators, schoolchildren, and civic organizations. Some have even created new communities based on educational philosophy, shared values, or special needs (for example, charters have been founded to serve dropouts, addicts, deaf children, and so on). Though some charter schools appeal to certain racial or ethnic groups (some schools are heavily African American, Hispanic, or Native American), charters by law must accept all comers. When demand outpaces a school's available slots, admissions are usually by lottery.

When critics suggest that little is happening in charter schools that is not found elsewhere in U.S. education, they are partly correct, but many charter innovations are situational—providing children and families with educational approaches not otherwise available in their communities.

While charter laws can cause dollar signs to light up in people's eyes, the specter of profiteering is limited. Most profit-seeking charter operators work closely with grassroots groups, typically utilizing a structure in which the local group holds the charter—and is accountable for the school's results—while outsourcing the school's day-to-day work to the private firm. In all such arrangements, the public's most important safeguard is that no one can profit for long from a bad school that nobody wants to attend. The surest way to make money from charter school management over time is to attract and retain customers by providing an effective education. It is also important to recall that the profit motive is not new to public education. Private firms have made money from public education for years by selling textbooks, tests, bus service, food, computers, chalk, and many other goods and services to school systems.

Finally, though the politics of vouchers and charters are sometimes intertwined, they need not be.[34] Charter schools differ from vouchers in crucial ways, beginning with the fact that they are public schools; that is, open to all comers, publicly financed, and accountable to a public authority for their results. Some charter advocates support vouchers while others are opposed, and vice versa.[35] The charter idea transcends party and ideology.

What Is Not Known

With all the policy wonks, education practitioners, and journalists watching charter schools at every turn, there is no shortage of reports, articles, and websites brimming with information about this high-profile school reform movement. However, a few areas in the charter world exist in which analysts still find themselves in the dark, frustrated and still grasping for answers.

Will Charter Schools Boost Academic Achievement?

Definitive data on the academic performance of charter schools are not yet available. Of the data at hand today, however, much is positive. The U.S. Department of Education commissioned a multiyear study of the academic achievement of charter schools, matching a thousand charter students in twenty-two schools in seven states with a thousand similar students. The researchers collected longitudinal data from a criterion-referenced test from grades three to nine. They found that "charter school students gained a half-year's more growth in one year in reading achievement compared to non-charter public school students. For math, charter students had a slightly greater achievement growth than non-charter students, but the difference generally was not statistically significant. The achievement of charter students of color improved more than the achievement of white charter school students."[36] The limited sample does not allow a generalization to all charter schools, but the news certainly points in a positive direction.

Several states have also sought to appraise the educational effectiveness of their charter schools. For example, the 1999 California Academic Performance Indicator (API) revealed good news about charter school performance. Based on the Stanford 9 achievement test, the API showed that a greater percentage of charter schools than of noncharter schools scored in the top half of all public school rankings. More specifically, 58 percent of charter elementary schools and 65 percent of all charter high schools were in the sixth through tenth deciles, as compared with 50 percent of all noncharter elementary schools and 50 percent of all noncharter high schools.[37]

In Colorado, a state study found that charter performance (in the thirty-two schools that had been operational for at least two years by the 1998–99 school year) "is stronger than state averages, stronger than sponsoring district averages and stronger than the average performance of other public schools in the same socioeconomic classification level." Moreover, the "great majority" of Colorado charter schools "were meeting—or exceeding—the performance goals they identified in their individual charter applications and in subsequent school improvement plans."[38]

A 1999 study found that 40 percent of charter pupils in Minnesota met the state's graduation requirements for math (compared with 71 percent of students statewide) and that 43 percent of charter pupils met the state standards for reading (compared with 68 percent statewide). Attendance and graduation rates were also lower for charter schools. But Minnesota officials note that half their charter students were economically disadvantaged (compared with 24 percent statewide), that at least half were new to their charter school, and that most were from the Minneapolis-St. Paul area, and thus not representative of the entire state.[39] The results are mixed in Arizona, too, leading one analyst of that state's data to conclude that "overall, . . . charter schools are not performing very differently than other regular public schools."[40]

Will charter schools furnish compelling evidence that they provide superior education? Many people are asking that question, but it may turn out to be the wrong question.[41] A better one might be, superior to what? Superior to all other schools in America, to the state's average test scores, or to the schools that charter pupils would otherwise be attending? Unfortunately, with all the different testing and assessment mechanisms now in use, with many districts and states changing them so often, and with controversies over which students and schools to compare against, finding reliable, comparable, clear, and useful data can be a Herculean task. That is why consensus is growing among charter watchers that these schools should make vigorous use of "value-added" assessments, which allow schools to measure the progress of individual children over time. However, good longitudinal data will take time to amass.

Will Charter Schools Be Able to Innovate in Special Education?

Some analysts say that charter schools do not adequately serve disabled children, alleging that some lack the staff or resources to operate a quality special education program while others attempt to deter families with disabled children from enrolling. The data on special education enrollment in charters are hazy, with percentages varying depending on how one defines "disabled" and with numbers skewed by the fact that many parents seek charter schools precisely because they want to give their child a second chance, free from the "special education" label.

Nancy J. Zollers of Boston College's School of Education, in a 1998 article coauthored with Arun K. Ramanathan, asserts that for-profit firms running charter schools in Massachusetts "have done a decent job of including students with mild disabilities, [but] . . . have engaged in a pattern of disregard and often blatant hostility toward students with more complicated behavioral and cognitive disabilities."[42]

It is perhaps unavoidable that some charter schools do not meet all their students' special needs. Part of the reason may be stinginess, malfeasance, or insensitivity, but mostly it is due to lack of experience, expertise, or resources. The proper solution is to make sure before issuing a charter that the proposed charter operators have addressed this issue in a reasonable way; that is, that the school has the staff it needs to do what it says it will do and that no one is denied admission because of disability. That does not mean every school must accommodate every need of every disabled child. Regular public schools do not do that, either. And a double standard must not be used to judge charter schools in the area of special education. Regrettably, many district schools do not adequately serve children with disabilities.[43]

But this line of reasoning may be missing the fundamental issue: Will charters be allowed to handle special education differently if they and their students' parents believe this is called for? These schools are meant to be different, even in special education.[44] Yet federal regulations issued in March 1999 require them to serve children with disabilities in the same manner as district schools, regardless of whether the charter school receives the requisite funds.[45] To insist that they model themselves on conventional schools in their treatment of disabled youngsters is shortsighted. If they cannot be different, there is not much point in having charter schools, at least not for youngsters with disabilities. Allowing charter schools to experiment with innovative approaches to special education could lead to progress in a field that has been stagnant, despite honorable intentions, for a long time.

Will Charter Schools Put Educational Accountability on the Map?

Charter accountability is, by and large, clearer and stronger than that in district public schools, but it is still underdeveloped. This should not be surprising, because many of the essential gauges and performance indicators remain to be developed. Much progress to date in charter accountability still is

recorded in terms of the old public school paradigm of regulatory compliance—leavened by consumer satisfaction and heightened emphasis on student achievement. It is a much better car but it is not yet a jet plane. Perhaps
a different paradigm would work better. We believe that a carefully designed
information-based approach that requires mandatory disclosure fits the bill.
Mary Graham terms a version of this method "regulation by shaming."[46]

A world that offers such a model can be found in the financial sector—
surely an imperfect one, but one with an undeniable track record of success.
We describe such a system in detail in our book *Charter Schools in Action.*[47]
Schools would benefit from something akin to the Generally Accepted
Accounting Principles (GAAP) by which private sector firms (and many nonprofit organizations) report their activities and results using standardized formats, taxonomies, and independent audits that embody uniform definitions
and common information categories. This could be termed Generally
Accepted Accountability Principles for Education (GAAPE). It borrows the
central premises and best attributes of the accounting principles while recognizing key differences between schools and private firms and going well
beyond financial matters.

Charter accountability can be thought of as a system of checks and balances that maintains public oversight and authority, maximizes the virtues of
market forces, and minimizes the vices of bureaucratic regulatory systems. In
a lightly regulated education environment, however, ample information is
essential for securing trust, both from clients and from sponsors. The idea
behind GAAPE is that, even as individual schools have wide-ranging freedom
to govern themselves, they also remain accountable via the marketplace—and
to sponsors and policymakers—thanks to their transparency. GAAPE affords
everyone concerned with a school a picture window through which to see
what is happening there and how well it is working. Instead of a brick wall
around such information, the school is surrounded by glass.

If vital information is made available about individual schools, in formats
that are clear and useful to multiple constituencies and comparable from one
school to the next, genuine accountability becomes possible. Accountability-
via-transparency is a systematic approach to providing parents, educators,
policymakers, taxpayers, and others with information that shows whether the
charter approach is working. Such information is not just the responsibility of
individual schools, but also the obligation of their sponsors and monitors, to
obtain, analyze, and use in their capacities as stewards and then to amass, distill, and report to the public. Reporting it is more than inscribing it on a government form and putting it in a file, or disclosing it when someone asks a
question. The information should be voluntarily, energetically, and regularly
pumped out into view, such as by newspaper notices and website postings.

With schools, as with private firms, there is a bottom line. But with schools it is a bit tricky. In the commercial sector, the primary interest is profitability. In education, student achievement is paramount, but it is not the only product of a good school—consider also the fostering of citizenship and character—and it is not the same in all schools. A school working with disabled youngsters or former dropouts, say, may be more successful than an advanced science and math school, even though its test scores are lower. Thus the bottom line is not as easy to track, report, and compare in education as in the private sector. All the more reason for maximum feasible transparency.

If charter schools can master accountability-via-transparency, perhaps their most valuable legacy will turn out to be their service as laboratories for better education accountability systems in general. At this point, however, it remains an open question.

Will Policymakers Sufficiently Lower the Barriers to Entry So That Charter Schools Attain a Critical Mass?

How big will the charter movement get? It remains unknown how copious is the supply of tireless individuals willing to take this risk. Clearly, there are hundreds, but are there tens of thousands? Early signs of burnout are apparent among charter leaders and teachers who work round-the-clock and often round-the-calendar to make their schools succeed. From where will their successors come?

The barriers to entry (legislative, financial, and political) remain high in many states. The federal study of charter schools identified a mind-boggling array of obstacles facing charter schools (see table 2-2).

The most pressing of these barriers is fiscal. Most charters have skimpier funding than conventional schools because many do not receive the full per pupil allocation or any capital money.[48]

That charter schools are able to generate demand, innovate, and—more often than not—produce achievement gains given these tight resource constraints is impressive, but numerous factors still inhibit their growth. Thus the supply of charter schools is a far more serious issue than the demand, because these barriers to entry (many of which are inscribed in state charter laws) are so mountainous. If this remains so, charter schools will not be able to serve all those who crave them, much less transform public education.

Nobody is certain yet what will constitute a critical mass of charter schools when it comes to effecting lasting change in a school system. David Armor and Brett Peiser studied the impact of interdistrict choice in Massachusetts for the Pioneer Institute and concluded that it took a loss of just 2 to 3 percent of the students to awaken a district and catalyze meaningful innovation in it.[49] Don Shalvey, former superintendent of the San Carlos School District

Table 2-2. *Estimated Percentage of Charter Schools Reporting Difficulties in Implementing Their Charter*[a]

Barriers	Total (percent)
Lack of start-up funds	48.5
Inadequate operating funds	37.4
Lack of planning time	34.5
Inadequate facilities	32.0
State or local board opposition	20.0
District resistance or regulations	18.2
State department of education resistance	12.3
Internal processes or conflicts	11.9
School administration and management	10.7
Health and safety regulations	10.5
Hiring staff	10.3

Source: RPP International, *The State of Charter Schools: Fourth-Year Report* (U.S. Department of Education, 2000), p. 44.

a. Ten other difficulties have a response total of less than 10 percent.

in California, estimates that a critical mass is about 10 percent of the pupil population. He has launched a string of 100 charter schools run by a non-profit organization called University Public Schools. As reported in the *Wall Street Journal*, "When enrollment reaches 10 percent of the local student population, he calculates, the district schools will have lost so many students and so much state funding . . . that they will be forced to improve their own programs or, better yet, adopt his."[50]

Will Charter Schools Reinvent Public Education?

Charter school growth does not have to be incremental. Hugh B. Price, president of the National Urban League, argues that "what's urgently needed is truly radical reform that structures public education so that its raison d'etre is student success." His four-point plan for transforming all urban schools into high-performing schools includes "charterizing" all urban schools.[51] David Osborne takes this a step further and implores others to "imagine, for a moment, a public education system in which *every* school is a charter school."[52]

Osborne's approach is consistent with a report from the Education Commission of the States (ECS), calling for bold new approaches to school governance and suggesting two models. One of these would create a system of publicly authorized and funded but self-governing and independently operated schools, with the district board relinquishing all day-to-day school control.

Under this scenario, the board no longer determines class size, hires principals, oversees curriculum, negotiates job rights, builds and repairs schools, and so forth. It gives up its exclusive franchise to operate schools and, instead, contracts with a variety of self-governing entities (for example, nonprofit and for-profit organizations, cooperatives, sole proprietorships) to run schools. This approach makes chartering a requirement for all schools, shifting the board's responsibility from providing educational services to purchasing them.

Hugh Price, David Osborne, and ECS have suggested their own versions of "charterizing" public education itself. We have also portrayed such a vision and laid it out in considerable detail in the final chapter of *Charter Schools in Action,* where we help the reader to imagine how that concept, put into practice, would work.[53]

Not everyone finds that prospect alluring. For example, Edward B. Fiske and Helen F. Ladd argue that charter schools should "remain limited in number and not become the norm."[54] But we believe that a fully developed charter mechanism foreshadows a new vision of public education itself.

Two visions of public education are competing today. One is that public education is a collection of institutions and programs run by government, managed by a superintendent and school board, staffed by public employees, and operated within a public sector bureaucracy where oversight is mostly a matter of compliance with rules and regulations. Public education in this familiar sense is not very different from a public library, public park, or public housing project.

An alternative understanding sees public education as a set of institutions and programs that are open to the public, paid for by the public, and accountable to the public for results. So long as this system satisfies those three criteria, it is providing a public education. Government need not run schools for them to be public. That is the great insight afforded by the charter phenomenon.

In conclusion, the charter idea—schooling based on freedom, innovation, choice, and accountability—can point to a new model for public education. It is rooted in the principle and ideal of public education but calls for a top-to-bottom makeover of its ground rules and institutional practices.

Notes

1. Joseph Lieberman, "Schools Where Kids Succeed," *Readers' Digest,* January 1999. Senator Lieberman was the sponsor of the first federal Charter School Grant Program and cosponsored the 1998 Charter School Expansion Act.

2. This paper is derived from Chester E. Finn Jr., Bruno V. Manno, and Gregg

Vanourek, *Charter Schools in Action: Renewing Public Education* (Princeton University Press, 2000).

3. These states are Arizona, California, Florida, Michigan, Minnesota, New Jersey, North Carolina, Ohio, Pennsylvania, Texas, and Wisconsin. See RPP International, *The State of Charter Schools 2000: Fourth-Year Report* (U.S. Department of Education, 1999), pp. 11, 15.

4. Center for Education Reform, "Charter School Highlights and Statistics."

5. June Kronholz, "Defying Convention, Superintendent Takes a Chance on Charter Schools," *Wall Street Journal,* April 11, 2000, p. A1.

6. Lynn Olson, "Gauging the Impact of Competition," *Education Week,* May 24, 2000.

7. RPP International, *The State of Charter Schools 2000: Fourth-Year Report,* pp. 14–15.

8. Center for Education Reform, *Charter Schools Today: Changing the Face of American Education* (Washington, D.C.: Center for Education Reform, 2000).

9. RPP International, *The State of Charter Schools 2000: Fourth-Year Report,* pp. 20–21.

10. Bryan C. Hassel, "Charter Schools: Politics and Practice in Four States," in Paul E. Peterson and Bryan C. Hassel, eds., *Learning from School Choice* (Brookings, 1998), p. 250. See also Bryan Hassel, *The Charter School Challenge: Avoiding the Pitfalls, Fulfilling the Promise* (Brookings, 1999).

11. Bryan Hassel, "Charter Schools: Policy Success Story Begins to Emerge," *Progressive Policy Institute Policy Brief* (August 1999), p. 2.

12. Center for Education Reform, "Charter Schools: Evidence of Success," http://edreform.com/pubs/chartiv.htm.

13. RPP International, *The State of Charter Schools: Third-Year Report* (U.S. Department of Education, 1999), p. 10. The quote comes from RPP International, *A Study of Charter Schools: Second-Year Report* (U.S. Department of Education, 1998), p. 97.

14. See Chester E. Finn Jr., Bruno V. Manno, Louann A. Bierlein, and Gregg Vanourek, *Charter Schools in Action: Final Report* (Washington, D.C.: Hudson Institute, July 1997), especially part I.

15. Julia E. Koppich and others, *New Rules, New Roles?: The Professional Work Lives of Charter School Teachers* (Washington, D.C.: National Education Association, 1998), p. 132.

16. Strictly speaking, these are not enforceable requirements for a public school, but charter schools are able to bring considerable moral suasion and peer pressure to bear—as well as coming up with extraordinarily imaginative volunteer options.

17. RPP International, *The State of Charter Schools 2000: Fourth-Year Report,* pp. 48–49.

18. Pioneer Institute, "Poll Finds Higher Satisfaction Rate among Charter School Parents," *Policy Directions,* no. 3 (June 1998), available at http://www.pioneerinstitute. org/research/policy/piodrct3.cfm.

19. Pioneer Institute, "Poll Finds Higher Satisfaction Rate among Charter School Parents," p. 42. However, this varies widely by school type: 64.4 percent of the founders of newly created schools cited this as their most important reason for founding the school, compared with 43.5 percent for the founders of preexisting public schools and 38.9 percent for the founders of preexisting private schools.

20. R. G. Corwin and J. Flaherty, *Freedom and Innovation in California's Charter Schools* (Los Alamitos, Calif.: SWRL, 1995).

21. Rosenblum Brigham Associates, *Innovation and Massachusetts Charter Schools* (Boston: Massachusetts Department of Education, 1998), p. 6.

22. Matt Richtel, "California District Puts Public School Online," *New York Times,* August 23, 1997.

23. See Anna Bray Duff, Charter Schools' Ripple Effect," *Investor's Business Daily,* August 31, 1999; "Charter Competition Helps Public Schools Improve, Says MSU Study," *Michigan Education Report,* no. 3 (Winter 2000); Priscilla Pardini, "Charters as Tools of Reform," *School Administrator* (August 1999), pp. 19–23; David Osborne, "Healthy Competition: The Benefits of Charter Competition," *New Republic,* October 4, 1999, www.tnr.com/archive/1099/100499/osborne100499.html; Robert Maranto, Scott Milliman, Frederick Hess, and April Gresham, "Do Charter Schools Improve District Schools?: Three Approaches to the Question," in Robert Maranto, Scott Milliman, Frederick Hess, and April Gresham, eds., *School Choice in the Real World: Lessons from Arizona Charter Schools* (Boulder, Colo.: Westview Press, 1999), pp. 129–41; Robert Maranto, Scott Milliman, Frederick Hess, and April Gresham, "Desert Bloom: Arizona's Free Market in Education," *Phi Delta Kappan* (June 2000), pp. 751–57; Lynn Olson, "Gauging the Impact of Competition," *Education Week,* May 24, 2000, pp. 1, 18–20; and Paul Teske, Mark Schneider, Jack Buckley, and Sara Clark, "Does Charter School Competition Improve Traditional Public Schools?" *Manhattan Institute Civic Report* (New York, June 2000). See also in this volume, Frederick M. Hess, "Hints of the Pick-Axe: Competition and Public Schooling in Milwaukee."

24. Robert Maranto, Scott Milliman, and Frederick Hess, "Does Public Sector Competition Stimulate Innovation?: The Competitive Impacts of Arizona Charter Schools on Traditional Public Schools," unpublished paper, University of Virginia, 1998, p. 19.

25. Eric Rofes, *How Are School Districts Responding to Charter Laws and Charter Schools?: A Study of Eight States and the District of Columbia* (Berkeley, Calif.: Policy Analysis for California Education, April 1998). See also Eric Rofes, "The Catalyst Role of Charter Schools," *School Administrator* (August 1999), pp. 14–18.

26. RPP International, *Charter Schools: A Challenge or an Opportunity?: The Impact of Charter Schools on Districts* (U.S. Department of Education, October 1999), p. 4.

27. RPP International, *Charter Schools,* pp. 13–14. These changes in operations and programs may be foreshadowing a different perspective on the way that school districts and other charter authorizers relate to and support individual schools. On

this possible new role for districts and other charter granting agencies, see Anthony S. Bryk, Paul Hill, and Dorothy Shipps with Michael J. Murphy, David Menefee-Libey, and Albert L. Bennett, *Improving Community Schools Connections: Moving toward a System of Community Schools* (Baltimore, Md.: Annie E. Casey Foundation, 1999); Katrina Bulkley, "Charter School Authorizers: A New Governance Mechanism?" *Educational Policy* (November 1999), pp. 674–97; Bryan C. Hassel and Sandra Vegari, "Charter-Granting Agencies: The Challenge of Oversight in a Deregulated System," *Education and Urban Society* (August 1999), pp. 406–28; and Bryan Hassel and Paul A. Herdman, *Charter School Accountability: A Guide to Issues and Options for Charter Authorizers* (Baltimore, Md.: Annie E. Casey Foundation, 2000).

28. RPP International, *Charter Schools,* pp. 45, 47.

29. RPP International, *The State of Charter Schools: Fourth-Year Report,* pp. 50–53.

30. RPP International, *The State of Charter Schools: Fourth-Year Report,* pp. 50–55. See also Jeff Archer, "Accountability Measures Vary Widely," *Education Week,* May 17, 2000, pp. 1, 18–20.

31. For a chronicling of some of these, see Thomas L. Good and Jennifer S. Braden, "Charter Schools: Another Reform Failure or a Worthwhile Investment?" *Phi Delta Kappan* (June 2000), pp. 745–50.

32. RPP International, *The State of Charter Schools: Third Year Report,* p. 42. Also see "Forum: School Colors: The Racial Politics of Public Education," *The Nation,* June 5, 2000, pp. 13–18 and Jonathan Schorr, "Giving Charter Schools a Chance," *The Nation,* June 5, 2000, pp. 19–23; Lynn Schnaiberg, "Charter Schools: Choice, Diversity May Be at Odds," *Education Week,* May 10, 2000, pp. 1, 18–20.

33. RPP International, *The State of Charter Schools: Third-Year Report,* pp. 2, 30–32.

34. For an important analysis of the two different constituencies that support charters and vouchers, see Bryan C. Hassel "Politics, Markets, and Two Choice Reform Movements: How Charter Schools and Voucher Programs Interact," unpublished paper, Harvard University, John F. Kennedy School of Government, A. Alfred Taubman Center for State and Local Government, 2000.

35. For example, Bryan Hassel supports charter schools but not vouchers. See Bryan C. Hassel, "The Case for Charter Schools," in Paul E. Peterson and Bryan C. Hassel, eds., *Learning from School Choice* (Brookings, 1998), p. 33; and "Politics, Markets, and Two Choice Reform Movements." Renowned economist Milton Friedman supports vouchers but is not enamored with charter schools (see Finn, Manno, and Vanourek, *Charter Schools in Action,* chapter 8).

36. RPP International, *Are Charter Schools Improving Student Achievement? Findings from the National Study of Charter Schools* (U.S. Department of Education, 2000), p. 1.

37. California Network of Education Charters, "API Announcement," June 5, 2000, http://www.canec.org.

38. Colorado Department of Education, *1998–99 Colorado Charter Schools Evaluation Study: The Characteristics, Status, and Performance Record of Colorado Charter Schools* (Denver, Colo., January 2000), p. i.

39. "Minnesota Study Finds Charter Schools Don't Measure Up," *Education Daily*, January 7, 1999. See also *Comparisons of Minnesota State-Wide Test Results for 1998* (Minnesota Department of Education, 1999).

40. Lori A. Mulholland, *Arizona Charter School Progress Evaluation* (Arizona State University, Morrison Institute for Public Policy, March 1999), p. 42.

41. Some charter researchers argue that because charter schools are an institutional innovation, not a pedagogical one, it is foolhardy to ask whether charter schools will boost academic achievement. According to this line of reasoning, it would depend on which educational intervention or treatment charter schools chose to offer, not their institutional arrangements.

42. Nancy J. Zollers and Arun K. Ramanathan, "For-Profit Charter Schools and Students with Disabilities: The Sordid Side of the Business of Schooling," *Phi Delta Kappan* (December 1998), p. 298. See also "Massachusetts Charters Assailed for Excluding Disabled," *Education Daily*, December 8, 1998.

43. Doug Struck and Valerie Strauss, "D.C. Special Ed System Still in Disarray, Report Says," *Washington Post,* July 20, 1998, p. B1. See also Doug Struck and Valerie Strauss, "FBI Probes Special-Ed School Used by School," *Washington Post,* July 29, 1998, p. B1. The *Washington Post* reported in July 1998 that the District of Columbia's special education program is "in disarray," with thousands of disabled children on long (and illegal) waiting lists, backlogs for hearings reaching almost a thousand youngsters, many special education students being sent to private schools, and soaring program costs. Boston College's Nancy J. Zollers also concedes that "public schools have not had a good track record with children with behavioral needs."

44. Some observers have noted a fundamental tension between the compliance-driven approach of special education legislation and the issue of autonomy that is so central to the charter concept.

45. U.S. Department of Education, *I.D.E.A. '97 (Part B Final Regulations)* (Washington, D.C., March 1999). See also U.S. Department of Education, *Applying Federal Civil Rights Laws to Public Charter Schools: Questions and Answers* (Washington, D.C.: Office for Civil Rights, May 2000).

46. Mary Graham, "Regulation by Shaming," *Atlantic Monthly* (April 2000), p. 36. Graham discusses how this information-based approach is applied in the private sector: It forces "companies to disclose . . . information [that] can improve customer choices and industry practices." See also the following on information-based regulation: Archon Fung, "Smart Regulation: How Government Is Marshalling Firms and Citizens to Protect the Environment," *The Taubman Center Report for 2000* (Harvard University, John K. Kennedy School of Government, A. Alfred Taubman Center for State and Local Government, 2000), pp. 2–3; David Weill, "Controlling Sweatshops: New Solutions to an Intransigent Problem," *The Taubman Center Report for 2000* (Harvard University, John F. Kennedy School of Government, A. Alfred Taubman Center for State and Local Government, 2000), pp. 4–5; and Mary Graham "Putting Disclosure to the Test," *The Taubman Center Report for 2000* (Har-

vard University, John F. Kennedy School of Government, A. Alfred Taubman Center for State and Local Government, 2000), pp. 6–7. Another strategy that has instructive lessons for an information-based approach is found in an inflation targeting approach to monetary policy. See the following for a discussion that presents the main elements of this strategy: Ben S. Bernanke, Thomas Laubach, Frederic S. Mishkin, and Adam S. Posen, *Inflation Targeting* (Princeton University Press, 1999), especially chapters 1, 2, 3, and 11.

47. See Finn, Manno, and Vanourek, *Charter Schools in Action,* chapter 6.

48. How do many charters do more with less? We have witnessed four techniques to realize savings or create efficiencies: using parental "sweat equity"; paring administrative personnel to a bare minimum; eschewing the extra, nonacademic often "extra curricular" programs that regular schools normally offer; and "outsourcing" some of the school's functions to external providers. According to the federal charter study, 54.1 percent of charter schools use a nondistrict outside provider for legal services, 52.8 percent for insurance, 45.6 percent for payroll, and 42 percent for social services. RPP International, *The State of Charter Schools: Fourth-Year Report,* pp. 48–49.

49. David J. Armor and Brett M. Peiser, *Competition in Education: A Case Study of Interdistrict Choice* (Boston: Pioneer Institute, 1997).

50. June Kronholz, "Defying Convention, Superintendent Takes a Chance on Charter Schools," *Wall Street Journal,* April 11, 2000, p. A1.

51. Hugh B. Price, "Urban Education: A Radical Plan," *Education Week,* December 8, 1999.

52. David Osborne, "Make 'Em All Charter Schools," *Washington Post,* November 14, 1999, p. B3. See also "Reinventing Our Public Schools: A Six Part Series Reprinted," *Christian Science Monitor,* 1999, available at http://www.csmonitor.com.

53. In the final chapter of *Charter Schools in Action,* we take the reader on an imaginary tour of a future metropolis (called Met City), circa 2010, that has basically gone "all charter." See also Chester E. Finn Jr., Bruno V. Manno, and Gregg Vanourek, "What If All Schools Were Schools of Choice?" *Weekly Standard,* June 19, 2000, pp. 26–29.

54. Edward B. Fiske and Helen F. Ladd, *When Schools Compete: A Cautionary Tale* (Brookings, 2000), p. 298. See also Edward B. Fiske and Helen F. Ladd, "The Invisible Hand as Schoolmaster," *American Prospect,* May 22, 2000, pp. 19–21, and their essay in this volume. We believe that their comparison of the New Zealand experience with the U.S. charter movement is faulty. The authors admit that the kind of charter granted to New Zealand schools under its move to a full choice system of "chartered" schools representing a three-way partnership of the state, the school, and the community never materialized. As they say in their book, "not only have school communities played a smaller role in the charter development process than had been envisioned, but charters have also ended up more bland and general and have not played the role within the schools that was anticipated" (p. 107).

3

School Choice in Michigan

MICHAEL MINTROM AND
DAVID N. PLANK

Across the United States, public schooling is increasingly being provided in a quasi-market. As pointed out by Charles M. Tiebout and then others, public service delivery by multiple local jurisdictions combined with a mobile citizenry of "consumer-voters" has long ensured a degree of choice and competition in the delivery of public services including schooling.[1] But recent policy changes have served to break the tight connection between residential location and schooling options. Parents dissatisfied with the schooling that their children receive in nearby public schools are now free to vote with their feet, moving their children to other schools that better satisfy their demands and expectations. Traditional public schools are obliged to compete with one another and with new entrants including charter schools to attract students and revenues. The array of schools from which parents can choose has been significantly expanded, and further increases in the variety of choices available to them appear inevitable.

The move to expand school choice has emerged partly in response to two powerful social trends. First, Americans have increasingly demonstrated a preference for social and spatial differentiation.[2] This preference has manifested itself in the proliferation of new suburbs, commonly appealing to (and often developed for) specific demographic groups. Authors including Christopher Lasch and Robert Reich have commented on the "secession" of various constituencies, such as the prosperous and the religious, from common institutions, among them public schools.[3] Spatial and social sorting has been accompanied by a growing emphasis on the importance of schooling as a private consumption good, which can improve a student's competitive position in the labor market.[4]

Second, citizens' confidence in the efficiency and competence of public sector bureaucracies has declined, and markets and quasi-markets have had to fulfill a variety of public purposes. Among other things, this has entailed a move away from the direct provision of public services by government agencies toward increased reliance on subsidies, incentives, and accountability frameworks as policy instruments to encourage private actors to accomplish policy goals.[5]

The acceleration of these trends has coincided with a rise in public dissatisfaction with the traditional public school system. This originates both in the failure of public school systems to address the educational necessities of poor children, including especially urban and minority children, and in the schools' perceived failures to provide students with the academic and intellectual skills that they will need to compete in a global economy with better-schooled Asians and Europeans.[6]

The introduction of school choice policies responds to each of these trends. First, it facilitates social sorting, by encouraging the establishment of schools addressing themselves to niche markets. Second, it reflects widespread disenchantment with the capacity of government to provide public services and introduces market pressures into a previously protected public monopoly. Third, as claimed by advocates of choice policies, increased competition in the educational system holds the potential to address quality concerns, as the need to compete for students obliges all schools to raise their standards and enhance their performance.

Taken together, these trends have induced significant policy changes in the past decade, including the adoption of charter school laws in more than thirty states and the expansion of open enrollment policies in many others.[7] Michigan and other states have seen increasing pressure to establish public voucher programs that would further expand the array of choices available to parents to include private and religious schools. Ohio and Wisconsin already have limited public voucher programs in place.

Until recently, the political debate on school choice has typically been framed in ideological terms, with advocates and critics advancing rival claims as to whether choice is "good" or "bad." This is in large part attributable to the novelty of school choice policies. In the absence of evidence about how the market for schooling works, strong claims about the advantages of choice could not be effectively challenged. Many of the advocates of choice have consequently exaggerated the benefits of choice and minimized the potential disadvantages.[8] By the same token, opponents' dire warnings about the catastrophic consequences of dismantling the public school system could not be refuted.[9]

As more and more school choice initiatives have been implemented, claims for and against its merits can be scrutinized against appropriate evidence. Instead of putting an end to present debates, analysis of emerging evidence will force a shift in discussions of school choice, making it harder for proponents and opponents to make sweeping claims for or against market-like arrangements in the delivery of public schooling.

Among the many jurisdictions that have recently embraced school choice initiatives, Michigan presents an important case. Because a range of policies designed to expand school choice has been extensively and enthusiastically introduced by Michigan policymakers, choice policies are now sufficiently well established in the state that the full range of consequences can be taken into account. While the rapid adoption of school choice initiatives is not unique to Michigan, the nature of the policy controversy is. With the consequences of school choice becoming more evident in Michigan, the political debate has begun to change. Initially, discussions about school choice involved talk of "unleashing" individuals and organizations through competition and the development of an educational marketplace. As competition among schools has become a reality, however, the metaphor has shifted. Instead of "unleashing" choice, policy debates in Michigan and elsewhere increasingly focus on "harnessing" market forces, so that the positive consequences of competition among schools can be realized and negative effects can be minimized. As discussion of the effects of school choice begins to take hold in Michigan, the rapid pace of expansion in the educational choices available to parents that has occurred in the past decade is unlikely to be sustained. This turn in both the language of policymaking and the focus of policy design marks what we call "the new politics of school choice." Cautious participants in school choice debates should take heed of what has been happening in Michigan. The emerging political battles there might prove emblematic of what is to come elsewhere in the United States.

School Choice Politics in Michigan

Michigan provides an especially interesting case study of the politics of school choice. Since 1994 Michigan's public schools have been financed almost entirely by the state, on the basis of per pupil capitation grants that are fully portable among public schools. Under this system of school finance, state funding "belongs" to students, not to schools or school districts, which is one of the essential conditions for the emergence of a market for schooling. Partly as a result, Michigan has been one of the three leading states in the charter school movement, with more than 170 charter schools—referred to formally in Michigan as Public School Academies—in operation and a substantial number waiting to open.[10] The state has also adopted an open enrollment law that permits students to transfer freely among neighboring school districts, subject to the availability of space in the receiving district. In addition, a vigorous campaign in Michigan to remove constitutional obstacles to public funding for private and religious schools and to provide public vouchers for students in selected school districts was recently defeated at the polls.

After five years of steady progress toward increased parental choice in the Michigan education system, however, the political momentum in support of further expansion among the choices available to parents has recently diminished. At the end of 1999, the legislature failed to lift the limit (or "cap") on the number of charters that can be issued by public universities, effectively preventing new charter schools from opening in 2000–01. The Republican Party was profoundly divided over the question of public vouchers, with Gov. John Engler opposing a ballot initiative sponsored by the Chamber of Commerce and other party stalwarts. Legislation permitting the establishment of charter schools and interdistrict transfers of students is unlikely to be reversed, but the apparently inexorable move toward the further expansion of market mechanisms in the state's education system appears to have stalled.

The shift in political dynamics on school choice issues in Michigan portends a similar shift in choice politics elsewhere. As experience with school choice policies accumulates, the effects of these policies are increasingly visible. Policy arguments have consequently begun to turn on the interpretation of evidence about how school choice policies work. Accompanying this shift is an increasing focus on the question of how to make the emerging market for schooling work better, maximizing the gains from choice while minimizing the potential harms. Designing effective rules to govern competition in the educational system is harder work than simply "unleashing" market forces or "protecting public schools." As this point has become increasingly apparent to practitioners and policymakers, the pace of change has slowed.

Background to School Choice Policies

With strong support from Governor Engler, the Michigan legislature adopted a charter school law in December 1993. At the same time, the legislature proposed a new school funding mechanism to be introduced subject to voter approval. In March 1994 Michigan citizens approved the ballot initiative known as Proposal A, which shifted the main burden of school funding from local property taxes to the state sales tax.[11] As a result, school districts now receive more than 80 percent of their funding from the state, on the basis of the number of pupils that they enroll. A lawmaking provision for interdistrict open enrollment across public schools was adopted the following year. The funds that schools and school districts receive from the state are fully portable; that is, students moving from one school to another take their funding with them.

Because of the changes introduced by the open enrollment law, the introduction of charter schools, and Proposal A, Michigan's school funding system is now "voucher ready." Students may take the funds that the state provides to a variety of schools, including schools in their own school district, schools in neighboring school districts, and charter schools. Perhaps inevitably, as the range of choices available to families has been expanded, the ways in which policy decisions serve to demarcate legitimate choices have received increasing scrutiny. Boundaries that might have seemed natural and impermeable in the past have come to seem increasingly arbitrary.

The demand for public alternatives remains strong. Charter schools now enroll more than 50,000 students (about 3 percent of all Michigan students), and total enrollments have grown by more than 60 percent in each of the 1999–2000 and 2000–01 school years.[12] Many charter schools have waiting lists, and there is a reported backlog of more than 100 charter applicants who cannot open schools because of the cap. An additional 15,000 students have transferred to other school districts under interdistrict choice policies.

Public policy debates now focus on two issues, both of which relate to the scope of school choice and, by implication, the extent to which schooling should be treated as a public or a private good. The first issue concerns whether the array of schools in which students' vouchers can be redeemed should be expanded to include private and religious schools. This question is complicated in Michigan by the fact that the state constitution includes an airtight prohibition against public funding for nonpublic schools. Any further move toward a public voucher system will therefore require a constitutional amendment, which must be approved by the state's voters. The matter is further complicated by the potential cost of a voucher program. A second provision in the Michigan Constitution (the so-called Headlee Amendment) prevents the state government from collecting tax revenue that exceeds an amount equivalent to 9.49 percent of total personal income in the state in any given year. It also prohibits the state from imposing unfunded mandates on local governments. As state expenditures are already constrained by the Headlee limit, it is not clear how any additional expenditures associated with vouchers would be borne.

The second issue at the center of policy debate in Michigan concerns whether the array of public sector alternatives available to students should be expanded and, if so, under what conditions. This question has two dimensions. On the one hand, a heated political debate has arisen about whether the cap that was imposed on the number of charters that could be granted by public universities should be lifted or removed. On the other hand, a somewhat quieter debate has taken place about whether present boundary restrictions on interdistrict transfers should be further loosened.

Charter Schools

In Michigan, most charter schools are located in metropolitan areas, in districts where household incomes and standardized test scores are below the state average.[13] Charter schools enroll a larger percentage of minority students than does the public school system.[14] Charter schools attract students from neighboring public school districts, but also from private and parochial schools, from home schooling, and increasingly from other charter schools. Many charter schools in Michigan target niche markets. Some of these schools are organized around the ethnicity, language, and culture of specific groups of students, including Armenians, Arab Americans, African Americans, and Native Americans. Others focus on distinctive curricula, including Montessori, basic academic skills, vocational programs, and "traditional" values.

Under current policies, the number of charters that can be issued by public universities is limited to 150, with no more than half to be issued by any single university.[15] A substantial number of prospective charter school operators cannot open schools because of the cap, and the demand for educational alternatives among parents appears to be strong. Raising or removing the cap is consequently a priority for the governor and for the Republican leadership in the Michigan legislature. In November 1999, however, at the end of the legislative session, bipartisan opposition blocked the governor's proposal to raise the cap in the House of Representatives. Last-minute efforts to strike a bargain, either with African American Democrats from Detroit or with the eleven Republicans who opposed the bill, came to nothing. Following the November 2000 election, the party composition of the Michigan legislature remained virtually the same as before. Thus moves to raise the cap do not seem imminent.

The critical feature of the current debate on increasing the number of charter schools in Michigan is that it has come to turn on the question of how to ensure that the emerging market for schooling works efficiently and effectively. The legitimate presence of charter schools in the public school system is taken for granted by both sides. The point at issue is whether changes are needed in the state's policy framework to ensure that choice advances public instead of only private purposes. Those who oppose raising the cap declare that they are prepared to do so in exchange for increased oversight and accountability in charter schools. The governor and others who favor expanding the number of charter schools minimize the need for policy changes but nevertheless appear ready to bargain.

Interdistrict Choice

Compared with the emergence of charter schools, interdistrict choice in Michigan has been less controversial. The number of students who participate is smaller, and public school educators are more comfortable competing with one another than with independent charter schools. Controversy that has arisen originated mainly in fears about the flight of white or middle-class students from urban school districts and in reciprocal anxieties about the transfer of poor and black students to prosperous and mostly white suburbs.[16] The available data suggest that these fears are not ungrounded. The net flow of students under interdistrict choice policies is from districts with relatively low household incomes, relatively low standardized test scores, and relatively high enrollment of minority students to nearby districts where incomes and test scores are somewhat higher and the percentage of minority students is lower.[17]

Interdistrict choice is also a significant phenomenon in rural parts of Michigan, where school districts are large and the population is dispersed. In rural areas the number of students who move among districts is relatively small, but in many cases those who move represent a substantial share of total district enrollment. In combination with steady out-migration and declining birth rates, interdistrict choice has exacerbated the financial problems of rural school districts in the Upper Peninsula and elsewhere.

The legislature recently relaxed the boundary restrictions on interdistrict transfers to allow students to enroll in contiguous school districts outside their county of residence. Proposals that would permit students to transfer to any school district in the state have thus far been blocked, however. In many parts of the state, local school districts have sought ways to work together to manage the potentially disruptive consequences of household choice of schools.

Public Vouchers

The Michigan Constitution contains an ironclad prohibition against public funding for private or parochial schools. Voters added this provision to the constitution in the early 1970s, after the conclusion of an acrimonious campaign for "parochiaid." Providing public vouchers in Michigan would consequently require a constitutional amendment to remove this bar, which would have to be approved in a popular referendum.

A proposal to remove the bar, and to fund a voucher program in selected school districts, was defeated by Michigan voters in November 2000. The proposed ballot initiative would have removed language from the state constitution that prohibits public funding for private and religious schools. In addition, the initiative would have required the state to provide publicly funded vouchers worth up to half of the average per pupil capitation grant for students in districts where dropout rates exceed 33 percent. Other districts could have joined the voucher program on the basis of a vote by the school board or a popular referendum. The ballot language also required that per pupil state funding be maintained at present levels in all Michigan school districts.

The campaign to win approval of the voucher initiative was led by Richard DeVos, a powerful figure in the Republican Party in Michigan. Key supporters included the Catholic Church, the Chamber of Commerce, and some sections of the African American community in Detroit and other cities. Their campaign was vigorously opposed by organizations representing key constituencies in the public school system, including the teachers unions, the school boards association, and the Parent-Teacher Association, as well as by the American Civil Liberties Union. Opinion within the charter schools community was deeply divided over the issue of vouchers.

The prospects for winning approval for a constitutional amendment declined dramatically in September 1999, when Governor Engler declared himself opposed to the voucher initiative.[18] According to the governor, the Michigan initiative was "bad public policy," with "no chance of passing." The governor's early declarations that he did not support the initiative and would not sign a petition to put the measure on the ballot were followed by the announcement that he would "work to defeat" the initiative if it reached the ballot. In addition, Governor Engler prevented the Michigan Republican Party from endorsing the ballot initiative at its annual convention in 1999 by insisting that the party defer its endorsement until a commission that he appointed had studied the issue and made its report.

Explaining his opposition to the proposed ballot initiative, Governor Engler initially declared that it would undermine his administration's efforts to improve public schools through the introduction of reform initiatives including charter schools. He also expressed the view that the ballot initiative was so badly crafted that it would "set the cause of vouchers back ten years." The initiative was roundly defeated in the November 2000 election.

Political Impasse

The politics of school choice in Michigan cut across traditional political boundaries, dividing both Democrats and Republicans. Among Democrats, there is considerable support for choice among African Americans and Catholics, especially in metropolitan Detroit, while the labor unions and other core constituencies remain strongly committed to the traditional public school system. Among Republicans, the voucher initiative has placed Republican governor Engler at cross-purposes with the Chamber of Commerce and other groups with whom he has been closely aligned in the past. In addition, a significant group of moderates has broken with the governor and refused to remove the cap on the number of charters that can be granted by public universities.[19]

Current debates also reveal political divisions among the supporters of charter schools. On the one hand are those who see charter schools as a strategy for breaking down the public school monopoly and inaugurating a market-based educational system; on the other are those who see charters as a source of innovation and new energy that will ultimately make the public school system work better.[20] Because its members are divided on this question, the Michigan Association of Public School Academies—which represents the state's charter schools and advocates on their behalf—has not taken a position on vouchers. Governor Engler has based his opposition to vouchers partly on the argument that a campaign for vouchers will diminish support for charter schools and thereby undermine his efforts to improve public education.

These political divisions portend significant changes in the politics of school choice, both in Michigan and nationally. Republicans control all three branches of the Michigan government, and after a decade in office Governor Engler's mastery over the machinery of state government is virtually complete. Despite these advantages, however, profound disagreements within the party over both charter schools and vouchers have virtually halted efforts to further strengthen Michigan's choice policies. If the supporters of school choice cannot push through new policies under these circumstances, then expanding opportunities for choice in the future is likely to require different political strategies.

The New Politics of School Choice

The opponents of choice have exaggerated the dangers that providing parents with more educational alternatives pose for the traditional public school system. At the same time, the advocates of choice have been extravagant in their claims for what choice policies can deliver, thus overloading the political debate and leaving themselves vulnerable to empirical refutation.

Charter schools have been heralded as a means for improving educational performance. But when assessed using students' standardized test scores, no evidence suggests that charter schools are doing better than their traditional counterparts in the same districts.[21] In addition, charter schools have long been claimed to have both the incentives and the freedom to innovate with school management and pedagogy. However, a recent comparative assessment of innovation in charter schools and traditional public schools offers a serious challenge to this claim. Michael Mintrom reports that most innovative practices now in place in charter schools are not new to the broader education system in Michigan. Some charter schools are using old policies and practices in new ways, but many are using old approaches in old ways. Given this finding, Mintrom not surprisingly also found limited evidence of charter schools having any systematic "ripple effects," causing changes in the policies and practices of nearby traditional public schools.[22] While the presence of charter schools is definitely having some effect on the actions of nearby traditional public schools, the dynamics are complex and the outcomes indeterminate—some districts may be encouraged to improve, but others are launched on a terminal cycle of decline.[23]

The apparent benefits of school choice are yet to be realized in Michigan, and some of the gains promised by advocates of choice may be mutually incompatible. This might help explain why the evidence on apparent benefits is either nonexistent or muted at present. Choice is expected to simultaneously encourage accountability to centrally defined standards and to foster diversity and innovation among schools. It is expected to free parents to choose the schools that they believe are best for their children, while improving educational opportunities and outcomes for all children.

Choice makes some children better off, but at least potentially at the cost of making other children worse off. The policy debate has consequently tended to divide its attention between two different sets of children. Advocates have focused insistently on choosers, who were previously held captive in the public monopoly system and who are unarguably made better off if offered nontraditional choices. Opponents have focused single-mindedly on nonchoosers, who gain nothing from choice and may be made worse off by the departure of significant numbers of their fellow students.[24]

The policy framework established to govern choice (in Michigan, at least) has some significant flaws that require legislative remedy. For example, the funding system established by Proposal A makes it especially attractive for charter schools to educate the least costly and least difficult students, while leaving more costly students in the public school system. How this will improve the performance of public schools is not clear. Similarly, the rapid emergence of private, for-profit education management organizations (EMOs) in Michigan has raised questions about financial transparency in the management of charter schools, about the institutional autonomy and public accountability of "corporate" charter schools, and more generally about the appropriate boundary between private and public sectors in the education system. Policy debate is now beginning to focus on these issues of policy design, rather than simply pitting choice advocates against defenders of the traditional public school system.

The politics of school choice is thus at a turning point in Michigan. The movement to expand the choices available to parents has stalled, and reviving it is likely to require the advocates of choice to adopt a different rhetorical and political strategy than they have favored in the past. For one thing, the new politics of school choice will require a fuller acknowledgment and assessment of the positive and negative features of the emerging market for schooling and a less charged rhetorical stance. The anticipated benefits of introducing school choice and charter schools in Michigan can still be realized. To ensure this happens, however, more effort will need to go into thinking through issues of policy design. In particular, policymakers will need to move beyond ideological certainties and begin to design rules and central coordination mechanisms that raise the likelihood that market-like arrangements will generate the intended gains. These observations also suggest that building support for choice can no longer be accomplished on ideological grounds alone. It will require coalitional politics of a kind that the current generation of Republican leaders in Michigan is unused to practicing.

The most hopeful scenario for the medium-term future of school choice in Michigan is a thoughtful debate on the particular advantages and disadvantages of specific policies, with a corresponding assessment of the policy framework that now governs the emerging market for schooling, aimed at making the market work more efficiently and effectively. Such a debate may now be in prospect, as the advocates of expanded choice are increasingly obliged to build coalitions to support specific policy moves.

In considering how best to introduce policy innovations such as school choice, decisionmakers face a dilemma. On the one hand, potential problems can be avoided by the gradual introduction of a new program such as charter schools, as has been the case in many states (Minnesota and Colorado, for example). Initially, only a few charter schools were allowed in these states, but the numbers have been steadily increasing and, politically, the momentum for charter schools has steadily grown as well. This might be construed as a sound approach to policy implementation, because problems may be found and dealt with prior to widespread adoption. On the other hand, small-scale policy innovation reduces the potential for political support to build and leaves the new program vulnerable to strangulation.

In Michigan, the loathing of charter schools by powerful enemies, such as the Michigan Education Association, was palpable from the outset. Thus building a vibrant, politically strong charter school movement was a top priority for supporters of the innovation. Governor John Engler went to considerable effort to ensure that many charter schools were authorized and established, even while legislative efforts were made to remove constitutional anomalies from the authorizing legislation, and as constitutionality issues were debated by state circuit court and supreme court justices. While many might dispute the added value of some of the charter schools now operating, and others might wince at some of the stories of charter schools that opened their doors before they were ready, few will deny that these schools now represent a permanent addition to Michigan's education community.

The effort to rapidly introduce school choice and charter schools in Michigan had both positive and negative consequences. On the positive side, it decisively shifted the tenor of policy debate. Charter schools are now an established fact in Michigan, enrolling significant numbers of students and taken for granted as important players in education policy debates. Discussion focuses on the pace of future expansion and on modifications to the present policy framework, and not on whether charters should be part of the public school system. On the negative side, this political strategy risked the potential of fueling political controversy and the loss of momentum as the costs of expanding choice became more visible. We call this "policy blowback," and its significance in the charter school debate is steadily increasing in Michigan.

Policy blowback from the rapid expansion of charter schools features two main elements. The first is the sudden emergence of powerful and largely unexpected policy consequences, including the proliferation of for-profit management companies among charter schools and the potentially terminal decline of some public school districts that have lost large numbers of students to charter schools or to neighboring school districts. The second is wide variance among the more than 170 newly established charter schools, which increases the risk that some schools will perform poorly or fail.

The urgent question in Michigan is whether the momentum can be reversed or whether it has simply stalled. Private, for-profit education management organizations that had based their business strategies on continued expansion in Michigan may now be at risk, which could have a permanent depressing effect on future growth in the state's population of charter schools.

Conclusion

Many observers view recent school choice initiatives as clear evidence that a market for schooling is emerging and that the market's inexorable logic will have positive, transformative effects on public schooling. While appealing, this view is faulty primarily because it heavily discounts the ways that political dynamics so often serve to put the brakes on policy change.

Some thinking that has guided the development of Michigan's school choice policies, while not mistaken, might have been misguided. Some design choices have betrayed a naive faith in markets and an ideologically driven belief in the virtue of competition. Policymakers would do well to remember that even straightforward exemplars of market-based delivery of goods and services (for example, supermarkets and the airline industry) are affected on a day-to-day basis by a combination of private and governmentally devised policies and practices. Education is a more socially contingent product than most others. Thus the claim that the delivery of public education would necessarily be improved by placing it in the hands of private organizations should not go unchallenged.[25] The increasing presence of privately managed charter schools in the emerging market for schooling is likely to prompt further interest in using school choice and the private delivery of education services to transform public schooling. But, for now at least in Michigan, the rapid move toward the introduction of a broad system of public vouchers has run into major political problems. Further, these problems have not been caused simply by the opposition of those who from the outset could have been predicted to fight tooth-and-nail against market-like reform.

If occasional political impasses force both opponents and proponents of school choice to rethink their positions with the aid of both improved theory and careful analysis of relevant evidence, then this is surely a good thing. Policy design should be deeply informed by a clear understanding of what does and does not work in particular contexts. Recognizing that market processes and political processes are inextricably bound, future efforts to design the market for schooling must be more heavily informed by reflective political analysis than has been the case in the past.

Policy scholars and policymakers must think carefully about what set of institutional arrangements would strike the appropriate balance between harnessing private interests for public purposes and preserving a lively public space for democratic deliberation of how public policies can improve our lives. The debate over open enrollment plans, charter schools, and public vouchers provides an opportunity for—indeed, necessitates—serious thought about these broader issues of public sector management. Thus, aside from indicating that supporters of market-like approaches to educational delivery will need to rethink their coalition-building strategies, the new politics of school choice calls for renewed intellectual leadership on the part of policy scholars. Cheerleading for opponents or proponents of particular policy reforms has never been an especially laudable behavior on the part of academic researchers. They can do much better than that. Right now, a serious need exists for policy scholars to engage in sophisticated theorizing about the design of new institutions for the governance and delivery of public schooling. To date, work of this sort has been rudimentary at best, showing limited appreciation for the ways in which political practices shape policymaking and, in turn, how policy outcomes shape political practices. A need also exists for academic researchers to draw careful interpretations from the growing body of evidence on school choice and its consequences. The new politics of school choice will frustrate true believers who think they hold all the solutions to contemporary educational policy dilemmas. But for those with a more skeptical cast of mind this situation is genuinely exciting. Present conditions provide considerable scope for the advancement of theoretically driven, research-intensive policy learning.

Notes

1. Charles M. Tiebout, "A Pure Theory of Local Expenditures," *Journal of Political Economy*, vol. 64 (1956), pp. 416–24.

2. Ira Katznelson and Margaret Weir, *Schooling for All: Class, Race, and the Decline of the Democratic Ideal* (Basic Books, 1985).

3. Christopher Lasch, *The Revolt of the Elites and the Betrayal of Democracy* (W.W. Norton, 1995); and Robert Reich, *The Work of Nations: Preparing Ourselves for 21st Century Capitalism* (Knopf, 1991).

4. See David F. Labaree, *How to Succeed in School without Really Learning: The Credentials Race in American Education* (Yale University Press, 1997); and Nicholas Lemann, *The Big Test: The Secret History of the American Meritocracy* (Farrar Straus and Giroux, 1999).

5. See John D. Donahue, *The Privatization Decision: Public Ends, Private Means* (Basic Books, 1989); Harvey Feigenbaum, Jeffrey Henig, and Chris Hamnett, *Shrinking the State: The Political Underpinnings of Privatization* (New York: Cambridge University Press, 1998); Richard C. Hula, ed., *Market-Based Public Policy* (St. Martin's Press, 1988); and David Osbourne and Ted Gaebler, *Reinventing Government: How the Entrepreneurial Spirit Is Transforming the Public Sector* (Reading, Mass.: Addison-Wesley, 1993).

6. See Eric D. Hirsch, *The Schools We Need and Why We Don't Have Them* (Doubleday, 1996); National Commission on Excellence in Education, *A Nation at Risk* (U.S. Department of Education, 1983); and Harold W. Stevenson, *The Learning Gap: Why Our Schools Are Failing and What We Can Learn from Japanese and Chinese Education* (Summit Books, 1992).

7. See Michael Mintrom, *Policy Entrepreneurs and School Choice* (Georgetown University Press, 2000), for a detailed analysis of the rise of school choice in the United States.

8. See, for example, John E. Brandl, "Governance and Educational Quality," in Paul E. Peterson and Bryan C. Hassel, eds., *Learning from School Choice* (Brookings, 1998), pp. 55–81; John E. Chubb and Terry M. Moe, *Politics, Markets, and America's Schools* (Brookings, 1990); Milton Friedman, *Capitalism and Freedom* (University of Chicago Press, 1962); and Paul T. Hill, Lawrence C. Pierce, and James W. Guthrie, *Reinventing Public Education: How Contracting Can Transform America's Schools* (University of Chicago Press, 1997).

9. See David C. Berliner and Bruce J. Biddle, *The Manufactured Crisis: Myths, Fraud, and the Attack on America's Public Schools* (Reading, Mass.: Addison-Wesley, 1995); and Ernest R. House, *Schools for Sale: Why Free Market Policies Won't Improve America's Schools, and What Will* (New York: Teachers College Press, 1998).

10. Arizona and California each have more charter schools in place than Michigan.

11. A detailed analysis of these changes to Michigan's system of educational finance is provided by Sandra Vergari, "School Finance Reform in the State of Michigan," *Journal of Education Finance*, vol. 21 (1995), pp. 254–70.

12. David Arsen, David N. Plank, and Gary Sykes, *School Choice Policies in Michigan: The Rules Matter* (Michigan State University, 1999).

13. Arsen, Plank, and Sykes, *School Choice Policies in Michigan*.

14. Jerry Horn and Gary Miron, *Evaluation of the Michigan Public School Academy Initiative* (Western Michigan University, The Evaluation Center, 1999); and Public Sector Consultants and Maximus, *Michigan's Charter School Initiative: From Theory to Practice* (Lansing, Mich.: Public Sector Consultants, 1999).

15. The number of charters that may be issued by public school districts and community colleges is not capped, but the number that these agencies have issued is relatively small.

16. The superintendent of a wealthy suburban district reports that his district has benefited financially from interdistrict transfers, but "we're worried that it's going to hurt our MEAP [Michigan Educational Assessment Program; that is, standardized test] scores," which are among the highest in the state. Another suburban superintendent worried publicly that too many interdistrict transfers would "change the complexion" of her district.

17. Arsen, Plank, and Sykes, *School Choice Policies in Michigan*.

18. He subsequently allowed some prominent Republicans, including his lieutenant governor, to support the proposal publicly.

19. Most members of this group were endorsed and supported in the last election by the Michigan Education Association, the state's main teachers union. In addition,

many of these Republicans opposing the expansion of the charter schools movement represent suburban school districts with excellent public schools, whose citizens have little to gain from expanded school choice policies.

20. For more discussion of the potential that exists for differences to emerge among supporters of charter schools, see Amy Stuart Wells, Cynthia Grutzik, Sibyll Carnochan, Julie Slayton, and Ash Vasudeva, "Underlying Policy Assumptions of Charter School Reform: The Multiple Meanings of a Movement," *Teachers College Record*, vol. 100 (1999) pp. 513–35.

21. For evidence from Michigan, see two evaluation reports commissioned by the legislature: Jerry Horn and Gary Miron, *An Evaluation of the Michigan Charter School Initiative: Performance, Accountability, and Impact* (Western Michigan University, The Evaluation Center, July 2000); and Robert Kleine, Colleen Scott, and Richard White, *Issues in Michigan's Public School Academy Initiative, Phase II* (Lansing, Mich.: Public Sector Consultants, July 2000).

22. Michael Mintrom, *Leveraging Local Innovation: The Case of Michigan's Charter Schools* (Michigan State University, 2000). The main findings of this report are also available in Michael Mintrom, "Policy Design for Local Innovation: The Effects of Competition in Public Schooling," *State Politics and Policy Quarterly*, vol. 1 (2001) pp. 343–63.

23. Arsen, Plank, and Sykes, *School Choice Policies in Michigan*.

24. This point has been made by Varun Gauri in *School Choice in Chile: Two Decades of Educational Reform* (University of Pittsburgh Press, 1999).

25. Problems of opportunism and regulatory costs can erode potential distinctions in the cost-effectiveness of for-profit, nonprofit, and publicly provided schools. See Byron W. Brown, "Why Governments Run Schools." *Economics of Education Review*, vol. 11 (1992) pp. 287–300.

4

Lessons from New Zealand

EDWARD B. FISKE AND
HELEN F. LADD

The rapid expansion of the charter school movement in the United States during the 1990s was impressive. At the beginning of the decade, no state had laws enabling charter schools; by the end of the decade, thirty-four states had such statutes and more than 1,700 charter schools were operating. Public support was extensive in many states, and enthusiasm for the idea extended to the Clinton administration, which made promotion of charter schools part of its educational policy.

Various studies have provided useful information about the politics that shaped charter school laws, how charters work in practice, and key policy issues that surround them, such as accountability, funding, and equity.[1] Nevertheless, understanding of the movement and its likely impact on education in the United States is still limited. Many advocates of charter schools support them not only because of the benefits they might bestow on children who enroll in these educational alternatives but also because of the potential improvement in the traditional public school system they might promote. Such improvement would occur if the charter schools served as laboratories for innovative ideas that were then transferred to the public schools or if they provided sufficient competition to the public schools to induce them to increase the quality of education they offer. Other advocates have even more ambitious hopes for the movement and look forward to a time when the traditional public school system is replaced by a whole system of charter schools.[2]

We use New Zealand's ten-year experience with self-governing schools and parental choice to provide a different perspective on certain aspects of the U.S. charter school movement. In particular, we use that experience to offer some observations about the desirable scale of the movement, how to organize access to charter schools, and how to hold such schools accountable to the public. The analysis draws heavily on our book *When Schools Compete: A Cautionary Tale.*[3]

New Zealand differs from the United States in that it is a country of only 3.8 million people—and one where sheep outnumber people by more than twelve to one. However, its population is the same as that of the median American state, which makes the New Zealand Ministry of Education the functional equivalent of a state department of education in the decentralized U.S. system. In addition, New Zealand has similar social, cultural, and political traditions, and, perhaps most important, it has a significant minority population, notably Maori (14 percent) and Pacific Islanders (6 percent). The urgent educational and other problems faced by urban Maori and Pacific Islanders are similar to those faced by minorities in the United States.

New Zealand Education Reforms

In 1989, under a plan known as Tomorrow's Schools, New Zealand abolished its national Department of Education, which had overseen state schools for decades, and turned control of its nearly 2,700 primary and secondary schools over to locally elected boards of trustees.[4] Virtually overnight, legal responsibility for governing and managing New Zealand's state schools shifted from professional bureaucrats to boards dominated by lay volunteers, and one of the world's most tightly controlled public education systems became one of the most decentralized. The Labour Government in power at the time also installed new systems for financing state schools and holding them accountable, and it replaced the department with a much smaller Ministry of Education charged primarily with making policy recommendations instead of running schools.[5]

Two years later New Zealand ratcheted the stakes of school reform up another notch. A newly elected National Government committed to New Right social principles abolished neighborhood enrollment zones and gave parents the right to choose which schools their children would attend. Primary and secondary schools found themselves competing for students against other schools in an educational marketplace. Public relations and marketing skills became as integral to the job description of principals as knowledge of curriculum and the ability to manage a faculty.

Under the reformed system, each school is run by a board of trustees elected at the school level, and each has a charter. The boards are controlled by parents and have the authority to hire and fire the principal and the teachers and to allocate funds received from the state. In the spirit of self-governance, schools that are at capacity are given the authority to set their own enrollment policies regarding which students they will accept.

The government provides each school with an operations grant, much of which is distributed on a per pupil basis, plus an entitlement of a specific number of teachers. The teacher entitlement reflects the government's policy decisions about appropriate teacher-pupil ratios by grade level and varies by school in line with the number of students in each grade. Schools hire their own teachers and allocate them among classes as they see fit. To the distress of some proponents of the reforms, salary schedules continue to be centrally determined, and in most schools teachers continue to be paid directly by the government. Some schools, however, responded favorably to financial sweeteners offered by the Ministry to switch to a system of bulk funding of salaries in which the school receives a block grant to be used for teacher salaries.

Comparisons to the U.S. Charter School Movement

The educational system established by the Tomorrow's School reforms in New Zealand bears some striking similarities to the U.S. charter school phenomenon. Each school is self-governing and therefore, in principle, free to innovate and to respond to its local community. It receives funding from the government that varies directly with the number of students in the school and, through its charter, specifies its mission and objectives. However, there are also some significant differences.

Most important, all New Zealand schools now have charters and operate with a high level of operational autonomy. This situation contrasts with the United States, where charter schools constitute a small minority of all schools and operate on the fringes of the various state educational systems. Second, and closely related, the Tomorrow's Schools reforms forced all schools to become self-governing regardless of whether they wanted to do so or had the demonstrated capacity to take on this responsibility. Significantly, elected members of school boards in New Zealand do not usually come together around the sort of common educational vision that would characterize the founding boards of most charter schools in the United States.

Another difference is that in New Zealand the boards of individual schools have not had to deal with the capital funding challenge faced by many charter schools in the United States. Because New Zealand's schools converted from existing public schools, the facilities were already there and the government retained ownership of them. In that sense the New Zealand schools are comparable to the two-fifths of U.S charter schools that were converted from public or private schools. In the United States any charter school that starts from scratch faces the serious challenge of generating the capital funds needed to establish a new school.

Because of these differences it would not be accurate to characterize the reformed New Zealand system as a whole country of charter schools. Nevertheless, sufficient parallels exist to ask what insights Tomorrow's Schools might offer proponents and critics alike of charter schools in the United States and elsewhere. In particular, the evidence from New Zealand provides some important lessons for the U.S. charter school movement about innovation and diversity, equality of access and accountability.

Freedom to Innovate and to Respond to Community Preferences

Although the Tomorrow's Schools reforms did introduce some diversity into the educational offerings of the New Zealand school system, innovation has been limited. Several factors account for this outcome. The main one is that the incentive system of the competitive model established in New Zealand does not encourage boards and principals of existing schools to look for niche markets. The strategic objective is to maximize roll numbers—at least up to the school's capacity—and thereby to maximize funding, which is closely tied to enrollment, and then, when capacity is reached, to gain control of the mix of students. As a result, boards turned out to be more interested in offering broad traditional programs aimed at attracting as many students as possible than in designing a program targeted to particular types of students and families.

Another reason is that establishing a school from scratch requires significant capital. It is not coincidental that the best example of such a start-up, the Hutt International Boys School near Wellington, serves a prosperous clientele. Other groups interested in starting new schools were not likely to have access to the necessary resources.

Finally, the limited amount of diversity in educational offerings can be attributed in part to the quick reassertion of the state's role. The original architects of the New Zealand reforms envisioned that each school would have its own unique educational vision and objectives. However, as the reforms proceeded it soon became clear that while the government was happy to encourage local school communities to develop some of their own local educational goals, such local goals would be secondary to those imposed from the center. The story of this shift in New Zealand thinking is instructive.

The Controversy over Charters

The concept of school charters took center stage in the 1988 report of the Picot Task Force that provided the blueprint for the initial reform effort. That report describes the local charters as the "lynchpin" of the new structure of compulsory education. Charters would provide each school with "clear and explicit objectives" reflecting "both national requirements and local needs." They would constitute a "contract between the community and the institution, and the institution and the state."[6] Under this three-way contract the various parties would have different responsibilities but would relate as equals. The state would fund schools and provide national guidelines, while boards of trustees would make local policies and run the schools in line with community interests.

Given the importance of contractual relationships to other parts of the public sector reform efforts in New Zealand at that time, the government policy paper that evolved from the task force report not surprisingly maintained the language of the three-way contract.[7] But the wording glossed over some built-in ambiguities and tensions. With primary and secondary education compulsory, how much control over missions should the state cede to schools? Could the charter ever be a contract in the sense of imposing enforceable responsibilities and obligations on all parties? If so, how would it be enforced? Could the government commit itself to provide sufficient funding for a school to achieve the objectives in the charter? Working out such details was the task of an implementation group, which circulated a draft framework for charters in March and a final version in May 1989. These documents addressed the ambiguities by substantially altering the design laid out in the earlier documents.

The March draft clearly stated that local school communities (that is, parents connected with the school) would have little or no say over about 80 percent of the contents of the school charter because, to protect the government's interest in educational outcomes, the government was planning to require that every charter include a commitment to the National Educational Guidelines.[8] The May 1989 framework further weakened the power of parents by changing the three-way contract to a bilateral agreement between a school's Board of Trustees and the minister of education, leaving no formal governance role for the local community in the form of obligatory opportunities for parental input.

Partly out of concern about the Ministry's insufficient capacity to negotiate and approve 2,700 new charters in a short period of time, and partly because the Picot Task Force had overestimated the ability of local boards to develop meaningful charters that were explicit enough to be used as accountability documents, the charter framework was further modified in January 1990. First, the relationship between the two parties, downgraded to an "agreement" in the May 1989 document, was further redefined as an "undertaking." Second, the new document removed the Ministry's legal obligation to provide adequate funding to schools, thus turning the former partnership into what amounted to a one-way obligation of boards to the state. A subsequent final change acknowledged that schools might not have adequate funding to achieve the goals and objectives of their charters and hence altered the language to require only that the schools make reasonable efforts to do so with the resources available to them.

Thus in a few months the charter went from being a three-way contract or partnership to a two-way "agreement" to a one-way "undertaking." As Liz Gordon, an academic critic who subsequently became a member of Parliament as part of the small left-wing Alliance Party, wrote shortly afterwards, "The state had taken the first step in regaining the power that had been given away in the Picot Report."[9] The ground had been laid for moving from a system in which communities worked alongside central authorities to set and implement goals for state schools to one in which boards of trustees essentially acted as agents in carrying out purposes established by the state. "This principal-agent relationship clearly lies at the heart of the charter changes announced in January 1990," wrote Gordon, "and is a marked departure from the model of community power that constituted one of the central principles of the educational reforms."[10] As a result, school communities played a smaller role in the charter development process than had been envisioned and the content of charters was homogenized. Charters have not become the force for innovation and quality within the schools that reformers anticipated.

Lessons for the U.S. Charter School Movement

The New Zealand experience demonstrates that governments have a clear interest in assuring that their own national (or state) purposes will be served and that they will use their powers of funding and accountability to vigorously assert this interest. This point may help explain the existence of many "weak" charter school laws in the United States; that is, laws that provide little freedom for charter schools to operate differently from traditional public schools.

The New Zealand experience also suggests that, as charter schools proliferate, state governments or other authorizing agencies may find it difficult to carry out that obligation without imposing greater limits and uniformity on the schools. In a related context, some proponents of permitting the use of vouchers for religious schools in the United States have warned about the possibility that this could lead to greater government regulation of such schools. The evolution of the Tomorrow's Schools reforms suggests that such fears are justified.[11] We would, however, be more inclined to emphasize the other side of the coin, namely, that the state has an obligation to assure that alternative schools are spending public tax dollars in a responsible way.

For charters to fulfill their function as a spur to innovation, it is thus probably best that they not become the norm. When charter schools are limited in number, they can be given the flexibility to be innovative, to offer alternative educational environments, and to take risks. Some new schools will be successful; others will not. The risks to the public or to individual children of such schools are not large when there are only a few of them because the government can assure that if a school does not meet the needs of a particular child, that child will have a guaranteed place in a traditional public school over which the government has direct operational control. Such a guarantee would seem to be important in a compulsory education system.

If charter schools operate on the fringes of the state system, chartering agencies can, in principle, assure that the founders of each school have the managerial capacity, fiscal responsibility, and educational experience to have a reasonable chance of succeeding while resisting the temptation to engage in the sort of heavy-handed regulation that would defeat the reasons for establishing charter schools in the first place.

Assuring Fair Access

Another consideration related to defining the appropriate scale of the charter school sector emerges from the interaction of self-governing schools with parental choice. The initial New Zealand reformers embraced self-governing schools primarily as a way to strengthen the collective voice of parents through the vehicle of elected boards of trustees in the schools to which their children were assigned and not so much to enhance the range of schooling options available to children. Not until the conservative National Party gained power and introduced full parental choice in 1991 was the concept of self-governing schools combined with parental choice.

American charter schools are choice schools. That is, families are in principle free to choose whether to send their children to any particular charter school. In terms of admissions restrictions that the schools may impose, federal civil rights laws prohibit charter schools from discriminating among students on the basis of certain protected characteristics such as race, sex, or disability, and many state laws include the same prohibition. Some state laws go further and explicitly prohibit charter schools from discriminating among students based on their intellectual or athletic ability. However, several state laws do allow schools to set admissions criteria that relate to the mission of the school and that give preference to certain groups of students, such as siblings of enrolled students or local residents.[12] Many charter schools enjoy significant leeway in selecting their students, and in some cases their selection criteria may work to the detriment of students from disadvantaged families. For example, some charter schools in California require firm commitments from parents about becoming involved in the school, commitments that some groups of parents may not be in a position to make.[13]

In principle, as part of the public school system, charter schools should be equally accessible to all students. To achieve this end, most charter school proponents argue that oversubscribed charter schools should be required to allocate their scarce spaces among applicants using a random lottery process. At least one scholar—Bryan C. Hassel—cites that requirement as a defining characteristic of the charter school phenomenon that distinguishes it from voucher systems. Private schools using vouchers, he maintains, would not face such constraints.[14]

Potential Magnitude of the Allocation Challenge

Although we have no way of knowing how a significant expansion of charter schools would play out in any particular U.S. state, the Tomorrow's Schools reform process offers lessons regarding the magnitude of the potential allocation challenge. Elsewhere we have documented the large shifts in enrollment patterns that accompanied the introduction of full parental choice in New Zealand.[15] In each of the three urban areas on which we focused our analysis we found a tendency for parents, including parents of minority students, to move their children from schools serving large concentrations of disadvantaged and minority students to schools serving more advantaged students. Because the New Zealand government owned the schools and was reluctant to bear the cost of expanding or replicating the popular schools as long as there were openings in the unpopular schools, the most popular schools quickly reached their physical capacity. In the spirit of local self-governance, New Zealand dealt with the oversubscription problem by allowing the schools that had reached capacity to establish their own enrollment policies and, thus, to play a large role in determining which students would attend the school.

As of 1997, over 50 percent of the primary students were enrolled in oversubscribed schools in Auckland and Christchurch, and about 24 percent of the students were in such schools in the slower growing Wellington area. The percentages were even larger for secondary school students. Over 60 percent of such students were in schools with enrollment schemes in both Auckland and Christchurch.[16] Thus the system of parental choice was quickly transformed into one in which schools do much of the choosing.

In practice, the prevalence of oversubscribed schools will vary with the amount of initial overcapacity of schools (there was more initial capacity in Wellington than in Auckland or Christchurch) and in the distribution of parental preferences among schools. For example, a school system that offers a wide range of educational choices to a population that places a high value on diversity could conceivably end up with relatively few oversubscribed schools as parents distribute their children evenly among schools. Such was not the situation in New Zealand, where preferences appeared to be single-dimensional and where the diversity of educational offerings was not extensive. While some people might argue that preferences are likely to be less single-dimensional in the United States, data on parental preferences from Cambridge, Massachusetts, collected in connection with that city's controlled choice program, clearly indicate that that some schools are much more popular than others.[17] Hence, we have no reason to believe the problems associated with oversubscription are unique to New Zealand.

Policy Options for Allocating Spaces in Oversubscribed Schools

Given that any system that involves parental choice of schools is likely to result in oversubscribed schools, the question becomes one of how to allocate the scarce spaces.

NEW ZEALAND'S SOLUTION TO OVERSUBSCRIBED SCHOOLS. New Zealand's decision to let oversubscribed schools have enrollment schemes over which the Ministry exerted no control was consistent with that country's model of self-governing schools. While the power for schools to choose their students could be desirable and productive to the extent that it generates a better match between the school offerings and student preferences, in practice it is undesirable because of its distributional effects. Disadvantaged students are adversely affected by the fact that the number of schools available to them is limited. In addition, New Zealand's approach favors the schools with enrollment schemes by permitting them to offer coherent and well-defined education programs to targeted groups of students.

Another downside of New Zealand's approach is that some parents may not be able to find schools for their children within reasonable commuting distance of where they live. This problem turned out to be especially acute in heavily populated and fast-growing Auckland, where students would sometimes have to travel past several schools before arriving at one willing to accept them.

By 1999, the practical problems created by enrollment schemes became so problematic that Parliament changed the law to require approval of school schemes by the Ministry of Education. Moreover, the Ministry will now grant this approval only if the proposed scheme has been worked out in consultation with parents, the community, and other schools likely to be affected by it. Satisfactory enrollment schemes must now take into account students' desire to attend a "reasonably convenient" school, a provision that includes students who arrive during the school year. Under the new arrangement, parents are still free to shop among schools, but they will be assured that the school in their locale will be available to their children. In effect, the government has now partially restored residential zoning as the basis of enrollment policy.

STRATEGIES FOR AVOIDING THE SHIFT FROM PARENTAL CHOICE TO SCHOOL CHOICE. New Zealand's solution of allowing oversubscribed schools to decide whom to admit is only one of several alternatives available to policymakers. For those who are committed to giving parents more control over which schools their children will attend but who also believe that this right should extend equally to all parents, the key question becomes: How can control of the process be kept from shifting from parents to schools? Several options have been discussed in New Zealand.

Require that schools accept everyone who applies. Such an approach would initially lead to overcrowded schools and the need either to expand capacity in such schools or to find informal ways of discouraging large numbers of students from attending particular schools. Expanding capacity to meet market demand would be expensive, wasteful, and impractical because the capital costs of expansion are not trivial and are hard to justify when there is excess capacity elsewhere.

Require random balloting. Employing a random balloting process to decide who will be able to attend oversubscribed schools has obvious appeal. Such a method is transparent and seems fair in that it appears to give equal opportunity to all parents. Random selection through balloting, however, is not free from problems, particularly when applied to a system in which all students—or at least a large proportion—are choosing schools and when all schools are essentially choice schools, as became true in New Zealand after 1991.

Consider, for example, the Auckland area in which some of the fast-growing suburbs have an abundance of students, many of whom might be interested in competing for several of the best schools. Assuming the process of matching students and schools was implemented at the school level, the process could end up being time-consuming and wasteful. Would students have to apply to many schools to assure acceptance by at least one school? As a school implemented its random selection process, how would it determine how many students to accept given that it would not be able to predict how many of the students it accepted would enroll? If the selection were implemented centrally instead of at the school level, some of the alleged benefits of school choice might be lost. That would be the case if unpopular schools were assigned a full allotment of students.

Implement some form of managed or controlled choice. Managed or controlled choice is a logical extension of the centralized random balloting approach but differs in that it would require some conscious balancing of competing interests. Under this approach, students and families would specify their preferences, and district officials would make student assignments using a formula that balanced the preferences of families against the interests of other students and the community as a whole. These community interests might vary from place to place. Some communities, for example, might deem it crucial to maintain ethnic or racial or socioeconomic balance among schools. That was the community interest, for example, in the development of one of the best-known programs of controlled choice, that of Cambridge, Massachusetts. Alternatively, or in addition, a community might place weight on maximizing the use of the existing facilities or resources. For example, it might want to assure that the schools that offer Japanese language and culture programs are allocated enough students with those interests to make the programs viable.

Controlled choice, however, brings its own set of requirements and trade-offs. The requirements for a fair system of controlled choice have been laid out elsewhere.[18] A well-designed system of controlled choice would maintain many of the benefits that choice offers to students and parents as educational consumers. However, it could also undermine some alleged benefits of choice because unpopular schools would not lose as many students as they would under an unmanaged system.

The bottom line is that it is impossible to sustain a system in which all parents are completely free to select the schools their children will attend.

Some mechanism must be devised for rationing places in popular schools, and this will inevitably involve constraints on choice. The challenges are to keep the constraints from falling disproportionately on students from disadvantaged families, as is likely to occur when schools can select their students, and to implement the system in a way that appropriately balances the interests of competing groups.

Lessons for the Charter School Movement

The implications for the charter school movement should be clear. Introduction of parental choice and the fact that this will inevitably lead to oversubscribed schools raise significant issues of fairness. As long as charter schools are relatively few in number, fairness can be assured by requiring schools to allocate their scarce places through some form of random balloting. If charter schools were to become the norm, however, assuring fair access would become a problem. Because balloting may not work well for a whole system of schools, some form of controlled or managed choice would most likely have to be introduced, a move that could undermine in various ways the intent of the charter school movement. Thus we conclude that U.S. charter schools are likely to better serve the goal of diversity and innovation in a fair way if they remain limited in number and do not become the norm.

Accountability for Charter Schools

Although general agreement exists in the United States about the importance of holding charter schools accountable for results, a good deal of uncertainty remains about how well states can or will succeed in doing so. Scholars on both sides of the charter school debate have looked at accountability and found it wanting.[19] The power to revoke school charters is available and has been used in a few cases on grounds of financial mismanagement and educational inadequacies, but it is likely to be too crude a tool for true accountability. Charter documents are often too vague to serve as the basis for charter revocation, and states frequently have no good means of holding their regular public schools, much less their charter schools, accountable for performance. Even in states with sophisticated test-based accountability systems for all their schools, authorities cannot use the system to make decisions about charter renewals or about major interventions unless they are willing to specify up front clear standards for such renewal, something that no state has yet done.

Even more so than in the U.S. charter school movement, accountability to the public was a central element of the New Zealand reform. The idea was to move toward a tight-loose-tight governance system—one in which the missions of the schools were clear (the first tight), the schools would be free to operate with autonomy and flexibility (the loose part), and schools would be held accountable (the second tight). The centrality of accountability to the New Zealand reform makes it a source of potential lessons for the U.S. charter school movement.

How Accountability Works in New Zealand

Given its roots in the British education system with its long tradition of school inspectors, New Zealand opted for an inspectorate model for holding its newly self-governing schools accountable. For this purpose, the initial reform legislation established a new agency, the Education Review Office (ERO), that would be independent of the Ministry of Education and charged with monitoring the schools.[20] The main function of the agency was to provide an independent and arm's-length evaluation at least every two years of how well each school was performing. To that end, the ERO sends a review team made up of former teachers to each school. The teams, which have from two to five members, visit classes, pore over school documents and records, discuss draft reports with the schools, and issue final public reports laying out both the school's strengths and any deficiencies that need to be addressed. Significantly, the ERO has no enforcement authority. Although the ERO got off to a halting start, the agency gained respect and credibility after the 1991 appointment of a strong and effective new chief review officer, Judith Aitken.

Because the original 1989 reforms did not include parental choice, the concept of market accountability did not emerge until 1991. The introduction of that form of accountability has not challenged the government's view that some form of accountability to the public, not just to parents, is still needed.

The inspectorate system has in general worked reasonably well in New Zealand. It is effective in part because of its independence from the Ministry of Education. In addition, it has credibility because of the high quality of the professionals on its staff and because of its strong leadership. However, a number of issues and concerns have arisen over the years.

Focus on Processes versus Outcomes

The intent of the reformers was for the ERO to monitor how well each school was meeting the "clear and specific aims and objectives, expressed as outcomes" included in each school's charter.[21] However, the charter failed to emerge as the definitive document envisioned by members of the task force.

As a result the ERO had to determine for itself what it should be monitoring. Aitken's solution was to introduce two distinct types of audit: assurance and effectiveness. The assurance audits, which began in 1992, were designed to verify that the boards of trustees were meeting their legal obligations to the Crown as specified in the schools' charter, including adherence to the National Education Guidelines, and that they were fulfilling other agreements between the state and the schools, such as the schools' property agreement.[22] In retrospect, such audits clearly were necessary, especially during the start-up period. During 1992–93, only 12 percent of the boards of trustees were operating in a fully lawful way. By 1998, the proportion was up to 90 percent.

In 1993 the ERO added the second type of audit—the effectiveness audit—to its arsenal as a means of shifting attention toward student achievement. Because New Zealand has no national compulsory tests, the ERO has no good way to compare student achievement in one school either with that of other schools or with national standards. Instead, effectiveness audits are primarily process-oriented and pose two specific questions to local boards of trustees: What do they expect the children in the school to learn? And how will they know that learning has occurred?[23]

Despite this effort to focus more on educational outcomes, the ERO has been criticized for directing attention to administrative and educational processes instead of student outcomes. To be sure, some of the processes are related to outcomes, such as whether the curriculum is being delivered and whether boards of trustees have any way of knowing what the students are learning. Nonetheless, the reviews often became mechanistic, were heavily focused on management procedures, and did not necessarily foster better educational outcomes. Moreover, the ERO provided no evidence in support of its general view that "the quality of school governance and management is a reliable indicator of the quality of educational service provided."[24] At the same time, the reviews were undoubtedly useful to many schools. A 1999 survey of primary schools, for example, indicated that 56 percent of the principals found them helpful and another 21 percent very helpful. In addition, most (72 percent) of the schools made minor changes as a result of the review, and 13 percent made major changes, mainly in the areas of assessment, curriculum, and performance management.[25]

Most people, including Judith Aitken of the ERO, acknowledge that the absence of compulsory national tests hinders the accountability process. At the same time, New Zealanders have some serious concerns about introducing such tests. They fear that they will narrow the curriculum and that they will be misused by both the ERO and the public in evaluating schools. The concern about misuse springs from the observation that average test scores across schools are highly correlated with the socioeconomic mix of students in the school. Unless sufficient testing is done to permit value-added calculations or comparisons are made only between schools with a comparable mix of students, test results may provide misleading information on a school's effectiveness. Efforts by the government in 1999 to introduce national tests at the elementary school-level ran into political obstacles and in 2000 were being introduced only on a pilot basis.

Even if national test results were available, a strong case can still be made for the inspectorate model. One reason for this is that the concepts of outcomes and school processes may not be as distinct as the tight-loose-tight governance structure would require. The public has an interest in assuring good processes as well as good outcomes and in strengthening the links between the two. For example, although a healthy and safe school environment is not a measure of educational outcomes, it is of considerable importance to the public. In addition, the public has an interest in assuring that a school is complying with the terms of its charter.[26] Is it offering the type of instruction specified in the agreement? Is it able to assemble the appropriate staff? Are its interactions with parents consistent with the agreement?

While part of the challenge for the U.S. charter school movement is to make sure that the chartering agencies are vigilant in assuring that prospective charter schools have adequate managerial capacity, that by itself is not sufficient. Inexperience in running a school, or changes in school leadership or personnel, could lead to managerial and process deficiencies that are best identified by an external monitor. Ideally such a review agency would pay attention both to educational processes and to student outcomes, and it would take heed of those outcomes that are measured by government-mandated student tests and of those specified by the local school community through its board of trustees. Thus we believe that the New Zealand review agency (or the relatively comparable English agency, Office for Standards in Education) provides a useful model for an external monitoring agency for U.S. charter schools.[27]

The Limits of Arm's-Length Accountability

Before the Tomorrow's Schools reforms, schools in New Zealand were accustomed to visits from school inspectors, most of whom were former teachers, with whom the schools developed close relationships.

In contrast, the new agency's sole function was to provide an arm's-length evaluation of how well the schools were performing. In recommending such a setup, the task force in effect abandoned a professional model of accountability aimed primarily at helping teachers deal with the teaching and learning process. Instead, it opted for a more management-oriented model that would minimize the possibility of monitors being unduly influenced—critics use the term "captured"—by the groups they were evaluating. Under the management approach, the focus is on good management practices. The major purposes are to inform boards of trustees about how well they are doing, to provide the government with information on the performance of schools, and to make information available to groups outside the system.[28]

Consistent with this arm's-length managerial approach, a recent study found that 75 percent of primary school principals viewed ERO team members as either reasonably or highly professional, yet only 32 percent felt that the review team had sufficient understanding of the particular needs of their school. A general view among teachers and principals seems to be that ERO reports are not particularly helpful on important issues relating to teaching and learning.[29]

In addition, school officials in New Zealand complain about the absence of advice and counseling in the new system. In partial recognition of this shortcoming, a recent review of the Education Review Office recommended that, as a normal part of its reporting procedure, the ERO include a section on the sources of advice and guidance available in the local area. More significantly, it recommended that the Ministry of Education "establish a range of actions to assist schools where action is required to improve the management and delivery of education."[30]

Arm's-length accountability by an outside agency minimizes the problem of provider capture but does not by itself offer the support that some schools may need to correct their deficiencies. The lesson from New Zealand for charter schools is that both functions—external monitoring and school support—are important and that separate institutions need to be in place to accomplish both of them. However, while a public agency must assume direct responsibility for the monitoring function, the support functions could be provided by one or more outside agencies, either nonprofit or profit-making. The government's role is to assure that such support is available to all schools.

Public Information as a Policy Lever

One of the first changes that Judith Aitken brought about when she assumed leadership of the ERO was to make all of its reports public and to encourage the local newspapers and television stations to publicize them. Given that the ERO had no enforcement power, she viewed public information as the main policy tool available to her to induce the schools to improve. Schools would be more apt to try to assure positive ERO reports, she reasoned, if they knew that they were going to be affected by what the reports said. For ambitious principals and teachers, being at a school with positive ERO reports has major benefits. It could have a big impact on how attractive the school is to potential students and their parents.

One problem with this approach is that negative publicity can be unfair. To the extent that the reports focus on the symptoms of much larger problems outside the control of the schools, they may do a disservice to the school community. That helps explain the tremendous collective anger of the South Auckland principals at the release of a major ERO report that summarized the problems of a whole group of struggling schools in the low-income area of South Auckland. The principals argued that their failure as measured by market criteria was largely due to factors beyond their control, a judgment with which a number of outside academic experts would concur.[31] The principals also argued that follow-up reports by ERO on troubled schools tended to stress continuing deficiencies while minimizing steps that had been taken to deal with them.

Two recent reviews of the ERO came to opposite conclusions about the relative benefits and costs of the use of public information as a policy lever. One report commissioned by the teachers union highlighted the concerns of teachers that media reporting tends to be fragmentary, negative in tone, and "crisis-oriented." It argued that public reports on failing schools, many of which serve disadvantaged students, are likely to exacerbate the departure of students from such schools, thereby compounding their problems.[32]

The second report, an official review of the ERO, fully endorsed the agency's legal obligation to make all final reports available to the media and suggested procedural changes designed to minimize adverse effects of the sort that have occurred in the past. These changes would include a longer time for schools to respond to the initial report so that they can be ready with action plans to address the report's recommendations. The final version would include not only schools' action plans, but also an introduction prepared by the schools describing the context in which they operate, brief details of significant achievements since the last review, and issues on which the schools were working.

With respect to U.S. charter schools, we would support having the media publicize any official evaluations but with the provisos just mentioned. It is hard to argue against public reports given the public funding involved. However, care should be taken that the reports maximize the chances that the schools will improve.

Tensions between Providing General Guidance and Promoting Innovation

Under Judith Aitken, the Educational Review Office has also come to see itself as the provider of general information on education to help schools do their jobs more effectively. It uses the information it gleans from its individual school reports to distill what works and what does not work in the teaching and learning process. Some of its periodic reports were written for principals and teachers and for members of boards of trustees who must oversee them (*Professional Leadership in Primary Schools, Core Competencies for School Principals,* and *The Capable Teacher*). Others were addressed to parents (*Choosing a School for a Five-Year-Old* and *Choosing a Secondary School*), while still others were focused on general issues related to teaching and learning (*Addressing Barriers to Learning* and *Students at Risk*). All are public documents available on the Internet.

The official review of the ERO in 1997 praised these publications and reported that they are highly regarded and seen as helpful in describing best practice and in generating debate on a variety of issues.[33] An alternative perspective on these reports criticizes the ERO for promoting a "good practice" model of schooling that may encourage complacency instead of a "best practice" model that would stimulate pedagogical innovation.[34] These two viewpoints highlight one of the tensions that inevitably arises in a decentralized system. On the one hand, the government says it wants the schools to be innovative and creative. On the other, many schools could undoubtedly benefit from some guidance about what approaches might make sense. The danger is that, in providing that guidance, the government may be thwarting innovation by sending signals about what it expects the schools to do.

Who Holds the Government Accountable?

Finally, one can turn the accountability question around and ask who holds policymakers accountable?

Judith Aitken has chosen to use the power and visibility of ERO to challenge national education policies and to focus public attention on large structural problems encompassing groups of schools. Her method was to publish a series of high-profile reports on different aspects of the state education system. Between 1996 and 1998, the ERO released three reports on groups of schools facing considerable difficulties, those in the urban area of South Auckland, the East Coast, and Northland. In doing so, the ERO has sought to balance its narrow purpose of evaluating individual schools with the goal of addressing larger structural problems. As Aitken stated, "It has been a struggle to get the Ministry [of Education] to understand that the school is not a great unit to focus on. Compare the successful firm. It has a lot of vertical and horizontal linkages to other firms."[35]

These ERO reports undoubtedly had an impact on discussions within the Ministry. The report on the South Auckland schools, for example, ultimately prompted the government to establish a NZ$19 million program aimed at assisting troubled schools in that area. It is not unreasonable to suggest that any inspectorate set up in the United States to monitor charter schools should also be charged with keeping an eye on how central authorities were dealing with charter schools in their jurisdiction.

Accountability in the U.S. Charter School Movement

Accountability is the single greatest challenge for the U.S. charter school movement. A good accountability system is essential for assuring that taxpayer dollars are being spent in ways consistent with the public interest that serves as the justification for making K–12 education compulsory. While the inspectorate approach of New Zealand (or alternatively, the British version) to accountability will not solve all problems, it provides a model worth pursuing in the United States and a necessary and useful complement to the current system of accountability that is either undeveloped or likely to rely heavily on student test scores. For site visits to be productive, however, a state government must be prepared to pay for a professional team of inspectors. The high potential costs of a quality review process provide an additional argument for keeping charter schools on the fringe of the traditional education system.

Notes

1. See Bryan C. Hassel, *The Charter School Challenge: Avoiding the Pitfalls, Fulfilling the Promise* (Brookings, 1999); Chester E. Finn Jr., Bruno B. Manno, Louann Bierlein, and Gregg Vanourek, *The Birth Pains and Life-Cycles of Charter Schools, Charter Schools in Action, Final Report, Part 2* (Washington, D.C.: Hudson Institute, 1997); and UCLA Charter School Study (Amy Stuart Wells and others), *Beyond the Rhetoric of Charter School Reform: A Study of Ten California School Districts* (Los Angeles, 1998).

2. See Hassel, *The Charter School Challenge,* chapter 7, for an elaboration of these views.

3. We spent five months in early 1998 visiting almost fifty primary and secondary schools in New Zealand, gathering and analyzing data from the Ministry of Education and other public sources, and interviewing public officials.

4. "Tomorrow's Schools" is the name of the government policy report that led to the 1989 legislation reforming the school system.

5. During the mid-1970s, at a time when the Catholic school system was under substantial financial pressure, Catholic and other religious schools were allowed to integrate into the public school system. Although permitted to maintain their separate character, they became public schools with the same per pupil funding as the

government-owned public schools. Since then schools that were private could integrate into the public school system under the same terms.

6. Task Force to Review Education Administration, *Administering for Excellence: Effective Administration in Education* (Picot Report) (Wellington, New Zealand, 1988).

7. These other reform efforts are described in Jonathan Boston, John Martin, June Pallot, and Pat Walsh, *Public Management: The New Zealand Model* (Auckland, New Zealand: Oxford University Press, 1996); and Graham Scott, Ian Ball, and Tony Dale, "New Zealand's Public Sector Management Reform: Implications for the United States," *Journal of Policy Analysis and Management*, vol. 16, no. 3 (1997), pp. 357–81.

8. The National Education Guidelines include three components: national education goals, national administration guidelines, and national curriculum statements.

9. Liz Gordon, "The State, Devolution, and Educational Reform in New Zealand," *Journal of Education Policy*, vol. 7, no. 2, p. 195.

10. Gordon, "The State, Devolution, and Educational Reform in New Zealand," pp. 187–203, quote on p. 196.

11. Joe Loconte, "Schools Learn That Vouchers Can Have a Hidden Cost," *Wall Street Journal*, January 26, 1999.

12. National Education Association, *Charter School Laws: A State-by-State Comparison, 1999*.

13. UCLA Charter School Study, *Beyond the Rhetoric of Charter School Reform*.

14. Bryan C. Hassel, "The Case for Charter Schools," in Paul E. Peterson and Bryan C. Hassel, eds., *Learning from School Choice* (Brookings, 1998), pp. 33–51.

15. Edward B. Fiske and Helen F. Ladd, *When Schools Compete: A Cautionary Tale* (Brookings, 2000), chapter 7; and Helen F. Ladd and Edward B. Fiske. "The Uneven Playing Field of School Choice," *Journal of Policy Analysis and Management* (January 2001).

16. Fiske and Ladd, *When Schools Compete: A Cautionary Tale*, figures 8.1 and 8.2.

17. Cambridge Public School System, "The Process of School Choice in the Cambridge Public Schools," 1998.

18. Parents must have a range of high-quality alternative schools from which to choose, every child must have a chance at every school, all parents must be educated about their options, transportation must be made available to those who cannot afford it, all parties must acknowledge that choice will cost more, and districts must be ready with training. See Edward B. Fiske, *Smart Schools, Smart Kids: Why Do Some Schools Work?* (Simon and Schuster, 1991), pp. 195–97.

19. Finn and others, *The Birth Pains and Life-Cycles of Charter Schools;* and Task Force to Review Education Administration, *Administering for Excellence.* See also Bruno V. Manno, *Accountability: The Key to Charter Renewal* (Washington, D.C.: Center for Education Reform, 1999).

20. Before its start-up, the new office was called the Review and Audit Agency, but the name was changed at the last minute to the Education Review Office (ERO).

21. Task Force to Review Education Administration, *Administering for Excellence*, p. 60.

22. Early in the implementation process, the working group rejected a proposal that the ERO have a role in approving school charters, on the grounds that the charter should be a contract between the Ministry and the schools and that, if the ERO was to provide an independent audit of the school, it should not be a party to the contract.

23. In 1998, the ERO began to consolidate the two types of audit into a single combined accountability review.

24. Education Review Office, *Annual Report, July 1993–30 June 1994* (Wellington, New Zealand, 1994), p. 6.

25. Cathy Wylie, *Ten Years On: How Schools View Educational Reform* (Wellington, New Zealand: New Zealand Council for Educational Research, 1999), pp. 181–82.

26. Paul T. Hill, "Accountability under Charters and Other School-Centered Reforms." University of Washington, 1997.

27. A few jurisdictions have already started down this path. The best examples are the state board of education in Massachusetts and the District of Columbia Public Charter School Board.

28. Deborah Willis, "Educational Assessment and Accountability: A New Zealand Case Study," *Journal of Education Policy*, vol. 7, no. 2 (1992), pp. 205–21.

29. Wylie, *Ten Years On*.

30. Austin Report, *Achieving Excellence: A Review of the Education External Evaluation Services* (Wellington, New Zealand: State Services Commission, 1997).

31. Martin Thrupp, "Shaping a Crisis: The Education Review Office and South Auckland Schools," in Mark Olssen and Kay Morris Matthews, eds., *Education Policy in New Zealand: The 1990s and Beyond* (Palmerston North, New Zealand: Dunmore Press Ltd.), pp. 145–61; Kay Hawk, interview with the authors, 1998.

32. Auckland Uniservices Limited, *A Review of ERO: Final Report to the PPTA* (1997), p. 7.

33. Austin Report, *Achieving Excellence*, p. 7.

34. Auckland Uniservices Limited, *A Review of ERO*, p. 5.

35. Judith Aitken, chief review officer, Education Review Office, interview with authors, Wellington, New Zealand, 1998.

PART 2

School Vouchers

5

The Hidden Research Consensus for School Choice

JAY P. GREENE

A flurry of activity has taken place in school choice research in the last few years. As a result, where there were once only theories and limited evidence, there is now a relatively solid understanding of the likely effects of school choice. I say "relatively" because all research is necessarily imperfect and additional study can always improve the confidence with which conclusions can be drawn. But the research on school choice includes several random-assignment studies, the "gold standard" of research design in which subjects are randomly assigned to treatment and control groups such as in a medical study. I can think of only one other education policy issue (the effect of class-size reduction) that has been the subject of even one significant, random-assignment experiment, let alone several "gold standard" studies. The norm in education policy is to foist fads conjured up in education schools onto unsuspecting children and their families without having subjected the policy to any systematic, empirical examination. Compared with this common practice in education, school choice has been thoroughly and carefully studied.

In addition to the quality of recent research on school choice, this research has consistently positive results. One would never know it from the media coverage, but the findings of school choice studies, at least on some questions, have been uniformly positive. Groups with vested interests in the results of the studies, such as the teachers unions as well as their friends and allies, always prefer to describe results as mixed or inconclusive at best. Reporters also prefer covering controversy and are wary of crossing any interest group by drawing conclusions from school choice research, which leads them to describe results as mixed or inconclusive as well. And even researchers have incentives to highlight disagreements with each other as a matter of academic pride and professional competition, which helps obscure the generally positive results that a variety of researchers have been finding.

If one looks beyond the rhetoric and spin about school choice research results, one sees consistently positive findings on some questions and generally favorable results on others. The truth is that school choice has been better studied than almost any education policy and has produced remarkably positive results across those studies.

The research on school choice can be organized as addressing three questions: (1) Does school choice benefit those who receive a voucher to choose a school? (2) Does school choice benefit students who do not actively choose a school (or as it is sometimes negatively framed, "those left behind")? and (3) How does school choice affect integration and the democratic values that society may wish schools to promote? The research on the first question, does choice benefit choosers, is the strongest and most consistently positive. Whether choice benefits nonchoosers is more difficult to study and therefore the evidence is less conclusive on that question, although recent research certainly suggests benefits for choosers and nonchoosers alike. The last question, whether choice poses a threat to the U.S. democratic system, has been the least studied perhaps because it is so central to the popular faith in the public school. Like all central myths people prefer not to examine them too closely, but some recent research suggests that choice may enhance the ability of schools to promote democratic goals.

Does School Choice Benefit Choosers?

One indication of the academic effects of school choice on choosers is whether they report being more satisfied with their school experience than do nonchoosers. Here the evidence in support of school choice is unambiguously and overwhelmingly positive. One of the evaluators of the school choice program in Milwaukee, Wisconsin, John F. Witte, reported that "satisfaction of Choice parents with private schools was just as dramatic as dissatis-

faction was with prior public schools."[1] In Cleveland, Ohio, evaluator Kim
K. Metcalf found: "Across the range of school elements, parents of scholarship students tend to be much more satisfied with their child's school than
other parents. . . . Scholarship recipient parents are more satisfied with the
child's teachers, more satisfied with the academic standards at the child's
school, more satisfied with order and discipline, [and] more satisfied with
social activities at the school."[2] Also in Cleveland, Paul Peterson, William
Howell, and I found that after two years of the program choice parents were
significantly more satisfied with almost all aspects of their children's education than were the parents of a random sample of Cleveland public school
parents. [3] Nearly 50 percent of choice parents reported being very satisfied
with the academic program, safety, discipline, and teaching of moral values
in their private school. Only around 30 percent of Cleveland public school
parents report being very satisfied with these aspects of their children's
schools. Very similar results were obtained from the privately funded school
choice programs in Charlotte, North Carolina; Washington, D.C.; Dayton,
Ohio; New York City; and San Antonio, Texas.[4]

If this were almost any other policy realm or consumer issue, the strong
positive effect of school choice on parental satisfaction would likely be considered sufficient evidence to conclude that the program is beneficial to its participants. If, for example, people report that they are happier with the maintenance of public parks, this would be taken as sufficient proof that efforts to
improve the parks have succeeded. The number of items of trash and repair
problems would not have to be counted to verify reports of satisfaction.

But the standards for assessing programs in education are different. Many
in the education and public policy communities only give serious consideration to changes in standardized test scores and give little credence to parental
reports. To put it bluntly, many in the education and policy communities
suspect that parents are unreliable and that reports of parental satisfaction are
of little value, while test scores are the only meaningful indicator of program
success. To put it more politely, many suspect that parents are not informed
consumers of education or experience psychological pressures to justify their
choices, making their assessments of program success unreliable. Whether
put bluntly or politely, the bottom line is that despite the overwhelmingly
positive effects of school choice on parental satisfaction, these findings have
not moved the policy debate much.

Instead, the policy debate has focused mainly on the effect of school
choice on standardized test scores. The test score results have also been consistently positive. The fact that the results have been consistently positive,

especially from several "gold standard" random-assignment experiments, gives the results enormous credibility. In the last few years, several researchers have conducted seven analyses of random-assignment school choice experiments from five different programs. Every one of those analyses finds statistically significant benefits from school choice for those who are provided with opportunities to choose a private school.

For example, in New York, Washington, D.C., Dayton, and Charlotte, privately funded programs offered scholarships to families with which they could send their children to private school. Because there were many more applicants than scholarships available, scholarships were awarded by lottery, allowing for the "gold standard" random-assignment research design. Comparing the standardized test scores of those students who won the lottery for a scholarship to the scores of those who lost the lottery allows researchers to identify with confidence the effect of receiving a voucher because any difference in the academic achievement of the two groups can be attributed to the voucher and not any differences in their backgrounds or motivations, given that on average the two groups are alike in those respects.

The results from New York, Washington, D.C., and Dayton were contained in a report issued by the Harvard Program on Education Policy and Governance (PEPG).[5] The PEPG report found that after two years in private school African American recipients of the scholarships performed significantly higher on standardized tests than did the African American members of the control group that applied for a scholarship but were not offered one by lottery. The benefit of receiving one of these privately funded vouchers in New York was about 4 percentile points; Dayton, about 7 percentile points; and Washington, D.C., about 9 percentile points. The report found no significant academic effect of receiving the scholarship, good or ill, for students of any other ethnic group.

Another group released a report of the results from the same New York scholarship program studied in the PEPG report.[6] Mathematica Policy Research, a research company that was involved in collecting the data in New York, conducted its own analyses of the New York data and issued its own report. Contrary to a misleading article in the *New York Times*, the findings from the Mathematica and PEPG studies were essentially the same.[7] Mathematica calculated the average benefit for African American students receiving a scholarship to be one-tenth of a percentile point higher than that reported by PEPG.

The only difference between the Mathematica and PEPG analyses of results from New York, a difference fully exploited by the *New York Times* in the throes of a presidential campaign, was the spin that each report placed on the findings. The Mathematica report preferred to emphasize the results broken out by grade, while the PEPG report focused on the average for African American students across all grades. Breaking out the results by grade produced very small samples for each grade, so that the effect of receiving a voucher was statistically significant only in sixth grade and positive, but not significant in two of the other three grades studied. Mathematica expressed worries that the benefit of the scholarship might not be widespread and therefore advised against drawing any conclusions. PEPG instead focused on the statistically significant benefit for African American students across all grades and, especially in light of the similar results from other cities, felt comfortable drawing a stronger conclusion than Mathematica did.

The difference between the two views can be illustrated by thinking about presidential campaign poll results. Say that a national poll found that 2000 Democratic nominee Al Gore was ahead of Republican candidate George W. Bush by 7 points. Someone then broke out the results by state, even though the sample in each state was fairly small, and found that Gore's lead was statistically significant only in California. Would it then be more reasonable to conclude that Gore and Bush were tied or that Gore was ahead? The PEPG interpretation of the results is analogous to focusing on the national poll results, while the Mathematica interpretation is analogous to focusing on breaking those results out by state, even though the number of subjects is small.

This discussion of the different interpretations of the results, however, obscures a basic truth: Both the PEPG and Mathematica analyses of results from a high-quality random-assignment school choice experiment in New York find statistically significant benefits from school choice. And the PEPG report finds statistically significant benefits from the other two programs it covered, in Dayton and Washington, D.C.

In addition, three other analyses of random-assignment choice experiments confirm the existence of academic benefits. My analysis of the privately funded scholarship program in Charlotte found that students given a voucher by lottery to attend private school outperformed their counterparts who failed to win a voucher by 6 percentile points after one year.[8] I was unable to determine whether benefits occurred exclusively for African American students because more than three-quarters of the students in the Charlotte study were African American, leaving too few students from other groups on which to draw any conclusions about possible academic benefits for those students.

Two analyses of random-assignment data from the publicly funded school choice program in Milwaukee also find significant gains for students who receive vouchers to attend private schools. One study, by myself, Paul E.

Peterson, and Jiangtao Du, found that students who won lotteries to receive a voucher scored 6 percentile points higher on their reading scores and 11 percentile points higher on their math scores than students who lost lotteries to receive a voucher.[9] Princeton economist and former member of the Clinton administration Cecilia Elena Rouse independently analyzed the data from Milwaukee and arrived at similar results, at least in math scores. After trying several analytical strategies, Rouse concluded: "Students selected for the Milwaukee Parental Choice Program . . . likely scored 1.5–2.3 percentile points *per year* in math more than students in the comparison groups." [10] Rouse also writes that her findings for math scores are "quite similar to those reported by Greene et al.," but she concluded that the results for reading were not robust.[11]

In addition to these seven random-assignment studies (PEPG's studies of New York, Washington, D.C., and Dayton; Mathematica's study of New York; my study of Charlotte; my study with Peterson and Du of Milwaukee; and Rouse's study of Milwaukee), three nonrandom-assignment studies have been conducted of publicly funded school choice programs. The quality of these nonrandom-assignment studies (including one I conducted) is so much lower than the quality of the random-assignment studies that less weight should be given to their results.

But it is striking that even these lower-quality studies are also generally positive in their findings. For example, in Milwaukee, John Witte compared the academic performance of choice students with a sample of Milwaukee public school students, controlling for a limited set of background characteristics. Based on this comparison, Witte writes: "The general conclusion is that there is no substantial difference over the life of the program between the Choice and MPS [Milwaukee Public School] students, especially the low-income MPS students. On a positive note, estimates for the overall samples, while always below national norms, do not substantially decline as the students enter higher grades. This is not the normal pattern in that usually inner-city student average scores decline relative to national norms in higher grades."[12] In other words, Witte, relying on nonrandom-assignment comparisons, found that choice did not significantly help or hurt students academically, while two other studies of the Milwaukee program relying on the more rigorous random-assignment comparison found significant academic benefits from choice. If these studies are mixed, as some like to say, they are mixed only to the extent that they are positive or neutral on the effects of choice on test scores.

Despite Witte's finding that choice neither helps nor hurts students academically, he has nevertheless endorsed school choice. Witte writes, "Choice can be a useful tool to aid families and educators in inner city and poor communities where education has been a struggle for several generations." He continues, "If programs are devised correctly, they can provide meaningful educational choices to families that now do not have such choices. And it is not trivial that most people in America . . . already have such choices."[13] Thus all three evaluations of the Milwaukee choice program conclude that choice has at least some significant benefits for its participants.

The Cleveland choice program also offers evidence on the academic effects of choice, but unfortunately the evidence from Cleveland is of lower quality because there are no random-assignment data nor are there sufficient data on the background characteristics of choice and public school families. Despite these data limitations, some analyses of test scores have been performed by Kim Metcalf of Indiana University School of Education and by myself, Paul Peterson, and William Howell. Both analyses find at least some significant academic benefits of the choice program in Cleveland.

After two years of the choice program's operation, Metcalf concludes: "The results indicate that scholarship students in existing private schools had significantly higher test scores than public school students in language (45.0 versus 40.0) and science (40.0 versus 36.0). However, there were no statistically significant differences between these groups on any of the other scores."[14] Metcalf's analyses were based on a comparison between one grade cohort of choice students and a nonrandom sample of public school students and had a limited set of controls for background differences, which could seriously bias results.

In addition to finding significant test score gains, Metcalf, like Witte, favors the expansion of educational opportunities offered by school choice: "The scholarship program effectively serves the population of families and children for which it was intended and developed. The program was designed to serve low-income students while maintaining the racial composition of the Cleveland Public Schools. . . . The majority of children who participate in the program are unlikely to have enrolled in a private school without a scholarship."[15] Overall, Metcalf has a positive assessment of the effects of the Cleveland choice program on its participants.

The analyses of test scores in Cleveland that I did with Peterson and Howell had serious data limitations as well. We only had test scores from two private schools, although those schools did contain nearly 15 percent of all choice students and nearly 25 percent of all choice students who had transferred from public schools. We were able to compare scores from students over time only relative to how they scored when they first entered these two schools. Based on the experience, described by John Witte, that inner-city students tend to have declining scores relative to national norms over time, we believed that any gains in test scores over time would be a strong indicator of academic progress for the choice students. We found that after two years students at the two schools we examined had gains of 7.5 national percentile points (NPR) in reading and 15.6 NPR in math.[16] These gains were achieved even though the students at these two schools were among the most disadvantaged students in Cleveland. We concluded that despite the shortcomings of the available data, there were indications of significant academic benefits for choice students in Cleveland.

Instead of getting lost in the details of these studies, it is worth stepping back and reviewing all of the results. There have been seven random-assignment and three non-random-assignment studies of school choice programs in the last few years. The authors of all ten studies find at least some benefits from the programs and recommend their continuation if not expansion. No study finds a significant harm to student achievement from the school choice programs. The probability that ten studies would find benefits and no significant harms if there were no benefit from school choice is astronomically low. Furthermore, the private schools participating in these various school choice programs tend to have per pupil operating costs that are nearly half the per pupil expenditure in the public schools. Even if no significant academic benefit came from school choice, the policy would find support because parents like it and it costs half as much money to produce the same level of academic achievement. Increasing student achievement significantly, while spending less money per pupil and making parents more satisfied, as the evidence from these ten studies consistently shows, provides strong support for school choice.

Does School Choice Benefit Nonchoosers?

If choice helps the choosers, does it do so at the expense of others? The suspicion is that choice programs "cream" the best students from the public schools, draining talent and resources from the public system. However, it is possible that creaming has largely already occurred in the public system. Higher achieving students and more affluent and involved families may have already chosen a public or private school that suits them, leaving "the rest behind." The U.S. Department of Education estimates that 59 percent of students currently attend "chosen" schools.[17] But many of the remaining 41 percent lack the financial resources to move to a desired public school attendance zone or pay private school tuition. Can vouchers exacerbate the situation in a way that harms nonchoosing families?

Evaluations of the Milwaukee and Cleveland programs have concluded that the programs successfully targeted very low-income families, offering them opportunities that they otherwise would not have. The average income of families participating in the Milwaukee program was $10,860.[18] In Cleveland, the mean family income was $18,750; New York, $10.540; Washington, D.C., $17,774; and Dayton, $17,681.[19] In Milwaukee, 76 percent of choice students were in single, female-headed households; Cleveland, 70 percent; Washington, D.C., 77 percent; and Dayton, 76 percent. The standardized tests of choice students before they began in private school showed that they averaged below the thirty-first percentile in Milwaukee, below the twenty-seventh percentile in New York, below the thirty-third percentile in D.C., and below the twenty-sixth percentile in Dayton. In other words, choice students were generally performing in the bottom third academically.

The most damaging thing that one could say about these choice programs with respect to creaming is that they probably attract the more capable of the disadvantaged poor. But if this is creaming, then food stamps, Temporary Assistance for Needy Families, and virtually all other antipoverty programs engage in creaming. Antipoverty programs generally fail to serve the most dysfunctional of the poor because those people have difficulty taking full advantage of the programs designed to help them. This is not normally seen as an indictment against antipoverty efforts, but as an unfortunate reality that all programs must face. Like these other antipoverty programs, school choice programs can be designed so that they target disadvantaged populations, even if they do not always reach the most disadvantaged of the disadvantaged.

But showing that school choice does not cream the best students does not address whether public schools respond effectively to the challenge of school choice to improve the quality of education for those who remain in traditional public schools. Studying this issue is difficult. None of the existing school choice pilot programs is large enough or has been around long enough to allow researchers to detect effects of choice programs on public schools with certainty. The Milwaukee public school district, home to the largest and longest-running choice program, has dramatically increased the number of public school choice programs to retain students who might be drawn to the private school choice program. The Milwaukee public schools have also promised parents that their children will read at grade level by grade three or they can receive individual tutoring. This promise was advertised on billboards and the sides of buses to make people want to "choose" the public schools. This attentiveness to the needs of students in Milwaukee suggests that the school district has constructively responded to the challenge of school choice to improve the quality of education for those who remain in the public schools. But these reports from Milwaukee are little more than anecdotes and not the kind of evidence that social scientists tend to require.

The evidence from a new evaluation I conducted of the A-Plus choice and accountability program in Florida provides stronger systematic evidence that the prospect of vouchers inspires significant academic improvement in public schools.[20] Under the A-Plus program, schools that had received two failing grades from the state would have vouchers offered to their students with which those students could attend a private or different public school. Comparing the change in test scores of schools that had previously received a failing grade with other schools reveals that those schools that faced the imminent prospect of vouchers if they did not improve achieved test score gains that were more than twice as large as the gains realized by other schools in the state. When schools in Florida had to improve or compete to retain their students under a choice system, they were able to make significant academic progress.

In addition, some studies recognize that there is variation in the amount of school choice already available to families to see whether areas with more choices available tend to have higher student test scores than areas with fewer choices available. The Harvard economist Caroline Minter Hoxby examined the effect of choice on the quality of public and private schools using an innovative research strategy.[21] Hoxby took advantage of the fact that some families currently exercise choice by moving to different school districts within a metropolitan area or by paying the tuition to send their children to private school. Some metropolitan areas have more choices available than others because some have more school districts and more private schools. For example, Boston has several school districts in the metropolitan area (Boston, Brookline, Cambridge, Waltham, and so on), while Miami has only one school district for the entire county.

Hoxby examined whether having more choices available is related to higher academic achievement. As one would expect from most economic theory and experience about competition and choice, she finds that the metropolitan areas with more choices available have higher academic performance at lower cost than do metropolitan areas with fewer choices. A one standard deviation increase in the available public school district choices results in a 3 percentile point improvement in test scores and a 4 percent increase in wages for students upon entering the work force, all for 17 percent less per capita expenditure.[22] A one standard deviation increase in choices offered by the private sector results in an 8 percentile point improvement in test scores and a 12 percent increase in wages for students upon entering the work force, without any significant change in per capita expenditure.[23] Hoxby concludes: "If private schools in any area receive sufficient resources to subsidize each student by $1,000, the achievement of *public* school students rises."[24] Choice appears to help the nonchoosers as well as the choosers.

A similar study that I conducted for the Manhattan Institute, called *The Education Freedom Index*, produced similar results.[25] I measured the extent of educational choices currently available to families in each state, including charter school choices, subsidized private school choices, home-schooling choices, and public school choices. Controlling for per pupil spending, median household income, class size, and racial composition, states that offered more choices to families in the education of their children had significantly higher student test scores. When parents have more choices, schools have greater incentives to attend to the needs of students or else families may withdraw their children and the accompanying resources.

More direct and conclusive research could be conducted than these three studies on whether school choice improves the quality of education for nonchoosers as well as choosers. To get that kind of evidence, several large-scale voucher programs that were in existence for several years would be needed. The overall educational achievement in those districts with large-scale school choice programs would have to be compared with comparable districts that did not have voucher programs to see if vouchers helped spur schools to improve. Enough positive evidence is available currently to suggest that such large-scale choice programs are worth trying. The mechanism by which some worry that choice will undermine the quality of public schools, creaming off the best students, has not occurred in the several choice programs that have been studied. Existing school choices, particularly the ability of wealthier families to move to different school districts or attendance zones, produce a considerable amount of creaming before voucher programs are introduced. Furthermore, studies of school choice that exists without vouchers show that when it is easier for more families to exercise such choices, school quality is higher.

How Does School Choice Affect Civic Values and Integration?

Even if some people were convinced that school choice could improve academic achievement for choosers and nonchoosers, they might still be wary of vouchers because of how they might affect the civic purposes of education. The U.S. system of government-operated schools was developed to ensure that desired civic values were transmitted to future generations as much as it was developed to impart economically useful skills.

Oddly, while promoting values is a central mission of public schools, virtually no systematic evidence exists to support the claim that government control of schools is important for achieving this goal. For many people, even academics, the importance of government control of schools to promote civic values is an article of faith.

Some recent studies in which I have been involved, however, cast doubt on whether government management of schools is necessary or even desirable for promoting civic values. In one study, colleagues and I analyzed responses from the Latino National Political Survey, which was a national sample of adult Latinos.[26] Subjects were asked whether they went to a public, private, or foreign school for each grade. They were also asked how willing they would be to let members of their least-liked group engage in political activities, such as running for office or holding demonstrations. The more willing people are to allow members of their least-liked group to engage in these political activities, the more tolerant they are said to be. Controlling for a variety of background characteristics, we found that adult Latinos who had been educated more in private school were more likely to be tolerant than those who had been educated more in public or foreign schools. The effect was moderate, but significant. Latinos who received their education entirely in private school were willing to tolerate the political activities of their least-liked group 50 percent of the time compared with 39 percent for Latinos who never attended private school, holding all other factors constant.

In another study, headed by Patrick J. Wolf of Georgetown University, a sample of college students were similarly asked questions about how willing they would be to allow members of their least-liked group to engage in certain political activities.[27] Again, controlling statistically for differences in the students' backgrounds, the more that students attended private school before college the more tolerant they were.

Harvard University researcher David E. Campbell examined a large national data set of secondary school students that contained a limited number of tolerance items that focused on antireligious activities.[28] These measures of tolerance are an especially hard test of whether tolerance is taught better at religious private schools, given their focus on tolerating antireligious activities. Despite this likely bias, Campbell found that Catholic school and secular private school students are more likely to be tolerant than are public school students. Secular, Catholic, and other religious private school students outperformed their public school counterparts on other civic measures, such as their experience with volunteering and their willingness to engage in public speaking or write letters on public issues.

Instead of being the bastions of intolerance they are sometimes imagined to be, private schools appear to be more successful than public schools at instilling tolerance in their students. And remarkably this private school advantage on tolerance appears to last into the adult lives of their students.

But does this tolerance in private schools extend to racial integration? School choice has a bad reputation on the issue of racial integration because people remember that vouchers were endorsed by some southern segregationists who wanted to use them to evade court orders to integrate schools. Vouchers do have this shameful history, but people seem to forget the shameful history of government-controlled public schools, which were segregated by law in much of the country for almost a century. The desirability of school choice with regard to racial integration should be judged by the policy's merits, not its pedigree.

In the last few years, a number of studies have examined the impact of school choice on racial integration. In one study, I examined the racial composition of a random sample of public and private school students' classrooms, collected by the National Education Longitudinal Study (NELS).[29] I found that private school students were significantly less likely to be in classrooms that were racially homogeneous. More than half (55 percent) of public school students were in classrooms that were almost entirely white or almost entirely minority in their racial composition, while 41 percent of private school students were similarly segregated. When all families choose their schools, as they do in the private sector, more had their children in racially mixed educational settings than when more families were assigned to schools, as they are in the public sector. Choice appears conducive to integration, while government assignment to public school appears conducive to segregation.

In another study, colleagues and I observed a random sample of public and private school lunchrooms in Austin and San Antonio, Texas, and recorded where students sat by race.[30] We found that private school students were significantly more likely to be in racially mixed groups at lunch than were public school students. After adjusting for the city, seating restrictions, school size, and student grade level, we found that 79 percent of private school students were in racially mixed groups compared with 43 percent of public school students. Sitting in a racially mixed group was defined as having any one of five adjacent students being of a different racial or ethnic group. We found that religious, private schools were better integrated than were secular schools, suggesting that the low tuition typically found at religious schools helped contribute to racial integration. If vouchers or tax-credits further reduced the financial barriers to private school attendance, integration in private schools might be even better.

We also found that public schools with more students from outside their attendance zones—that is, with more magnet programs or transfer students—had higher rates of integration. Choice systems, where schooling is detached from housing, seem better able to transcend racial segregation in housing patterns. Traditional public schools, however, appear to replicate and perhaps reinforce racial segregation in housing.

Recent work by Stanford economist Thomas Nechyba, with Michael Heise, arrives at similar conclusions about segregation by income. Based on policy simulations, they found that "by removing education-related incentives for high-income households to separate themselves from poor neighborhoods, vouchers introduce a desegregating force into society. [And] by reducing housing prices in high quality public school districts and raising them in low quality districts, vouchers help more low-income families afford to live in areas with better public schools."[31] In other words, the public school system of attaching schooling to housing has created distortions in housing segregation and pricing. Housing prices are artificially high in areas with desirable public schools and artificially low in areas with undesirable public schools, contributing to more severe sorting of housing patterns by income (and race). By detaching schooling from housing, school choice makes it easier for wealthier families to stay in economically mixed neighborhoods by giving them easier access to desirable schools. And by reducing the premium placed on housing in areas with good schools, vouchers make it easier for poorer families to move into those areas. It is no wonder that vouchers are most supported by poor inner-city residents and most opposed by well-to-do suburbanites.

But these findings are based on examinations of existing private schools or policy simulations. What would the effects of an actual choice program be on integration? Some evidence from the Cleveland and Milwaukee school choice programs addresses this question. Following a strategy similar to that used to examine the data from NELS, I looked at whether choice students in Cleveland were more likely to attend schools that were racially representative of the broader community and less likely to attend racially homogeneous schools than were public school students.[32] I found that nearly a fifth (19 percent) of recipients of a voucher in Cleveland attend private schools that have a racial composition that resembles the average racial composition of the Cleveland area (defined as having a proportion of minority students in the school that is within 10 percent of the average proportion of minorities in metropolitan Cleveland). Only 5 percent of public school students in the Cleveland metropolitan area are in comparably integrated schools. More than three-fifths (61 percent) of public school students in metropolitan Cleveland attend schools that are almost entirely white or almost entirely minority in their racial composition. Half of the students in the Cleveland Scholarship Program are in comparably segregated schools. The amount of integration is not great in either system, but it is markedly better in the choice program.

When Howard Fuller and George Mitchell examined racial integration data from Milwaukee, their findings were similar to those from Cleveland.[33] In 1998–99, they observed that 58 percent of Milwaukee public elementary students attended schools with more than 90 percent or less than 10 percent minority students. Only 38 percent of elementary school students at a large sample of Milwaukee Catholic schools were in similarly segregated schools. In 1998–99, Catholic schools accounted for more than half of the growth of choice students in the Milwaukee voucher program.

The public systems in Cleveland and Milwaukee, despite years of busing and other forced desegregation efforts, produce highly segregated schools. Desegregation has failed in those districts because white parents lacked faith in the public school's ability to manage integration successfully and fled to the suburbs. The school choice programs in those cities, however, allow families to transcend racial segregation in housing to select a racially mixed school in which they have confidence. And families are more likely to pick racially mixed schools when their choices are enabled by a voucher than when their choices are enabled by their ability to purchase housing in areas with desired schools.

Contrary to popular myth, private schools are bastions for neither intolerance nor segregation. Private control of schools appears to promote these civic purposes of education more effectively than government control of schools. Given the strong presumption that public purposes of education are best served by public control, considerably more research needs to be done on these questions before opinions might be changed.

Conclusion

Reviewing the recent evidence on the effects of school choice leaves a few basic conclusions:

—There is a positive consensus among all seven random-assignment studies and three non-random-assignment studies. Differences do exist among these studies, but all have found important benefits of choice for the families that participate in them.

—Choice does not appear to cream the best students. In all studies of existing choice programs, the evidence shows that participants have very low family incomes, predominantly come from single-mother households, and have a prior record of low academic performance.

—The existing choice programs are not large enough and they have not operated long enough to address definitively the effects, positive or negative, on the public school system. However, the results from the A-Plus program in Florida suggest that the prospect of vouchers may inspire significant improvement in public schools. And Caroline Minter Hoxby's work finds that metropolitan areas with more choices available have significantly better outcomes at lower cost. My work on the Education Freedom Index similarly finds that states that offer more choices to parents enjoy higher student achievement. From these examinations of choice systems that currently exist, choice is likely to improve public schools.

—Private schools are more likely to promote political tolerance than are public schools.

—Private schools are more likely to be integrated than are public schools.

The finding of positive effects of choice on its participants is remarkably consistent across all studies of existing choice programs and is something that should be regarded with reasonably high confidence. The finding of the absence of creaming is also something that is consistent across all studies of existing choice programs and is something that should be regarded with confidence. The conclusion about the positive effects of choice on public schools is based on three innovative studies, but more studies could confirm their findings. The best current evidence supports the view that choice should help improve public schools, but this conclusion cannot be drawn with greater confidence unless more choice programs are instituted on a larger scale.

The findings that choice contributes to higher levels of racial integration and civic values are consistent across several studies with appropriate analytical designs. These conclusions are so at odds with conventional wisdom on the matter, however, that they probably need additional studies to confirm the results with higher confidence. Yet, they are the most solid conclusions that can be drawn given the available evidence.

But perhaps the most striking finding from the review of school choice research is the absence of evidence about how school choice harms students or society. Given that vouchers cost about half as much as conventional public education, the absence of harms is proof enough that school choice is an attractive option. Perhaps significant damages caused by school choice will be detected or perhaps the benefits will diminish when programs are attempted on a larger scale. Without attempting larger-scale programs, society will have a hard time knowing.

Notes

1. John F. Witte, "The Milwaukee Voucher Experiment," *Educational Evaluation and Policy Analysis*, vol. 20, no. 4 (Winter 1999), p. 237.

2. Kim K. Metcalf, "Evaluation of the Cleveland Scholarship and Tutoring Program, 1996–1999," Indiana University, 1999, p. 20.

3. Paul E. Peterson, William G. Howell, and Jay P. Greene, "An Evaluation of the Cleveland Voucher Program after Two Years," Working Paper (Harvard University, Program on Education Policy and Governance, 1998), available at http://www.ksg.harvard.edu/pepg/. See also Jay P. Greene, William G. Howell, and Paul E. Peterson, "Lessons from the Cleveland Scholarship Program," in Paul E. Peterson and Bryan C. Hassel, eds., *Learning from School Choice* (Brookings, 1998), pp. 357–94.

4. Jay P. Greene, "Vouchers in Charlotte," *Education Matters*, vol. 1, no. 2 (Summer 2001), pp. 55–60; Paul E. Peterson, Jay P. Greene, William G. Howell, and William McCready, "Initial Findings from an Evaluation of School Choice Programs in Washington, D.C., and Dayton, Ohio," Working Paper (Harvard University, Program on Education Policy and Governance, 1998); Paul E. Peterson, David Myers, and William G. Howell, "An Evaluation of the New York City: School Choice Scholarships Program: The First Year," Working Paper (Harvard University, Program on Education Policy and Governance, 1998); and Paul E. Peterson, David Myers, and William G. Howell, "An Evaluation of the Horizon Scholarship Program in the Edgewood Independent School District, San Antonio, Texas: The First Year," Working Paper (Harvard University, Program on Education Policy and Governance, 1999). All of these papers are available at http://www.ksg.harvard.edu/pepg/.

5. William G. Howell, Patrick J. Wolf, Paul E. Peterson, and David E. Campbell, "Vouchers in New York, Dayton, and D.C.," *Education Matters*, vol. 1, no. 2 (Summer 2001), pp. 48–54. The report is also available at http://www.ksg.harvard.edu/pepg/.

6. David Myers, Paul E. Peterson, David Mayer, Julia Chou, and William G. Howell, "School Choice in New York City after Two Years: An Evaluation of the School Choice Scholarships Program," Working Paper (Harvard University, Program on Education Policy and Governance, 2000), available at http://www.ksg.harvard.edu/pepg/ and from Mathematica Policy Research.

7. Kate Zernike, "New Doubt Is Cast on Study That Backs Voucher Effects," *New York Times*, September 15, 2000.

8. Greene, "Vouchers in Charlotte."

9. Jay P. Greene, Paul E. Peterson, and Jiangtao Du, "School Choice in Milwaukee: A Randomized Experiment," in Paul E. Peterson and Bryan C. Hassel, eds., *Learning from School Choice* (Brookings, 1998), pp. 335–56. See also Jay P. Greene, Paul E. Peterson, and Jiangtao Du, "Effectiveness of School Choice: The Milwaukee Experiment," *Education and Urban Society*, vol. 31, no. 2 (February 1999), pp. 190–213.

10. Cecilia Elena Rouse, "Private School Vouchers and Student Achievement: An Evaluation of the Milwaukee Parental Choice Program," *Quarterly Journal of Economics*, vol. 113, no. 2 (May 1998), p. 593.

11. Rouse, "Private School Vouchers and Student Achievement," p. 578.

12. Witte, "The Milwaukee Voucher Experiment," pp. 236–37.

13. Joe Williams, "Ex-Milwaukee Evaluator Endorses School Choice: Opponents of Program Have Used His Earlier Work to Argue It Has Failed," *Milwaukee Journal-Sentinel,* January 9, 2000, p. 1.

14. Metcalf, "Evaluation of the Cleveland Scholarship and Tutoring Program," p. 15.

15. Metcalf, "Evaluation of the Cleveland Scholarship and Tutoring Program," p. 23.

16. Peterson, Howell, and Greene, "An Evaluation of the Cleveland Voucher Program after Two Years," table 12. See also Greene, Howell, and Peterson, "Lessons from the Cleveland Scholarship Program."

17. *Findings from the Condition of Education 1997: Public and Private Schools: How Do They Differ?* (U.S. Department of Education, National Center for Education Statistics, July 1997), available at http://nces.ed.gov/pubs97/97983.html.

18. Greene, Peterson, and Du, "School Choice in Milwaukee," p. 344.

19. Metcalf, "Evaluation of the Cleveland Scholarship and Tutoring Program," p. 9; Paul E. Peterson, David Myers, Josh Hamilton, and William G. Howell, *Initial Findings from the Evaluation of the New York School Choice Scholarship Program* (Mathematica Policy Research, 1997), table 2, available at http://www.ksg.harvard.edu/pepg; and William G. Howell and Paul E. Peterson, "School Choice in Dayton, Ohio: An Evaluation after One Year," Working Paper (Harvard University, Program on Education Policy and Governance, February 2000), available at http://www.ksg.harvard.edu/pepg/.

20. Jay P. Greene, *An Evaluation of the Florida A-Plus Accountability and School Choice Program* (Manhattan Institute for Policy Research, February 2001), available at http://www.manhattan-institute.org/html/cr_aplus.htm.

21. Caroline M. Hoxby, "Analyzing School Choice Reforms That Use America's Traditional Forms of Parental Choice," in Paul E. Peterson and Bryan C. Hassel, eds., *Learning from School Choice* (Brookings, 1998).

22. Hoxby, "Analyzing School Choice Reforms That Use America's Traditional Forms of Parental Choice," p. 144.

23. Hoxby, "Analyzing School Choice Reforms That Use America's Traditional Forms of Parental Choice," p. 148.

24. Hoxby, "Analyzing School Choice Reforms That Use America's Traditional Forms of Parental Choice," p. 148. Emphasis in original.

25. Jay P. Greene, *The Education Freedom Index,* Civic Report 14 (Manhattan Institute for Policy Research, September 2000), available at http://www.manhattan-institute.org/html/cr_14.htm.

26. Jay P. Greene, Joseph Giammo, and Nicole Mellow, "The Effect of Private Education on Political Participation, Social Capital and Tolerance: An Examination of the Latino National Political Survey," *Georgetown Public Policy Review,* vol. 5, no. 1 (Fall 1999), pp. 53–71, available at http://www.georgetown.edu/publications/GPPR/.

27. See chapter 13 in this volume, "Private Schooling and Political Tolerance" by Patrick J. Wolf, Jay P. Greene, Brett Kleitz, and Kristina Thalhammer.

28. See chapter 12 in this volume, "Making Democratic Education Work" by David E. Campbell.

29. Jay P. Greene, "Civic Values in Public and Private Schools," in Paul E. Peterson and Bryan C. Hassel, eds., *Learning from School Choice* (Brookings, 1998), pp. 83–106.

30. Jay P. Greene and Nicole Mellow, "Integration Where It Counts," *Texas Education Review*, vol. 1, no. 1 (Spring 2000), pp. 15–26.

31. Michael Heise and Thomas Nechyba, *School Finance Reform: A Case for Vouchers*, Civic Report 9 (Manhattan Institute for Policy Research, Center for Civic Innovation, October 1999). See also Thomas Nechyba, "School Finance Induced Migration Patterns: The Impact of Private School Vouchers," *Journal of Economic Theory* (1999); and "Mobility, Targeting and Private School Vouchers," *American Economic Review* (forthcoming).

32. Jay P. Greene, "The Racial, Economic, and Religious Context of Parental Choice in Cleveland," paper presented at the Association for Public Policy Analysis and Management meeting, Washington, D.C., November 1999, available at http://www.ksg.harvard.edu/pepg/.

33. Howard Fuller and George Mitchell, "The Impact of School Choice on Racial and Ethnic Enrollment in Milwaukee Private Schools," *Current Education Issues*, no. 99–5 (December 1999). See also Howard Fuller and George Mitchell, "The Impact of School Choice on Integration in Milwaukee Private Schools," *Current Education Issues*, no. 2000-2 (June 2000).

6

Going Private

TERRY M. MOE

America is engaged in a heated debate over school vouchers. At its heart is a controversy over the numbers and types of parents who want to go private, what motivates them, and what a shift of parents from public to private would mean for the larger society.

According to voucher advocates, parents are mainly concerned about school quality. In the absence of vouchers, only parents with enough money are able to seek out good schools by going private. But under a voucher system, they argue, with the cost of private education much reduced (or zero), many more parents would be able to—and would want to. This is particularly true for parents who are disadvantaged or trapped in failing public schools, for they have the most to gain from new opportunities. The upshot, advocates say, is that a voucher system would have very positive effects on society. It would get kids into better schools, give all schools incentives to perform, and promote social equity.

Critics dispute all this. In their view, going private has little to do with school quality. The real motivations are largely social and pernicious. Private schools have special appeal to people with money and education, who want their children separated from ordinary kids. They have special appeal to whites, who want to avoid blacks. And they have special appeal to the devoutly religious, who want schools of their own. So far, critics argue, the social downside has been limited because only 10 percent of American children go private. But if choice were expanded, pernicious motivations would be unleashed, and the education system would become more inequitable, more segregated, and more penetrated by religion.

These perspectives on parental choice could not be more different or more fundamental to an assessment of vouchers. The question is: How do they seem to square with the facts? I have carried out research, based on a nationally representative survey of American parents, that provides some tentative answers. The details are reported in my book *Schools, Vouchers, and the American Public* (Brookings, 2001). Here, I will briefly highlight some of the more basic themes and findings.

The Logic of Choice

Before turning to the data, let's begin by thinking rather abstractly for the moment about the demand for private schooling. There is a logic to it, and this logic should tell us something about what to expect.

Under the current system, going private is costly, and parental choice is governed by a simple calculus. Parents will tend to go private if they can afford the tuition, and if the value they associate with going private—whether it derives from performance, religion, ideology, race, or other concerns—exceeds the costs. This calculus does not tell us what parents actually value. They may value performance, or they may not. They may value racial separation, or they may not. These are empirical issues that can only be answered by looking at the data. The simple fact that parents must weigh the benefits of going private against the financial costs, however, points to certain implications that should guide our thinking.

Most obviously, private schools under the present system are more accessible to the financially well-off, because they are better able to afford the tuition. The same applies for the well educated, both because education is highly correlated with income and because better educated parents tend to be more motivated by educational concerns. For these reasons, the current system should indeed promote a class bias in the types of parents going private, much as the critics of choice contend (and as supporters recognize). This bias would only be enhanced, of course, if some of these parents were elitist and sought separation for its own sake. But even if none were elitist, a class bias would be an inherent part of the system.

Now let's consider what would happen if choice were vastly expanded, and parents were allowed—by means of vouchers, say—to send their children to private schools at no cost. The most immediate implication is that even the poorest parents—many of whose children, by no coincidence, are trapped in our nation's worst schools—would now find it within their means to pursue private schooling for their kids. Unless other factors (discrimination, for instance, or lack of information) prevent them from following through on their demand, many more low-income parents would probably go private than currently do, and the income biases associated with the current system would be reduced, perhaps drastically.

Biases due to education (controlling for income) might remain, because the better educated parents at all income levels would continue to be more motivated to seek out new opportunities. But in the aggregate, with income and education so highly correlated, and with information about private options increasingly available over time, many more people with low educations would tend to find their way into the private sector—lowering the average level of parent education in that sector, and thus leading to moderation on this score as well.

Here, too, we cannot say what parents might value about going private. But we can say that, whatever they value, the parents who currently go private are likely to be somewhat more extreme on these values than other parents are (because they care about them enough to pay for them)—and that, when the costs of choice are reduced, more people with these same values will be able to go private. It is reasonable to suggest, then, that the public parents who indicate an interest in going private should turn out to be similar on value grounds to the parents who already go private. They should also tend to be more moderate.

In sum, if we think in analytical terms about the demand side of school choice, there are logical reasons for having certain expectations about what would happen if choice were expanded. Under the current system, in which choice is costly, private school choice can be expected to produce social biases that mirror some of the concerns of voucher critics. An expansion of choice, however, should not make these biases worse, as critics tend to argue. Rather, it is more reasonable to expect that just the opposite will happen, and that the biases of the existing system will actually be moderated, perhaps substantially.

The Data

The analysis is based on a 1995 survey designed to explore the voucher issue. The sample consists of 4,700 randomly selected adults from across the United States, including oversamples of 1,200 parents and 1,000 inner-city parents. With statistical weighting, the sample as a whole yields a representative cross-section of the population. The survey is supplemented by a separately collected data set on the demographics and academic performance of the school districts in which each respondent lives.

With these data, the desire of parents to go private (or not) can be explored by reference to a range of possible influences. Among the more notable are the following (the actual analysis includes many more than are listed here):

—Background: income, education, religion, race, and political party.

—Context: how advantaged the school district is (as measured by an index of test scores and socioeconomic characteristics), and whether the respondent chose where to live based on the schools.

—Attitudes: support for diversity (racial integration), a perception of inequity (that the public schools provide a lower-quality education for low-income and minority kids), support for voluntary prayer in the schools, support for greater parent influence, desire for smaller schools, belief in what I call the "public school ideology" (which measures a normative attachment to public schooling and its ideals), a belief in markets (that choice and competition are likely to make schools more effective), and a concern that moral values are poorly taught in the public schools.

—Performance: an index of four items. One asks respondents whether the public schools are doing fine or are in need of major or minor change. Another asks them to rate the local public schools on a scale from one to ten. Another asks them whether their community is proud of its public schools. And still another asks them to compare the academic performance of the local public schools to private schools.

Who Goes Private under the Current System, and Why?

Now let's take a first look at the evidence. Even voucher advocates would agree that, because private-school choice is costly under the current system, parents who go private are likely to be more socially advantaged than parents who keep their children in the public schools. A simple descriptive comparison of parents in the two sectors documents as much. On average, private parents have higher incomes and more education than public parents, and they are more likely to be white. They also display the religious and partisan characteristics commonly associated with private schooling: they are more likely to be Catholic, born-again Christian, and Republican.

The existence of social biases, however, does not necessarily mean that the rest of the critics' indictment about pernicious motivations is supported by the evidence In fact, a multivariate (probit) analysis, incorporating all the background, context, attitude, and performance variables outlined earlier, suggests that it is not. Two findings stand out.

—Attitudes toward race (diversity) appear to have little to do with why parents go private. There is no indication that whites go private in order to flee blacks and other minorities.

—Of all the influences on parental choice, by far the most powerful is school performance. The less satisfied parents are with the performance of the public schools, the more likely they are to go private. The notion that private parents are really motivated by social concerns, and that performance matters little to them, misses the mark entirely.

This analysis also reveals that, aside from attitudes toward race, all the other attitudes in the model—inequity, public school ideology, prayer, moral values, school size, and markets (parent influence could not be included in this part of the analysis, for measurement reasons)—proved relevant to why these parents currently go private. The question is: Do these same sorts of values and beliefs seem to be relevant for public school parents who, given the choice, would be interested in switching to private schools?

Do Public Parents Want to Go Private?

Let's focus our attention now on public school parents, and see what we can learn about the reasons some of them are interested in going private.

The first step is to get a sense of how many public parents would like to go private if given a chance. What we are getting at here is a kind of hidden demand. For it is clear that parents who currently go private are doing so because they want to—but it is *not* clear that parents who currently send their kids to public school are doing what they want. Many might prefer to go private, but be unable to do so for cost reasons.

What is the extent of this hidden interest in private schools? The survey asks public parents the following question: "If you could afford it, would you be interested in sending your children to a private or parochial school?" The results are striking. They show that most public parents, 52 percent, would be interested in going private if money were not a problem, compared to 43 percent who say they would stay in the public sector. This is consistent with a 1999 survey by Public Agenda, which asked public parents a similar question and found that 57 percent were interested in going private.

The desire to go private is even stronger among low-income inner-city parents. In this group, 67 percent said they would be interested in leaving the public system. This is an early indication that, as advocates claim, choice has special appeal to the disadvantaged—and is not a policy whose support is grounded in elitism.

The notion that there is widespread interest among parents in going private is often disputed by critics. They cite figures that seem to show the opposite. A well-publicized report by the Carnegie Foundation for the Advancement of Teaching, for example, asked public parents the following question: "Is there some other school to which you would like to send your child? This could be public or private, inside or outside of your district, with your child's grade level." A full 70 percent said they would not switch, and just 19 percent indicated they would switch to a private school. Phi Delta Kappa (PDK) has included the same sort of question and gotten similar answers in its polls.

Properly interpreted, there is no conflict between these "opposing" sets of results. The Carnegie and PDK questions implicitly ask respondents if they know of some other school they regard as preferable to their current school. But most public parents have no incentive to be well informed about specific private schools (or even other public schools), so it is not surprising that they can't point to specific schools where they'd like to send their kids. When asked whether they are interested in going private, however, most parents make it clear that they are. Both measures are useful and valid. They are just measuring different things.

Why Do Public Parents Want to Go Private?

Now let's explore the desire to go private in greater depth. The question is: What would happen if choice were no longer costly, and all parents were given the option of sending their kids to private schools? Which parents would be most likely to go private, and why? Here are the highlights of a multivariate (probit) analysis that takes account of all the factors discussed earlier.

First, as the descriptive results for inner-city parents tend to suggest, an interest in private schools is especially high among low-income and minority (African American and Hispanic) parents generally. When choice is freely available and income no longer a constraint, private schools have disproportionate appeal to those who are less well off and whose need for new opportunities is clearly much greater. This association of choice with the disadvantaged is reinforced by the results for district context: It is the public parents in disadvantaged districts who are the most interested in going private.

Still, the more traditional influences associated with the current system continue to be relevant when choice is expanded. The public parents who are

better educated, Catholic, born-again, and Republican are especially interested in going private—suggesting that many of the same sorts of values and
beliefs are at work.

The education result, it is important to note, reinforces a basic theme
from the broader research literature: The parents who want to go private tend
to be low-income and minority, but also (controlling for income and race)
better educated. Choice advocates laud the equity-promoting effects of
expanded choice, and point to polls and programs showing that low-income
families have a strong interest in going private. Yet opponents point out that,
even within programs restricted to the poor, it is the better educated, more
motivated poor who take greatest advantage of choice. And this, critics
argue—not without reason—may give rise to certain inequities. These results
provide support for both sets of claims.

Now let's consider what values and beliefs seem to affect the desire to go
private among public parents. Several findings deserve emphasis:

—Racial attitudes do not appear to play a significant role. This suggests
that the critics' claims about the pernicious effects of race, while perhaps justified decades ago, are probably wide of the mark today.

—Aside from race, all of the attitudes in the model—regarding inequity,
public school ideology, prayer, moral values, parent influence, school size,
and markets—appear to have an influence, and in the direction choice advocates would expect. Public parents appear to be influenced by the same basic
values and beliefs that are important to current private parents. The consistent relevance of these concerns suggests that there is a common structure to
the way parents think about their choice of schools.

—Of all the attitudes in the model, attitudes toward inequity stand out as
the most salient. This dovetails nicely with our earlier results, which associate
choice with the plight of the disadvantaged. Overall, as perceptions of
inequity rise from low to high, the probability that a public parent will be
interested in going private increases by 17 percent. If we break respondents
down by income, moreover, we find that concerns about inequity are far
more important to parents who are disadvantaged than they are to other parents. Among low-income parents, a growing sense of inequity makes them
26 percent more likely to be interested in private schools, as compared to
comparable shifts of 12 percent for middle income parents and 11 percent
for upper income parents. The equity issue, then, seems to matter a great deal
to disadvantaged parents, and they appear to connect it to private-school
choice in a way that is entirely consistent with the argument voucher advocates have been making for the last decade: that choice is a way of promoting
social equity.

—For parents as a whole, public school ideology is almost as important as equity concerns in shaping the desire to go private. Parents who score high on public school ideology are 13 percent less likely to be interested in going private than parents who score low. This underlines the pervasive role that normative commitments play in wedding parents to the public system and making them resistant to arguments for vouchers.

—Performance is by far the most powerful influence on the desire to go private. When satisfaction with public school performance drops from high to low, the probability that a public parent is interested in going private increases by 37 percent—which dwarfs the effects of all other variables. Performance looms as the number one consideration for parents. The familiar arguments to the contrary appear to be quite wrong.

Low-Income, Inner-City Parents

Now let's take a closer look at inner-city parents. When we restrict the analysis to this population, one finding stands in sharp contrast to those we uncovered for parents generally. Among inner-city parents, it appears that race does matter, and in just the way critics have argued: White parents who are opposed to diversity are especially interested in going private. The obvious interpretation is that, because race is a more salient issue in the inner city than elsewhere, many whites see private schools as a way to avoid integration with minorities.

This is the first evidence (within my own study) that separatism and possibly even bigotry may be motivating some of the parental interest in private schools. And it makes sense that such effects would show up, if they show up anywhere, for low-income whites in the inner city—for these are the whites who are most directly affected by policies of diversity. Whites in the suburbs, and whites with money, are much more removed from the reality of integration.

There is a more benign interpretation, however. It may be that our diversity variable has little to say about racism per se, but is really measuring the extent to which respondents value diversity. People who score low are not necessarily racists. They just do not value diversity as much as people who score high. Thus the model's results may simply be telling us that whites who support diversity are especially inclined to stay in the public sector. Whites who lack that positive motivation are less wedded to the public schools and more open to private options, but this does not mean they are racists.

We should be careful, then, about jumping to conclusions. Nonetheless, it appears that race is relevant to the way inner-city whites approach going private, and this raises a red flag that choice advocates and program designers need to be concerned about. On this count, the critics may be right.

Aside from this finding about race, two other findings from this analysis of inner-city parents need to be underlined. The first is that their desire to go private is heavily influenced by their sense that the current system is inequitable. Indeed, race aside, inequity is far more powerful than any other attitude in the model—and indicates, once again, that disadvantaged parents make a strong connection between equity and school choice.

The second finding concerns performance. The critics of choice have long argued that low-income parents from the inner city are particularly unlikely to be guided by performance criteria. They construct an image of parents who need the help of school administrators and government agencies and, if left to their own devices, would make ill-informed decisions that are not motivated by school quality. The empirical results, however, again show that performance is the most powerful factor in the entire analysis. When satisfaction with school performance drops from high to low, the probability that a low-income parent expresses interest in going private increases by 30 percent, which is quite a large shift indeed. In this key respect, they look a lot like all the other parents. They are primarily interested in getting good schools for their children.

The New Public and Private Sectors

What would the public and private sectors look like under a system of expanded choice? Our analysis gives us a basis for drawing some provocative inferences.

Let's begin by recognizing that, in reality, only some of the "swing" parents—the public parents interested in going private—would actually make the switch. The fact is, of course, only some would want to: for they have merely indicated an interest in going private, not that they would actually do so, and there may be all sorts of reasons they would eventually stay put. Moreover, the private sector would have to expand tremendously to absorb them all, and it could not immediately do this. For the short run, demand would exceed supply, leaving many swing parents in the public sector.

In the analysis that follows, I assume that the *most* interested swing parents are the ones who make the switch. These I identify as the parents who, in the prior probit analysis, are estimated to be at the high end—the upper half—of the interest scale. Given this scenario, only half of the swing parents switch from public to private, the other half remain in the public sector—

and the public sector thereby retains about 75 percent of its families overall. Empirically, this seems very plausible.

Suppose now that the new private system consists of the existing private parents plus the swing parents most interested in going private, while the new public system consists of the swing parents who are less interested plus the remaining public parents. How do the new systems compare to the original ones?

Even when just half of the swing parents go private, an expansion of choice dramatically transforms the private sector along almost every social dimension. Compared to existing private parents, the new recruits are substantially lower in income and education, more likely to come from disadvantaged districts, and more likely to be black or Hispanic. When these recruits become part of the new private sector, the usual social biases associated with private schooling are vastly reduced. Indeed, minorities now make up 33 percent of the transformed private sector. As these changes almost dictate, there is also a shift in political partisanship: for with the socially disadvantaged comes a big influx of Democrats, and the original Republican bias is reduced considerably.

There is one social bias, however, that is reduced only slightly: religion. The parents making up the new private sector are almost as likely to be Catholic as current private parents are, and they are just as likely to be born-again. Even with the influx of disadvantaged parents, therefore, the private sector retains much of its religious character.

This same expansion of choice does not lead to major changes in the public sector. It remains pretty much as before, except that it is somewhat higher in income, contains proportionately fewer minorities, and retains more parents who are from better districts. Again, this happens because many of the disadvantaged choose to leave, and the parents who stay tend to be rather advantaged. But overall, the public sector is not affected by the expansion of choice to nearly the extent the private sector is—and the reason is pretty obvious. The current private sector is small and relatively select (due to the tuition requirement), and it is transformed by the influx of new recruits. The public sector is already large and heterogeneous, and it remains so even after many parents leave. It is affected at the margins.

Given the changes occurring in both sectors, how does an expansion of choice appear to affect the social gap between public and private? The transformation of the private sector does not succeed in eliminating all vestiges of the original gap. The new private sector is still somewhat higher in education and income than the public sector, and more Catholic and Republican. This is due to the fact that the new recruits (many of them disadvantaged) have been averaged in with current private parents (many of them fairly advantaged), and there are not enough of the former—under my assumption—to outweigh the latter.

Nonetheless, the changes are considerable. The effect of choice is to reduce the social differences between public and private—and thus to promote moderation—on every one of the dimensions we have considered. Moderation is weakest for religion, testifying to the tenacity of religion in the private school equation. But the degree of moderation is quite pronounced for income and education. The income gap, in particular, is dramatically reduced, leaving only slight differences between public and private. On other social grounds, moreover, the expansion of choice goes farther than this and reverses the traditional association of private schooling with social advantage. Most important, parents in the new private sector are actually more likely to be black or Hispanic than public sector parents are.

These results are not chiseled in stone. With somewhat different assumptions about how many parents switch from public to private and exactly who they are, the details of the analysis would be somewhat different. It is reasonable to suggest, however, that its basic thrust would remain essentially the same: that choice tends to break down existing biases of social advantage.

Conclusion

For the most part, the evidence from this study tends to support the claims of voucher advocates and contradict those of critics. The appeal of private schools is especially strong among parents who are low in income, are minority, and live in low-performing districts: precisely the parents who are the most disadvantaged under the current system. They would be the ones who disproportionately take advantage of an expansion of choice in education— and their shift from public to private should tend to produce a very substantial measure of social moderation, rather than the worsening of social biases that critics say would occur.

Critics also argue that performance has little to do with why parents find private schools attractive, and that the real reasons are rooted in elitism, racial separation, and religion. It is true that religious and moral values play important roles in the current system and would continue to do so under a system of expanded choice. But the evidence suggests that school performance is the single most important factor in the choice to go private—and that elitism and racial separation have little to do with it.

Some of the concerns critics raise, however, do find limited support in the data. One is that racial motives may play a role among low-income whites in the inner city. The other is that, even among the disadvantaged, those with higher levels of education are more likely to go private (although I should emphasize that, because disadvantaged people are so interested in going private, and because they are poorly educated as a group, the aggregate effect of choice is to lower the average education levels of private sector parents, not to raise them). Both of these results point to possible problems that choice advocates and program designers need to be aware of in pursuing voucher plans that are truly equitable.

We also need to recognize that there is more to the critics' argument than these data can address. The focus here has been on the demand for private schools, and thus on what parents want. But parents who want to go private might not be able to do so in their everyday lives for reasons that choice advocates too often dismiss. In the real world, even if everyone had the right to choose their schools, parents who are educated and financially well-off are likely to be more motivated than other parents, to have better information about their alternatives, to have more resources at their disposal for getting their way, to have better social connections and more attractive opportunities, and to have children who are easier and less costly to teach. On the supply side, moreover, private schools may find these advantaged parents (and their children) desirable, and may discriminate against poor and minority families.

These are legitimate concerns. Critics are right to emphasize them, and choice advocates need to take them into account as they think about the proper design of choice systems. With the right designs, these problems may be mitigated, and parental demand more freely pursued. In any event, the analysis here is an analysis of the demand side of the equation only, and what it has to tell us about the social effects of choice should be understood to hold as long as other things are equal. It tells just part of what must ultimately be a much larger story.

Nonetheless, the part that it tells is quite fundamental—and quite positive for the choice movement, which clearly has much to build upon in attracting parents to its cause.

7

School Choice and American Constitutionalism

JOSEPH P. VITERITTI

In December 2000 a federal appellate panel in Ohio handed down a 2-1 ruling affirming a lower court decision holding that the Cleveland voucher program in effect since 1995 violates the establishment clause of the First Amendment. The same program had been upheld on federal constitutional grounds by the Ohio Supreme Court. Attorneys representing the state and parents whose children participate in the program are taking their case to the U.S. Supreme Court.

In 1998 the High Court refused to hear a challenge to a similar program in Milwaukee after its legality was upheld by the Wisconsin Supreme Court; and in 1999 it declined to review a case from Maine after a state supreme court and a lower federal court found that religious schools could be excluded from participation in a statewide program. But the Ohio case is likely to be heard. The High Court signaled its interest in the Ohio dispute in 1999 when it intervened to halt an injunction issued by the trial court that would have suspended the program while the case was under review. In the meantime, voucher and tax credit cases are wending their way through the courts in Florida and Illinois, and half the state legislatures are considering new laws.

The anticipation of a landmark ruling has generated much speculation and argumentation within the scholarly community. Should the states be prohibited from granting financial assistance to families who send their children to religious schools? Does excluding parochial schools or their students from a universal voucher program constitute a form of discrimination that violates the free exercise clause of the First Amendment or the equal protection clause of the Fourteenth Amendment?

Several paths can be taken to assess whether a government program meets an acceptable constitutional standard, all of which are related, none of which suffices on its own. One might begin with the question of original intent, which asks what the framers had in mind when they drafted the Constitution more than two hundred years ago. It is a natural place to start such an inquiry, but it is of limited utility in addressing contemporary problems because the circumstances that existed in eighteenth-century America are hardly comparable to those that prevail at the threshold of the twenty-first.

Any capable lawyer knows that to figure out how the courts might treat a legal question today, it is also necessary to examine precedent. Discovering what the Court has said in past cases provides an insight into how it might act now. But precedent rarely provides a single standard for review, and it does not necessarily lead to a just conclusion. The U.S. Supreme Court has not been consistent in its opinions on great constitutional questions; its members are influenced by their own personal philosophies and dispositions; and First Amendment jurisprudence is among the most erratic areas of American law.

Then there is the Constitution itself. I am not referring here just to the words contained in one clause or another that might be relevant to a given question, but to the underlying political principles embodied in the document as a whole, those guiding lights that give the law of the land meaning through the ages. Such principles provide a standard of justice for judging either one case or an entire body of case law formed over time. Among these principles is that of constitutionalism itself, which requires government to be limited, that there are provinces of personal prerogative beyond the reach of public authority.[1]

This paper will utilize all three approaches, examining original intent, case precedent, and the broader Constitutional context. I will argue that providing families with an opportunity to attend private or religious schools with public support is not only permissible under the First Amendment, but also consistent with the principles of equality and political pluralism that underlie American constitutionalism.

First Amendment Jurisprudence

Opponents of school choice usually rest their legal arguments on three land-mark cases: *Everson* v. *Board of Education of Ewing, Lemon* v. *Kurzman,* and *Committee for Public Education and Religious Liberty* v. *Nyquist,* which were the foundation for a decade of jurisprudence through the 1970s that was strongly though not consistently separationist on church-state issues.[2] *Everson,* handed down in 1947, involved a New Jersey program that reimbursed parents for the costs of transporting children to parochial schools. What draws separationists to this decision is the opinion of Justice Hugo L. Black who, invoking the famous Jeffersonian metaphor, called for a "wall of separa-tion between church and state."[3] The case is of particular significance because it is the first in which the Court incorporated the establishment clause under the Fourteenth Amendment so that it could be applied against the states, much as the *Cantwell* v. *Connecticut* decision had regarding the free exercise clause seven years earlier. Before these two cases it was rightly assumed that the First Amendment served to limit only the actions of the federal government.[4]

What separationists fail to emphasize about *Everson* is that the landmark decision endorsed the claims of parochial school parents and underscored two fundamental principles of law that are crucially relevant to the choice question. Drawing on the "child benefit" concept that it originally articu-lated in 1930, the Court explained that a significant legal distinction exists between aid disbursed to religious schools, which is prohibited by the estab-lishment clause, and aid given to children, which is allowed.[5] It further explained that to deny parochial school students the same benefits entitled to others would amount to a form of discrimination that runs afoul of the free exercise protections guaranteed in the same First Amendment. As the opin-ion reads:

> New Jersey cannot consistently with the "establishment of religion" clause of the First Amendment contribute tax-raised funds to the sup-port of an institution which teaches the tenets of faith of any church. On the other hand, other language in the amendment commands that New Jersey cannot hamper its citizens in the free exercise of their own religion.[6]

The Court did not fully enunciate a separationist posture until the *Lemon* decision of 1971, when it set three criteria for reviewing First Amendment cases. It proscribed any government action that (1) has no "secular purpose,"

(2) has a "primary effect" of advancing or inhibiting religion, or (3) fosters "excessive entanglement" between church and state.[7] While *Lemon* supposedly represented an attempt to define clear standards for review, the majority opinion was incongruous and imprecise. Although warning against government sponsorship and financial support for religion, Chief Justice Warren E. Burger referred approvingly to the *Walz* v. *Tax Commission* decision handed down a year earlier, which upheld tax exemptions for religious institutions. At another point the chief justice remarked that prior holdings do not require a total separation of church and state, but this is the direction that the Court seemed to be moving.

In *Lemon* the Court struck down salary supplements for parochial school teachers who taught secular subjects. The decision prompted a dissent by Justice Byron R. White, who cautioned that the establishment clause coexists with the free exercise clause, which counsels against refusing support for students attending parochial schools simply because they are in a setting that provides them with instruction that is consistent with the tenets of their faith.

In 1973 the *Nyquist* decision invalidated a New York law that provided maintenance and repair grants for nonpublic schools, tuition allotments for poor children, and tax relief for parents. Although the prohibition of direct aid to the schools was consistent with prior decisions, the ban on assistance to children and parents seemed to contradict the "child benefit" concept that prevailed in prior holdings. The Court declared that "insofar as such benefits render assistance to parents who send their children to sectarian schools, their purpose and inevitable effect is to aid and advance those institutions."[8] In another decision handed down that same day the Court overturned a partial tuition plan enacted in Pennsylvania because, Justice Lewis F. Powell Jr. reasoned, the assistance furnished "an incentive for parents to send their children to private schools" and "the intended consequence is to preserve and support religion-oriented institutions."[9]

It was a remarkable leap of legal reasoning for the Court to equate an opportunity to attend parochial schools with a state incentive to do so or the intention of advancing religion. The criteria enshrined in the "*Lemon* test" were so vague that they furnished the Court with a tool for acting in an arbitrary manner. Thus it deemed that any benefit accrued to a religious institution, however incidental, provided grounds for concluding that such a benefit was not only the "primary effect" but also the "primary intent" of the action, completely overlooking the secular benefits that students might receive. But 1973 would prove to be a watershed year for First Amendment jurisprudence, with the Court handing down several opinions that would treat any form of assistance to parochial institutions or their students with grave suspicion. In *Levitt* v. *Committee for Public Education and Religious Liberty,* for example, the Court refused to allow New York State to reimburse parochial schools for expenses they incurred administering tests that the state itself had required, the same tests given at public schools and paid for with state funding.[10]

Although the Burger Court continued to move in a separationist direction through the 1970s, it did so in a confused and muddled fashion, with many of its fine-point distinctions on what was permissible defying reason. Textbook loans to parochial school students were permissible, but lending instructional materials and equipment was not. There was no problem with providing transportation for parochial school students from home to school, but a bus ride for a field trip was unconstitutional. Although the Court approved offering parochial school students transportation services from home to school comparable to those received by their public school peers, it imposed no obligation on the states to do so.

The legal tide began to turn in 1980, when the Supreme Court upheld a New York law that appropriated funds to nonpublic schools for the administration of state exams and the collection of data that the state required.[11] Then in 1983 the Court handed down the landmark *Mueller* v. *Allen* decision. The case involved a tax deduction for tuition and other educational expenses. Unlike the program that had been struck down in *Nyquist,* in which the benefits were not available to public school parents, the benefits in the Minnesota plan were made available to all parents and could be applied to costs for transportation, supplies, or equipment. The facts of the case clearly indicated that the overwhelming majority of those who took advantage of the tuition provision had children in Catholic schools.

Justice William H. Rehnquist, who wrote for the majority, noted that because aid flowing to parochial schools was the result of independent decisions made by parents, no "imprimatur of state approval" was conferred on any brand of religion or religion generally.[12] In so doing he revived the legal distinction between direct and indirect aid that lapsed in the prior decade as well as the child benefit concept that prevailed in cases dating back more than fifty years. As a signal of things to come, the future chief justice commented that it was about time to relax the "primary effect" test commanded by *Lemon.* In a subsequent opinion he asserted, "There is simply no historical foundation for the proposition that the framers intended to build the 'wall of separation' constitutionalized in *Everson.*"[13] He further opined that the *Lemon* test "has no basis in the history of the amendment it seeks to interpret, is difficult to apply, and yields unprincipled results."

In 1996 a unanimous Supreme Court in *Witters* v. *Washington Department of Social Services* approved the use of a public scholarship by a student attending a Bible college.[14] In drafting the opinion, Justice Thurgood Marshall emphasized that such aid was made available to a broad category of students from both public and nonpublic schools, and although some of the aid would inevitably wind up in religious institutions, that result was purely a function of independent decisions made by aid recipients. In a concurring opinion, Justice Powell, who had written for the majority in *Nyquist,* outlined three criteria that would guide future decisions. These require that (1) a program is neutral on its face, regarding any particular religion or religion in general; (2) assistance is equally available to public and private school students; and (3) any aid derived by sectarian institutions is the result of private decisions made by individuals who are the beneficiaries.

In 1993, *Zobrest* v. *Catalina Foothills School District* upheld the right of a Catholic high school student to receive the services of a sign language interpreter provided under a federally funded program.[15] Here again, the Court emphasized that when government offers a neutral service to children who attend religious schools it does not offend the First Amendment. In 1995 the Court sided with a student group at the University of Virginia when the college administration refused to allow it to use student activity fees to publish a newspaper with a religious message. Justice Anthony M. Kennedy drew a distinction between "government speech endorsing religion, which the Establishment Clause forbids, and private speech endorsing religion which the Free Speech and Free Exercise Clauses protect."[16]

If there could be any doubt that the Rehnquist Court was reversing the thinking that governed the jurisprudence of its predecessor, it was removed in 1997 by *Agostini* v. *Felton. Agostini* overturned *Aguilar* v. *Felton,* a 1985 decision holding that public school teachers cannot offer government-supported remedial instruction to poor children on the premises of a parochial school. In executing the reversal, the five-member majority explicitly declared that "more recent cases have undermined the assumptions upon which *Aguilar* rests."[17]

Agostini set the stage for *Mitchell* v. *Helms,* a far-reaching 6-3 ruling that overturned two prior decisions prohibiting religious schools from receiving federal assistance in the form of equipment and materials. Writing for a four-person plurality, Justice Clarence Thomas noted that the aid was available to a broad range of recipients and focused on the single criterion of neutrality. Dismissing the distinction between direct and indirect aid as arbitrary, and indicating that such funding is permissible even when it is used to advance a religious mission, Justice Thomas commented,

If the government is offering assistance to recipients who provide, so to speak, a broad range of indoctrination, the government itself is not thought responsible for any particular indoctrination.[18]

In a more moderate concurring opinion joined by Justice Stephen G. Breyer, Justice Sandra Day O'Connor took exception to the latter points. But she then went on to explain that funds diverted toward the religious mission of a school are not problematic in private choice programs in which the aid is indirect and "wholly dependent on the student's private decision" to attend the school.

A profound philosophical change has occurred on the Court over the last two decades. A working majority now exists that is more accommodationist on the question of religion and less suspicious of sectarian institutions as posing an inherent threat to constitutional norms. A sense of neutrality has emerged designed to assure that such institutions are treated fairly, that their members are not discriminated against in reaping the rewards of programs enacted for the general welfare. The underlying principle behind the new spirit of accommodation is equality. The egalitarian ethos, critically compromised during a brief ten-year period of judicial decisions, has deep roots in the American constitutional tradition.

American Constitutionalism

Originalism is an intriguing intellectual indulgence.[19] One cannot fathom the possibility of understanding the Constitution and at the same time resist the temptation to peek into the minds of those who wrote it. The prospect of applying eighteenth-century thinking to resolve twenty-first century problems is precarious, and it tends to invite selective interpretation by partisans in debate. Looking into the past, scholars can make some claims with great certainty, others that fall into the realm of informed speculation, and yet others that are purely a product of the imagination. The first task in such an inquiry is to understand the difference between these so as to proceed with due caution.

The Constitution was written by men who had deep fears of excessive government. Their motivation was to define a sphere of private life in which citizens would enjoy a maximum degree of freedom. Among the most cherished freedoms they sought to protect is that of religion. According to the conversations that took place during the First Congress, the framers were determined not to repeat the common European practice of joining ecclesiastic and government authority in an established church. Whether they sought to translate disestablishment into a rule for erecting a high, impenetrable wall of separation is questionable. The metaphor that Justice Black attributes to Jefferson in *Everson* is actually traceable to Roger Williams, who fled Congregationalist Massachusetts in 1636 to found Providence as a haven for religious freedom. While aware that intimacy could be risky for either side, Williams was more worried about protecting religion from civil authority than the other way around.[20]

Although the framers did not want to infuse government authority to advantage any one faith, evidence suggests that they were comfortable with maintaining a healthy interaction between the two spheres. On the same day that the First Congress adopted the Bill of Rights, it sent a message to President George Washington urging him to issue a proclamation of public Thanksgiving and prayer to "acknowledge the many signal favors of Almighty God."[21] Washington enthusiastically replied, "It is the duty of all nations to acknowledge the providence of Almighty God, to obey His will, to be grateful for His benefits and humbly to implore His protection and favor."[22] This is the same Washington who, as commander of the Continental army, petitioned Congress to authorize the hiring of military chaplains and the purchase of twenty thousand Bibles for his troops and who, as the nation's first chief executive, bid the country in his Farewell Address "reason and experience both forbid us to expect that national morality can prevail in exclusion of religious principle."[23]

The same Congress that drafted the First Amendment also adopted the Northwest Ordinance, deeming that "Religion, morality and knowledge being necessary for good government, schools and the means of education shall forever be encouraged."[24] This language had been taken from the Massachusetts Constitution written by John Adams in 1780 and eventually copied into the New Hampshire Constitution of 1784. Later the Ohio Company was given a land grant with the understanding that a substantial portion of it would be used for religious instruction among the Native American population. In pursuit of that mandate President Thomas Jefferson signed a treaty with the Kaskaskia tribe in which the federal government agreed to pay for the upkeep of a priest, a school, and a church.[25] The U.S. Supreme Court upheld the constitutionality of Jefferson's treaty in an opinion written by Chief Justice John Marshall.[26]

Some would portray the above examples as isolated occurrences that were out of step with the mainstream of life at the birth of the republic.[27] To the contrary they were in accord with a spirit of accommodation and cooperation that defined American civic life in towns and communities from the earliest of colonial times.[28] In most colonies, especially in New England, the religious congregation was the foundation upon which the political community was built.[29] Because there was no public school system at the time, education was a private manner. While some parents assumed direct responsibility for educating their children, in most cases the task was passed on to the local clergyman, who would offer general instruction along with religious instruction. The minister's expenses, as well as costs for the upkeep of the church, were paid for with local taxes. The integration of education with a proper religious upbringing continued through the middle of the nineteenth century, when Alexis de Tocqueville observed that in America "almost all education is entrusted to the clergy."[30]

Historically, it is difficult to reconcile a strict standard of church-state separation with the behavioral norms that prevailed at the time the Constitution was written or the thinking of its many authors. One must understand that the men who attended the Philadelphia convention and joined the First Congress were neither all of one mind nor consistent in their own thinking over time.[31] Granted, Jefferson was an avowed separationist. The separationist prescription he put forward in the famous letter to the Danbury Baptist Association was also apparent in his proposal to create a statewide system of public schools for Virginia, where he warned against Bible training and religious enquiries for children who were at an impressionable age. Notwithstanding his enormous influence, Jefferson did not speak for the majority of his contemporaries when it came to religion. Furthermore, he was not a party to the deliberations that resulted in the creation of the Constitution or the Bill of Rights. On these matters, James Madison, his fellow Virginian, is more illuminating.[32]

James Madison was the principal author of the U.S. Constitution and the chief architect of the government it brought into being. One cannot possibly comprehend American democracy without understanding Madison, but here, too, the historical record is not a consistent guide. Contemporary opponents of school choice are especially fond of citing two important essays of Madison in pleading their case, "Memorial and Remonstrance" and the "Detached Memoranda." The first, from 1785, was written in opposition to a bill in Virginia that would have made funds available to support "Teachers of the Christian Religion." The second, from 1817, was drafted to protest the celebration of Thanksgiving and the appointment of congressional chaplains. Both are important philosophical tracts, but their significance cannot be appreciated outside a larger theoretical framework that defined Madison's system of governance. The animating concept behind Madison's thinking was that of pluralism, which carried an explicit demand for equality of treatment before the law and commensurate pleas for political tolerance and the protection of minority rights.

No work better captures the genius of Madison's statecraft than Federalist Paper No. 10.[33] Madison explains how the best solution to the threat of tyranny is an extended republic composed of multiple factions. Such diversity in the political arena makes it difficult for any one group to dominate public affairs and protects against majority tyranny. The same rules of political science applied in No. 52, but this time with a particular reference to religion. Here Madison declares:

> In a free government the security of civil rights must be the same for that of religious rights. It consists in one case in the multiplicity of interests, and in the other the multiplicity of sects. The degree of security in both cases will depend on the number of interests and sects.[34]

It is difficult to overstate how Madison's concern with the fate of religious minorities conditioned his devotion to religious freedom, for he understood, as did many of his fellow patriots, that religious minorities are among the most vulnerable of political minorities. The bill he opposed in "Remonstrance" had been put forward by a group of Virginians that included Patrick Henry, George Washington, and John Marshall. They were worried that the disestablishment of the Anglican Church created an institutional vacuum that might lead to a declining public morality, which in turn could weaken the foundation of government. Madison joined Jefferson in opposition because he feared that the bill could inadvertently lead to a loosely structured Christian establishment, which was a distinct possibility in a state where there was so strong a consensus around religious propriety. Madison argued that each person deserves "equal title to the free exercise of religion according to the dictates of conscience," that "we cannot deny an equal freedom to those whose minds have not yielded to the evidence that has convinced us."[35] Madison's objective here was not only to safeguard the equality of religious minorities, but also the rights of nonbelievers.

Madison's resolve comes through again in the "Memoranda." It was curious that he opposed the Thanksgiving celebration or paying military chaplains, given that he endorsed both practices as president. It was he who reinstituted the former practice after it had been suspended by Jefferson. But one sees in the "Memoranda" a growing apprehension that the nation was in the process of cementing a majority consensus about religious belief into a diluted form of establishment that would adversely affect those of minority faiths. His warning is worthy of quotation:

> The establishment of the chaplainship to Congress is a palpable violation of equal rights. . . . The tenets of the chaplains elected (by major-

ity) shut the door of worship against the members whose creeds and consciences forbid participation in that of the majority. To say nothing with other sects, this is the case with that of Roman Catholics and Quakers who have always had members in one or both of the legislative branches. Could a Catholic clergyman ever be appointed a Chaplain?[36]

Madison's anxiety over the plight of religious minorities was symptomatic of a larger preoccupation that was at the heart of his constitutional scheme. Madison simply did not trust the venal instincts of those politicians who made their way into the state legislatures.[37] He was persuaded that an extended republic would attract men to the national government who were public-minded and less likely to trample on the rights of minorities. If Madison's constitutional plan was not a foolproof mechanism for offsetting political passions in the state legislatures, his fears would prove prophetic as the nation entered the nineteenth century.

The Common School

When Horace Mann opened the doors to his new public school in 1837, he set the stage for a struggle over religious freedom that continues today.[38] The common school would serve as the threshold for acculturating immigrant populations from Europe to an American way of life, fortifying American democracy, and offering each individual an opportunity for a better existence. Education became an essential part of the American dream, a social leveler unparalleled in the modern state. But the opportunity for a free public education would come at a price. The heaviest cost was imposed on the political and social pluralism that Madison found so essential to a healthy democracy; the most severe wounds inflicted upon religious minorities who soon realized that acculturation was a form of homogenization.

Mann believed that religion could play a role in cultivating morality and civic virtue among the immigrant masses. Although he pledged religious neutrality in the public schools, his academic curriculum was an instrument for inculcating the Protestant faith.[39] Students were required to recite prayers, sing hymns, and read the King James version of the Bible. For Mann, becoming an American meant adopting the cultural and religious mores of the Yankee culture that defined the mainstream of New England society. He claimed that reading the Bible without commentary was a neutral act, but he was persuaded that students would come to recognize the power of its truths. Thus in preparing his final report to the Board of Education in 1848, he confessed, "Our system earnestly inculcates all Christian morals."[40]

If there is any episode in American history that validated Madison's fears of majority tyranny, it was that period in the nineteenth century when the common school movement took hold. This tyranny showed its most ugly side to the smaller religious communities that stood on the fringe of political power. Mann's religious message was deeply resented, not just by Catholics and Jews, but also smaller Protestant denominations such as Baptists and Quakers who did not worship in the same churches as the ruling establishment. It was only the Catholics, however, who had the numbers to mount a formidable protest, which in turn stirred up a strong wave of anti-Catholic bigotry.

In 1852 an outburst by Catholics against Bible reading in the Cambridge public schools brought a blunt editorial in the *Common School Journal* that was indicative of the prevailing mentality.

> The English Bible, in some way or another, has, ever since the settlement of Cambridge, been read in its public schools, by children of every denomination; but in the year 1851, the ignorant immigrants who have found food and shelter in this land of freedom and plenty, made free and plentiful through the influence of these very Scriptures, presume to dictate to us, and refuse to let their children read as do ours, and always have done, the Word of Life. The arrogance, not to say the impudence, of this conduct, must startle every native citizen.[41]

Within the next year the Massachusetts legislature passed the nation's first compulsory education law. The law was sponsored by the nativist Know-Nothing Party as a way to discipline recalcitrant Catholics. Now education was no longer a private affair, but a public one. School attendance, once offered as an opportunity to those who did not have the means to educate their children, was transformed into an obligation. This free education was made available in government-run schools that still carried a religious message. When Catholic leaders demanded funds to operate their own schools, their petitions received a strong rebuttal. In 1854 the Massachusetts legislature passed a law prohibiting aid to religious schools. During the same year it instituted a Nunnery Investigating Committee and attempted to enact legislation that would limit the franchise and officeholding to native-born citizens.

Developments in Massachusetts were symptomatic of a growing national mood. While it was the only state with a law requiring Bible reading in public schools, the practice was followed by 75 to 80 percent of the schools in the country.[42] Most state courts at the time were unsympathetic to pleas by religious minorities to end the practice, accepting the argument that the

Bible was nonsectarian literature.[43] With growing urban congregations, Catholic leaders across the country lobbied state legislatures to acquire funds for their own schools.[44] Much of the rhetoric that surrounded the funding debates resembled the arguments heard today. When Catholics in Michigan proposed an aid bill, opponents portrayed their plan as a nationwide plot by the Jesuits to destroy public education. Parochial school advocates in Minnesota were accused of subverting basic American principles.

The sweep of local battles finally took on the patina of a national issue in 1875 when Rep. James G. Blaine of Maine proposed a constitutional amendment to prohibit funding of religious schools. Blaine's proposal was evidence of the widely held understanding at the time that the First Amendment did not prohibit such funding. Blaine's objective was to correct what he saw to be a "constitutional defect."[45] Harboring political ambitions, Blaine sought to use the issue to ride a wave of nativist, anti-Catholic sentiment right to the White House in a campaign against "rum, Romanism and rebellion."[46] Blaine's amendment got strong backing in both houses of Congress but fell four votes short of the two-thirds majority needed in the Senate.

Although Blaine's amendment failed in Washington, it became a model for bills hurried through the state legislatures where (as Madison feared) political passions held more sway. Within one year, fourteen states passed laws prohibiting aid to religious schools; by 1890 the number was up to twenty-nine.[47] While many choice opponents point to these amendments as provisions designed to protect religious freedom, the intent and effect were the opposite. Enacted in a storm of religious bigotry, they were designed to undermine the principles within the First Amendment. Coupled with compulsory education laws and a public school system that decidedly favored one religious tradition over others, Blaine's amendment marks a period in bold contrast to an earlier century when communities set up schools that reflected their own values.

The lowest point in the long episode came in 1922 when Oregon passed an initiative that required all children to attend public school.[48] Cooked up by the Ku Klux Klan and the Scottish Rite Masons, the plan was an undisguised attempt to close nonpublic schools. The measure was challenged by the Sisters of the Holy Names of Jesus and Mary as well as the directors of the Hill Military Academy. Their fight was eventually taken to the U.S. Supreme Court, where it resulted in a landmark decision. In *Pierce* v. *Society of Sisters*, a unanimous Court declared:

> The fundamental theory upon which all governments in this Union repose excludes any general power of the state to standardize its chil-

dren by forcing them to accept instruction from public teachers only. The child is not the mere creature of the state; those who nurture him and direct his destiny have the right . . . to prepare him for additional obligations.[49]

Pierce upheld the right of nonpublic schools to exist and that of parents to determine what education is appropriate for their children. Unfortunately, *Pierce* did not take up the important issue of funding. This left a regrettable arrangement in most states that commanded compulsory education for all students but supported only those who attended public school. The net result was a system that favored one group of students over another, furnished disincentives for parents to send their children to nonpublic schools, and, on a practical level, left the latter option open only to those who could pay their own way.

Modern Times

No one knows how Madison would have assessed the present situation, or how he would have deliberated if asked to judge the voucher case from Ohio. Much has changed, much remains the same; some for the better, and some for worse. The common school and compulsory education would have been difficult to anticipate at the birth of the nation. Religious life has been transformed in ways that alter the stakes of the contemporary debate. The kind of majoritarian consensus about religion that prompted Madison to write his "Remonstrance," or that reared its head at the Protestant pulpit a century later, no longer exists.

Americans are among the most avid churchgoers in the modern world, and when asked most will attest to their belief in God and the importance of their faith.[50] However, the old mainline Protestant churches that once dominated religious and political life in America now share the pulpit and the statehouse with other groups—not just Catholics, Jews, and Baptists, but also a growing population of Evangelical Christians, Muslims, Buddhists, and Hindus. American religious life has become diversified by a flow of immigration from outside of Europe and new patterns of worship. There has been no time in U.S. history when the threat of an established church has been so remote; and, as Madison would have it, the greatest assurance of that is a vibrant religious pluralism.

There are religious zealots today, mostly on the political right, who would marshal public authority to favor one religious perspective over another. But contrary to the situation that prevailed in more perilous times, they are in a distinct minority. On the whole Americans today are disinclined to impose their religious views on their neighbors and exhibit a strong sense of tolerance toward people of other faiths. As Alan Wolfe describes it, Americans tend to exhibit a "quiet faith," which they are reluctant to interject into public life.[51] If there is one characteristic that distinguishes public schools today from the institutions of Horace Mann it is their avid secularism. Although noble efforts are being launched to reverse the trend, secularism has been taken to such a point that religion remains a taboo topic within the public school curriculum.[52]

Most Americans accept this secularism in their public schools. Just because it is so widely taken for granted, it visits a tyranny of its own upon minorities who view religion differently. Schools have forbidden children to mention God in school presentations and religion in commencement exercises or to write about matters of faith in their assignments. The resounding message communicated in public schools is to "leave religion home." Many disagreements revolve around the issue of school prayer. In a recent case the Court ruled against officially sanctioned prayers at a football game.[53] In the past the Court has permitted students to pray in school so long as the prayers were not organized by school authorities. While the differentiation between voluntary and official prayer is an entirely reasonable standard, it can be difficult to apply when confronted by the facts of a particular case. At stake is the crucial determination between activities prohibited by the establishment clause and those protected by the free exercise clause.

Since public schools have become secularized, a more compelling argument can be made to provide alternatives to the minority of deeply religious families whose attitudes toward their faith are different from the majority's. Most people have an easy time separating religion from their daily lives. To use a term popularized by Stephen L. Carter, they do not feel compromised by the expectation to "treat religion as a hobby."[54] But religion imposes more exacting demands upon those who are devout observers. It may require a daily routine of prayers, the observance of strict dietary laws, or an unusual form of attire. These same devout observers may be offended by the idea of having their children partake in curricular activities that most people readily accept, such as teen counseling, sex education, or even coeducation.[55]

For the deeply religious, education is a way of inculcating values that cannot be conveyed in public schools. The only avenue for pursuing such a value-based education is through a religious school. Under the existing arrangement, that option is only available to those who have the private means to afford it; the rest are expected to fall into line with the majority. It is an unjustifiable burden to place on individuals as the price for practicing religion the way they see fit. Public mores, school finance schemes, and the law have conspired to conjure a standard of religious freedom in America that works well for all but those for whom religion is most important. Could that have been what the framers had in mind? Can you imagine reserving freedom of the press only for the illiterate or freedom of speech only for the quiet?

I am not suggesting that public school dispensations or private school vouchers be offered only to those who demonstrate that they are truly religious because that would involve a level of church-state entanglement that is far too meddlesome.[56] Needs-based plans such as the ones in Milwaukee and Cleveland that provide aid to students whose families cannot afford private school tuition make more sense. As research cited in the March 2000 Program on Education Policy and Governance conference indicates, many poor parents prefer to send their children to religious schools. Some may do so for strictly religious reasons, but many do so because they believe that the sense of community created in schools with strong religious values has collateral effects that translate into a safer learning environment and higher levels of academic achievement. These are sophisticated observations on the part of poor parents. I wonder whether social scientists would ever have figured it out themselves if James S. Coleman were not so bold as to suggest it back in 1982.[57]

The importance of Coleman's assertion and its confirmation by parents cannot be exaggerated. If the assertion is true, it means that school choice can be brought to bear on the root problem that perpetuates a larger social inequality: the continuing inability to sever the relationship between achievement and race.[58] The founders may not have anticipated the depth of that inequality two centuries ago. Contemporary research in political science has demonstrated, however, that the political equality that Madison and his colleagues aspired to cannot be achieved without closing the racial gap in education.[59] The Supreme Court spoke to this point when it declared in 1954:

Today, education is perhaps the most fundamental function of state and local governments. Compulsory school attendance laws and the great expenditures for education both demonstrate our recognition of the importance of education to our democratic society. . . . It is the very foundation of good citizenship. Today it is the principal instrument in awakening the child to cultural values, in preparing him for later professional training, and in helping him to adjust normally to his environment. In these days, it is doubtful that any child may reasonably be expected to succeed in life if he is denied the opportunity to an education. Such an education, where the state has undertaken to provide it, is a right that must be made available to all on equal terms.[60]

Accepting this proposition changes the stakes of the choice debate. I need to restate that, for reasons mentioned above (pluralism and secularism especially), I do not believe that contemporary America is at risk of setting up an established church. The racial inequality highlighted in *Brown* v. *Board of Education* (1954) is of much more immediate concern; its consequences are more profound.

Just Choosing

Many opponents of school choice acknowledge the central role of education in American life but do not accept the empirical assertion that parochial schools out-perform public schools. Many of these choice opponents change their tune, however, when put under oath in federal court and inadvertently rally the Coleman assertion to argue against choice. Picking up on the argument the Supreme Court accepted in 1973, they contend that choice provides parents with a compelling incentive to attend religious schools. (The federal appeals court in Ohio is a recent case in point.) They dismiss the possibility that parents may prefer parochial schools for religious reasons or that such schools may provide a setting that is supportive of their beliefs. The unspoken premise of the incentive argument is that parochial schools are so academically superior to public schools that when given a choice to send their children to religious institutions, parents find the offer irresistible.

There may be some truth to this claim. To the extent that it is true, it provides a persuasive argument for choice. But assessing how much of the attraction minority parents have to parochial schools is academic rather than religious remains difficult. As Coleman explained, the two factors are connected. Ultimately one's response to the question must turn on an assessment of the comparative academic strengths of parochial schools and public schools. Do choice opponents believe that parochial schools provide poor children with the only opportunity for a decent education? Or is it merely a better opportunity? How much better? At what point does the draw become a dangerous incentive for nonbelievers to get involved with religion? Who should decide that?

Since the *Mueller* decision of 1983, the Supreme Court has suggested that parents should decide. So long as children who attend parochial schools do so because their parents, for whatever reason, want them to, it is permissible. It is permissible even if the state has some role in supporting that choice.

Because the state supports the decisions of parents who choose to have their children in public schools, the implied formula appears equitable.

A policy in which the state supports the independent choices of parents would be fair even if parochial schools were the only reasonable academic option available to their children. The indignity of an inferior education is not cured by compounding it with the injustice of making it compulsory. But the landscape of American education has changed since *Mueller*. The range of choices has expanded for those who want to reach beyond traditional public schools.

The assortment of educational options within the public sector now includes magnet schools, interdistrict choice schools, and charter schools. Between 1982 and 1991, the number of students enrolled in magnet schools climbed from 441,000 to more than 1.2 million; the number of schools offering such programs climbed from 1,019 to 2,433.[61] Since 1985, eighteen states have implemented open-enrollment programs across district lines, and another nineteen have instituted choice programs at the local level.[62] Since 1991, another thirty-six states and the District of Columbia passed charter school laws, and there are more than 2,000 such institutions in existence today.

Perhaps the situation becomes clearer when reexamining Cleveland, the scene of the legal battle. There were 3,852 students enrolled in the Cleveland voucher program at the beginning of the 2000–01 school year. Of the fifty-seven private schools that participate in it, forty-seven are sectarian. Cleveland has twenty-three magnet schools that enroll more than 13,584 students. The city has nine charter schools that enroll 1,962 students, and two new ones are being planned, with a projected enrollment of 460.[63] Thus families in Cleveland who seek alternatives to the regular public schools have much to choose from beyond the parochial schools participating in the voucher program. The incentive argument is further weakened by the fact that students who enroll in the voucher program receive considerably less public funding than students in public schools. Per capita funding for children in the voucher program is $2,250 or less; for charter school students, $4,518; and for those in regular public schools, $7,746. Funding for magnet schools is generally at the same level as regular public schools and is occasionally higher because of the enrichment programs provided.

The range of options presents parents with an array of complex factors to weigh in deciding where to send their children to school. As difficult as the choice might be, it is preferable to no choice at all. But the most important decision to emerge from the Cleveland experience will be ultimately handed down by the U.S. Supreme Court. It now has a fair set of standards to guide its deliberations with the criteria set down by Justice Powell in *Witters* (1996) and reinforced in recent decisions. These criteria are based upon the principles of neutrality, equality, and freedom, all of which have a special meaning within the American constitutional tradition. If these criteria are followed, the Cleveland program will be upheld. If they are not, then religious freedom and educational opportunity will continue to mean different things to different people.

Notes

1. See Carl J. Friedrich, *Constitutional Government and Democracy*, rev. ed. (New York: Ginn and Co., 1950); and J. Roland Pennock and John W. Chapman, *Nomos XX: Constitutionalism* (New York University Press, 1979).

2. For a more detailed analysis of the case law, see Joseph P. Viteritti, *Choosing Equality: School Choice, the Constitution, and Civil Society* (Brookings, 1999), pp. 129–43.

3. *Everson* v. *Board of Education of Ewing*, 330 U.S. 1, 15–16 (1947).

4. *Cantwell* v. *Connecticut*, 310 U.S. 296 (1940). See also Joseph P. Viteritti, "Choosing Equality: Religious Freedom and Educational Opportunity under Constitutional Federalism," *Yale Law and Policy Review*, vol. 15 (1996).

5. *Cochran* v. *Board of Education*, 281 U.S. 370 (1930).

6. *Everson* v. *Board of Education of Ewing*, 330 U.S. at 16.

7. *Lemon* v. *Kurzman*, 403 U.S. 602, 614–15 (1971).

8. *Committee for Public Education and Religious Liberty* v. *Nyquist*, 413 U.S. 756, 793 (1973).

9. *Sloan* v. *Lemon*, 413 U.S. 825, 830, 832 (1973).

10. *Levitt* v. *Committee for Public Education and Religious Liberty*, 413 U.S. 472 (1973).

11. *Committee for Public Education and Religious Liberty* v. *Regan*, 444 U.S. 646 (1980).

12. *Mueller* v. *Allen*, 463 U.S. 387, 399 (1983).

13. *Wallace* v. *Jaffree*, 472 U.S. 38, 106 (1985).

14. *Witters* v. *Washington Department of Social Services*, 474 U.S. 481 (1986).

15. *Zobrest* v. *Catalina Foothills School District*, 509 U.S. 1 (1993).

16. *Rosenberger* v. *Rectors of the University of Virginia*, 515 U.S. 819 (1995).

17. *Aguilar* v. *Felton*, 521 U.S. 203, 222 (1997).

18. *Mitchell* v. *Helmes*, 120 S.Ct. 2530 (2000).

19. See, generally, Jack N. Rakove, *Original Meanings: Politics and Ideas in the Making of the Constitution* (Random House, 1996); Paul Brest, "The Misconceived Quest for the Original Understanding," *Boston University Law Review*, vol. 60 (1980); and Terrence Sandalow, "Constitutional Interpretation," *Michigan Law Review*, vol. 60 (1981).

20. See Mark De Wolfe Howe, *The Garden and the Wilderness: Religion and Government in American History* (University of Chicago Press, 1965).

21. Cited in Steven B. Epstein, "Rethinking the Constitutionality of Ceremonial Deism," *Columbia Law Review*, vol. 96 (1996), p. 2113.

22. Reprinted in Philip Kurland and Ralph Lerner, eds., *The Founders Constitution*, vol. 5 (University of Chicago Press, 1987).

23. George Washington, "Farewell Address," September 17, 1796.

24. Northwest Ordinance, Article 3, Articles of Confederation, July 13, 1787.

25. David Tyack, Thomas James, and Aaron Benavot, *Law and the Shaping of Public Education, 1785–1954* (University of Wisconsin Press, 1987).

26. *Worcester v. Georgia*, 31 U.S. (6 pet.) 515 (1832).

27. Isaac Kramnick and R. Lawrence Moore, *The Godless Constitution: The Case against Religious Correctness* (Norton, 1996).

28. Thomas J. Curry, *The First Freedoms: Church and State in America to the Passage of the First Amendment* (New York: Oxford University Press, 1986).

29. Barbara Allen, *Tocqueville on Covenant and the American Republic* (Johns Hopkins University Press, 2000); John G. West, *The Politics of Revelation and Reason: Civic Life in the New Nation* (University Press of Kansas, 1996); and Barry Alan Shain, *The Myth of American Individualism: The Protestant Origins of American Constitutional Thought* (Princeton University Press, 1994).

30. Alexis de Tocqueville, *Democracy in America*, vol. 1, Philips Bradley, ed. (Knopf, 1945), p. 320.

31. See Viteritti, *Choosing Equality*, pp. 118–29; Gary Rosen, *American Compact: James Madison and the Problem of Founding* (University Press of Kansas, 1999), pp. 126–55; and Jean M. Yarbrough, *American Virtues: Thomas Jefferson and the Character of a Free People* (University Press of Kansas, 1998), pp. 170–96.

32. See Michael W. McConnell, "The Origins and Historical Understanding of Free Exercise of Religion," *Harvard Law Review*, vol. 103 (1990); and Michael W. McConnell, "Muticulturalism, Majoritarianism, and Educational Choice: What Does Our Constitutional Tradition Have to Say?" *University of Chicago Legal Forum* (1991).

33. See David Epstein, *The Political Theory of the Federalist* (University of Chicago Press, 1984), pp. 59–146; and Rakove, *Original Meanings*, pp. 35–36, 310–16, 330–36.

34. See Ronald F. Thiemann, *Religion and American Public Life: A Dilemma for Democracy* (Georgetown University Press, 1996), pp. 72–144; and James Davidson Hunter, "Religious Freedom and the Challenge of Modern Pluralism," in James Davidson Hunter and Os Guinness, eds., *Articles of Faith, Articles of Peace: The Religious Liberty Clauses and the American Public Philosophy* (Brookings, 1990).

35. James Madison, "Memorial and Remonstrance against Religious Assessments," (1785), reprinted in Saul Padover, ed., *The Complete Madison* (Harper, 1953).

36. James Madison, "Detached Memoranda" (1817).

37. See Rakove, *Original Meanings*, pp. 48–51, 314–16, 335.

38. See, generally, Viteritti, *Choosing Equality*, pp. 145–79.

39. Charles M. Glenn, *The Myth of the Common School* (University of Massachusetts Press, 1988).

40. Horace Mann, "Twelfth Annual Report to the Board of Education" (1848).

41. "The Bible in the Public Schools," *Common School Journal*, vol. 14 (January 1, 1852), p. 9.

42. Tyack, James, and Benevot, *Law and the Shaping of Public Education*, p. 164.

43. Otto Templar Hamilton, *The Courts and the Curriculum* (New York: Teachers College, 1927).

44. Diane Ravitch, *The Great School Wars* (Johns Hopkins University Press, 2000); and Lloyd Jorgenson, *The State and the Non-Public School* (University of Missouri Press, 1980).

45. *New York Times*, November 29, 1875, p. 2.

46. See Stephen K. Green, "The Blaine Amendment Reconsidered," *American Journal of Legal History*, vol. 36 (1992); and Marie Carolyn Klinkhamer, "The Blaine Amendment of 1875: Private Monies for Political Action," *Catholic History Review*, vol. 42 (1957).

47. Green, "The Blaine Amendment Reconsidered," p. 43. See, generally, Joseph P. Viteritti, "Blaine's Wake: School Choice, the First Amendment, and State Constitutional Law," *Harvard Journal of Law and Public Policy*, vol. 21 (1998).

48. See William G. Ross, *Forging New Freedoms: Nativism, Education, and the Constitution, 1917–1927* (University of Nebraska Press, 1994), pp. 148–73; Jorgenson, *The State and the Non-Public School*, pp. 205–15; and David Tyack, "The Perils of Pluralism: The Background of the Pierce Case," *American Historical Review*, vol. 74 (1968).

49. *Pierce* v. *Society of Sisters*, 268 U.S. 370, 374–75 (1930).

50. *The Diminishing Divide . . . American Church, American Politics* (Washington, D.C.: Pew Research Center for the People and the Press, January 25, 1996).

51. Alan Wolfe, *One Nation After All* (Viking Books, 1998), pp. 39–87, 275–323.

52. Warren A. Nord, *Religion and American Education: Rethinking a National Dilemma* (University of North Carolina Press, 1995). But see also, Warren A. Nord and Charles C. Haynes, *Taking Religion Seriously across the Curriculum* (Alexandria, VA: First Amendment Center, 1996).

53. *Santa Fe Independent School District* v. *Doe*, 120 S.Ct. 2266 (2000).

54. Stephen L. Carter, *The Culture of Disbelief: How American Law and Politics Trivialize Religious Devotion* (Anchor Books, 1994).

55. See Rosemary C. Salomone, *Models of Schooling: Conscience, Community, and Common Education* (Yale University Press, 2000).

56. See Kent Greenawalt, "Five Questions about Religion Judges Are Afraid to Ask," in Nancy Rosenblum, ed., *Obligations of Citizenship and Demands of Faith* (Princeton University Press, 2000).

57. James S. Coleman, Thomas Hoffer, and Sally Kilgore, *High School Achievement* (Basic Books, 1982).

58. See Christopher Jencks and Meredith Phillips, eds., *The Black-White Test Score Gap* (Brookings, 1998); and Susan E. Mayer and Paul E. Peterson, eds., *Earning and Learning: Why Schools Matter* (Brookings, 1999).

59. See Norman H. Nie, Jane Junn, and Kenneth Stehlik-Barry, *Education and Democratic Citizenship in America* (University of Chicago Press, 1996).

60. *Brown v. Board of Education*, 347 U.S. 483, 493 (1954).

61. Rolf K. Blank, Roger E. Levine, and Lauri Steel, "After 15 Years: Magnet Schools in Urban Education," in Bruce Fuller and Richard Elmore, eds., *Who Chooses? Who Loses? Culture, Institutions, and the Unequal Effects of School Choice* (New York: Teachers College Press, 1996), p. 157.

62. Nina Shokraii Rees, *School Choice: What's Happening in the States?* (Washington, D.C.: Heritage Foundation, 2000).

63. All data concerning the Cleveland school district were obtained from the Ohio Department of Education. According to the decision rendered by the U.S. District Court in Northern Ohio, there were 3,761 students enrolled in the voucher program and fifty-six private schools participated, forty-six of which are religious.

8

Effects of School Vouchers on Student Test Scores

WILLIAM G. HOWELL, PATRICK J. WOLF,
PAUL E. PETERSON, AND DAVID E. CAMPBELL

I n the past decade considerable data have been collected on
school vouchers' effects on low-income families and their children.[1] Just ten years ago, the only information available about this
controversial issue came from an experimental public choice program conducted during the 1960s in Alum Rock, California.[2] But
in the early and mid-1990s, new voucher programs sprouted
across the country in such cities as Milwaukee, Wisconsin; Cleveland and Dayton, Ohio; Indianapolis, Indiana; New York City;
San Antonio, Texas; and Washington, D.C. And with their appear-
ance, ample opportunities for new research have arisen.

Initially, evaluations of these programs confronted numerous
limitations. Planning for the evaluations, for instance, often began
after an experiment was under way, making it impossible to gather
baseline data or to form an appropriate control group. As a result,
the quality of the data collected was not as good as researchers normally would prefer.[3]

Recent evaluations of voucher programs in New York City, Dayton, and Washington, D.C., have yielded the best available information on the student test-score outcomes of school voucher programs. Because vouchers in these cities were awarded by lot,
program evaluations could be designed as randomized field trials.

Before conducting the lotteries, the evaluation team collected baseline data on student test scores and family background characteristics. One and two years later, the evaluation team retested the students.[4] Because average student abilities and family backgrounds are similar at baseline, subsequent differences observed between those students offered a voucher and those not offered a voucher may be attributed to programmatic effects. This chapter reports on the estimated effects of switching from a public to a private school on the test-score performances of students after one and two years.

Prior Research on Vouchers and Test Scores

Studies on school sector effects generally find that low-income and African American students attending private schools tend to stay in school longer than their public school peers and (though the evidence on this account is more mixed) score higher on standardized tests. One recent University of Chicago analysis of the National Longitudinal Survey of Youth finds that, even when adjustments are made for family background characteristics, students from Catholic schools are 16 percentage points more likely to go to college.[5] This impact is greatest among urban minorities. The study's conclusions comport with many others.[6] After reviewing the literature on school effects on learning, John F. Witte concludes that studies of private schools "indicate a substantial private school advantage in terms of completing high school and enrolling in college, both very important events in predicting future income and well-being."[7]

Even the most careful of these studies, however, can account for only observed family background characteristics. Researchers cannot be sure that they have controlled for an intangible factor—the willingness of a family to pay for its child's tuition, and all that this implies about the importance it places on education. As a result, whether findings describe actual differences between public and private schools or simply differences in the kinds of students and families attending them remains unclear.[8] This self-selection problem arises whenever a population differentiates itself by freely selecting into a particular treatment condition—in this case, a private school.

The best solution to the self-selection problem is the random assignment of students to test and control groups. Until recently, evaluations of voucher programs have not utilized such a design. Privately funded programs in Indianapolis, San Antonio, and Milwaukee admitted students on a first-come, first-served basis. And in the state-funded program in Cleveland, though scholarship winners were initially selected by means of a lottery, eventually all applicants were offered a scholarship, thereby precluding the conduct of a randomized experiment. The public Milwaukee program did award vouchers by a lottery, but data collection was incomplete.[9]

As a consequence, the findings presented here on New York, Dayton, and Washington, D.C., provide a unique opportunity to examine the effects of school vouchers on students from low-income families who live in central cities. In contrast to prior studies, vouchers were awarded by lotteries conducted by the evaluation team, follow-up test-score information was obtained from about one-half to two-thirds of the students who participated in the studies, and baseline data provided information that allowed the analysts to adjust for nonresponse.

The Three Voucher Programs

In several key respects, the designs of the three voucher programs—the School Choice Scholarships Foundation (SCSF) program in New York City, the Parents Advancing Choice in Education (PACE) program in the Dayton metropolitan area, and the Washington Scholarship Fund (WSF) program in Washington, D.C.—were similar. All were privately funded; all were targeted at students from low-income families, most of whom lived within the central city; all provided partial vouchers, which the family was expected to supplement from other resources; all students included in the evaluation had previously been attending public schools. The programs, however, differed in size, timing, and certain administrative details. Table 8-1 summarizes the programs' most important characteristics.

The SCSF Program in New York City

In February 1997, SCSF announced its intention to provide 1,300 scholarships worth up to $1,400 annually for at least three years to children from low-income families. The scholarship could be applied toward the cost of attending either religious or secular private schools. After announcing the program, SCSF received initial applications from over 20,000 students between February and late April 1997.

To qualify for a scholarship, children had to be entering grades one through four, live in New York City, attend a public school at the time of application, and come from families with incomes low enough to qualify for the U.S. government's free school lunch program. To ascertain eligibility, families were asked to attend verification sessions during which their income and child's public school attendance were documented. Seventy-five percent of students offered scholarships found places in private schools.

Table 8-1. *Description of the Voucher Programs*

Characteristic	New York, N.Y.	Dayton and Montgomery County, Ohio	Washington, D.C.
Name of program	School Choice Scholarships Foundation	Parents Advancing Choice in Education	Washington Scholarship Fund
First year of program	1997–98	1998–99	1998–99
Maximum amount of scholarship (dollars)	1,400	1,200	1,700
Eligible grades	1–4	K–12	K–8
Income eligibility	Eligible for federal free lunch program	Up to 2 times federal poverty line	Up to 2.5 times federal poverty line
Number of students from public schools who were tested at baseline	1,960	803	1,582
Take-up rate in first year (percent)	62	54	53
Testing response rate in first year (percent)	82	56	63
Testing response rate in second year (percent)	66	49	50

The PACE Program in Dayton, Ohio

In the spring of 1998, PACE offered low-income families within the Dayton metropolitan area an opportunity to win a scholarship to help defray the costs of attending the private school of their choice. Students entering kindergarten through twelfth grade qualified for a voucher. For the 1998–99 school year, PACE offered scholarships to 515 students who were in public schools and 250 who were already enrolled in private schools.

Based on census data and administrative records, program operators estimated that approximately 32,000 students met the program's income and eligibility requirements; of these, 3,000 initially applied. PACE invited applicants to sessions in which administrators verified their eligibility for a scholarship. Over 1,500 applicants attended these verification sessions in February, March, and April 1998. The lottery was then held on April 29, 1998.

During the first year of the program, the PACE scholarships covered 50 percent of tuition at a private school, with the maximum award being $1,200.

Support was guaranteed for at least four years, with a possibility of continuing through high school, provided funds remained available. Scholarship amounts increased beginning in 1999 as a result of additional funds raised by PACE and the Children's Scholarship Fund, a nationwide school choice scholarship program. Of those students offered scholarships, 53 percent made use of them to attend a private school in the first year of the program.

The WSF Program in Washington, D.C.

The Washington Scholarship Fund was originally established in 1993. At that time, the program offered a limited number of scholarships to students from low-income families. By the fall of 1997, WSF was serving approximately 460 children at seventy-two private schools. WSF then received a large infusion of new funds from two philanthropists, and a major expansion of the program was announced in October 1997. Administrators relied upon general news announcements and paid advertising to publicize the enlarged school choice scholarship program. WSF announced that, in the event that applications exceeded scholarship resources, winners would be chosen by lottery.

To qualify, applicants had to reside in Washington, D.C., and be entering grades K–8 in the fall of 1998. Families with incomes at or below the poverty line received vouchers that equaled 60 percent of tuition or $1,700, whichever was less.[10] Families with income above the poverty line received smaller scholarships. No family with income more than two-and-a-half times the poverty line was eligible for support. WSF claims that it will attempt to continue tuition support for at least three years and possibly, if funds are available, until students complete high school.

Over 7,500 telephone applications to the program were received between October 1997 and March 1998. In response to invitations sent by WSF, over 3,000 applicants attended income verification sessions. The lottery selecting scholarship winners was held on April 29, 1998. WSF awarded over 1,000 scholarships, with 809 going to students not previously in a private school. Of those students offered scholarships, 53 percent made use of them to attend a private school in the first year of the program.

Evaluation Procedures

The evaluation procedures used in all three studies conform to those in randomized field trials. The evaluation team collected baseline data prior to the lottery, administered the lottery, and then collected follow-up information one and two years later.

Baseline Data Collection

At the income verification sessions attended by voucher applicants, students took the Iowa Test of Basic Skills (ITBS) in reading and mathematics.[11] Only students in kindergarten were not tested at baseline.[12] The sessions took place during the three months preceding the lotteries. These sessions generally lasted about two hours and were held in private school classrooms, where schoolteachers and administrators served as proctors under the overall supervision of the evaluation team. The producer of the ITBS graded the tests.[13]

While children were being tested, accompanying adults filled out surveys on their satisfaction with their children's schools, their involvement in their children's education, and their demographic characteristics. Students in grades four and higher completed similar surveys. Findings from these surveys have been reported elsewhere.[14]

Over 5,000 students participated in baseline testing in New York City. After vouchers were awarded, 960 families were selected at random from those who did not win the lottery to form a control group.[15] All of these students were attending public schools. In Dayton, 1,440 students were tested at baseline, of whom 803 were attending a public school at the time. In Washington, D.C., 2,023 students were tested at baseline, of whom 1,582 were attending a public school at the time. In all three cities, follow-up testing and survey information was obtained only from families with children in public schools at the time of baseline testing.

The Lottery

The evaluation team conducted the lottery in May 1997 in New York City and in April 1998 in Dayton and Washington, D.C. Program operators notified winners a couple of weeks thereafter. In New York City, the final lottery was held in mid-May 1997.

If a family was selected in a lottery, all children in that family entering eligible grades were offered a scholarship. Separate lotteries were held in Dayton and Washington, D.C., for students enrolled in public and private schools at the time. This procedure assured random assignment to test and control groups of those families participating in the evaluation.[16]

Because vouchers were randomly awarded, families offered scholarships did not differ significantly from members of the control group (those who did not win a scholarship).[17] In all three cities, the demographic characteristics and test scores of the treatment and control groups are identical to one another. Only in Dayton were minor differences in baseline test scores observed: Those students who were offered a voucher scored 6.5 percentile points lower in math and 3.1 points lower in reading than those not offered a scholarship, a statistically significant difference. Estimated effects of the program on subsequent test scores adjust for baseline test scores.

Collection of Follow-up Information

In all three cities, the procedures used to obtain follow-up data replicated those implemented at baseline. Students again took the ITBS in mathematics and reading. Caretakers accompanying the child completed surveys that asked a wide range of questions about the educational experiences of each of their children. Students in grades four and higher again completed a questionnaire that asked them about their experiences at school.[18]

To obtain a high participation rate in follow-up sessions, program administrators in all three cities financially compensated those families who either were never offered a voucher or had declined a voucher offered to them at baseline. In New York City and Washington, D.C., families who participated in the follow-up sessions also qualified for a new lottery. In Dayton, a new lottery was promised as a reward for participating in the first follow-up session but not for the second. Instead, families were given a higher level of compensation for participating in the second follow-up session.

In New York City, 80 percent of the students included in the evaluation attended the first-year testing sessions; 66 percent attended the second-year sessions. Detailed response rate information for the first and second follow-up surveys and tests is reported elsewhere.[19]

First-year follow-up test information was obtained from 995 students who had been tested at baseline in Washington, D.C., a response rate of 63 percent. In the second-year follow up, the response rate was 50 percent. In Dayton, 57 percent of families attended follow-up sessions after one year, and 49 percent after two years.

We are reasonably confident that these modest response rates do not undermine the integrity of our findings. First, response rates were virtually identical for treatment and control groups after one and two years in all three cities.[20] Had response rates differed noticeably between the two groups, then perceived treatment impacts might be spurious, assuming that the likelihood of attending follow-up sessions was correlated with test-score achievement. Second, comparisons of baseline test scores and background characteristics reveal only minor differences between the second-year respondents and nonrespondents in all three cities.[21] Finally, to account for the minor differences between respondents and nonrespondents that we did observe, we generated weights based upon the probability that each student, according to his or her baseline demographic characteristics, would attend follow-up sessions. Students who were more likely to attend follow-up sessions were weighted downward somewhat; and students who were less likely to attend these sessions, but nevertheless did attend, were weighted upward. Because only slight differences existed between the groups of respondents and nonrespondents, the weights had little effect on the results of the analysis.[22]

There remain two possible sources of bias. First, to generate the weights we could use only observable characteristics as recorded in parental surveys. To the extent that there are unmeasured, or unobservable, characteristics that encourage some families to attend follow-up sessions, but not others, these weights may not completely eliminate the bias associated with less-than-perfect response rates. Second, changes in academic performance over time (not baseline characteristics) could predict the likelihood that different subgroups within the treatment and control group populations attended subsequent testing sessions. If treatment group families that did not benefit from vouchers dropped out of the study, while control group families that were suffering most in the public schools continued to consistently attend follow-up sessions, then observed impacts may be somewhat inflated.

Data Analysis and Reporting Procedures

The evaluation takes advantage of the fact that a lottery was used to award scholarships. As a result, it is possible to compare two groups of students that were similar, on average, except that only members of the treatment group were offered a scholarship. Any statistically significant differences observed between the two groups, therefore, may be attributed to the voucher's impact.

To compute the impact on children's test scores of switching to a private school, we estimate a statistical model that takes into account whether a child attended a public or private school, as well as baseline reading and math test scores. Only students who attended a public school before the initial lottery were included in the study. Baseline test scores were used to adjust for minor baseline differences between the treatment and control groups on the achievement tests and to increase the precision of the estimated impact.

Because the randomization process concerned only the offer of a voucher, and not attendance at public and private schools, we cannot directly compare those who used a voucher with those who did not. Such a comparison would introduce bias and give up all the advantages that are part and parcel of a random-assignment evaluation. Instead, we used a familiar technique, often

Table 8-2. *Overall Impact of Switching to a Private School on Test Score Performances in Three Cities*[a]
Percentiles

Ethnic group	Year one	Year two
African Americans		
Overall	3.3	6.3**
Math	5.5*	6.2*
Reading	1.3	6.3**
All others		
Overall	0.2	−1.0
Math	−0.2	−1.2
Reading	0.4	−0.8

*Significant at the .10 level, two-tailed test.
**Significant at the .05 level, two-tailed test.
a. Figures represent the average impact of switching to a private school on test scores in New York City; Dayton, Ohio; and Washington, D.C. Averages are based upon effects observed in the three cities weighted by the inverse of the variances of the point estimates.

used in medical and econometric research, that preserves the essence of a random-assignment evaluation.[23] The outcome of the lottery, a random event, was used to create what statisticians refer to as an instrumental variable, which obtains consistent estimates of the effects of attending private school on student test scores.[24] According to the statistical theory that underpins the use of this technique, results from lotteries are powerful instrumental variables, because the lottery, being a random event, is not directly related to student test-score performance. Use of this statistical technique corrects for differences that arise from the fact that not all those offered a voucher made use of one.

Observed Effects of Switching from a Public to a Private School

The average impacts across all three cities of switching from a public to a private school are presented in table 8-2. Impacts are expressed in terms of National Percentile Ranking (NPR) points, which range from 0 to 100 and nationally have a median of 50.

When averaging across the three cities, impacts for all students are not statistically significant after one or two years. Impacts do differ, however, when breaking out the results by ethnic group. One finds no significant differences between the test-score performance of non–African American students switching from a public to a private school and the performance of students in the control group—either after one or two years. Nor were significant differences observed in the test-score performance of these students on reading and math tests, considered separately.

The effects of switching to a private school on African American students, however, differed markedly from the effects on students from other ethnic backgrounds. In the three cities, taken together, African American students who switched from public to private schools scored, after one year, 3.3 NPR points higher on the combined math and reading tests and, after two years, 6.3 percentile points higher than the African American students in the control group. Only the impact in year two is statistically significant.

Forty-two percent of the students participating in the second year of the evaluation in New York City were African Americans. The percentages in Dayton and Washington, D.C., were 74 percent and 94 percent, respectively. Hispanic students participating in the second year of the evaluation constituted 51 percent of the New York City population, 2 percent of Dayton's, and 4 percent of Washington, D.C.'s. Finally, 5 percent of the students participating in the evaluation in New York City were white, versus 24 percent in Dayton and 1 percent in Washington, D.C. The remaining students came from a variety of other ethnic backgrounds.

We place particular emphasis on the overall test scores, which simply represent the average of the math and reading components.[25] When student performance is estimated on the basis of one-hour testing sessions, the combined test-score performance on the reading and math sections is a better indicator of student achievement than either section separately. Theoretically, the more test items used to evaluate performance, the more likely it is that one will estimate performance accurately. Empirically, performances on the two tests are highly correlated with one another (r equals about .7). In addition, results from the two tests, when combined, were found to be more stable across time and from place to place, indicating that combining results from the two tests reduces what is probably random, idiosyncratic variations in observations of student performance.[26]

Although the overall test scores provide the most reliable point estimates, the data in table 8-2 also show that, for the three cities taken together, differences after two years are approximately the same for the reading and math components. On average, African American students in the three cities who switched from public to private schools achieved 6.3 percentile points higher than their peers in the control group on the reading portion of the test and 6.2 points higher on the math portion.

The findings for each city are reported in table 8-3. No effects on students from ethnic backgrounds other than African American were observed in any

Table 8-3. *Impact of Switching to a Private School on Test Score Performance*

City and ethnic group	Year one		Year two	
	Percentiles	Number	Percentiles	Number
New York City				
African Americans				
Overall	5.8**	623	4.3**	497
Math	7.0***	623	4.1*	497
Reading	4.6**	623	4.5**	497
All others				
Overall	−1.7	817	−1.5	699
Math	−2.1	817	−3.2	699
Reading	−1.3	817	0.2	699
Dayton, Ohio				
African Americans				
Overall	3.3	296	6.5*	273
Math	0.4	296	5.3	273
Reading	6.1	296	7.6*	273
All others				
Overall	1.0	108	−0.2	96
Math	−0.8	108	0.0	96
Reading	2.8	108	−0.4	96
Washington, D.C.				
African Americans				
Overall	−0.9	891	9.0***	700
Math	7.3**	891	9.9***	700
Reading	−9.0**	891	8.1**	700
All others				
Overall	7.4	39	0.1	44
Math	8.5	39	5.8	44
Reading	6.3	39	−5.6	44

*Significant at .10 level, two-tailed test.
**Significant at .05 level, two-tailed test.
***Significant at .01 level, two-tailed test.

Source: Robert Stine, "An Introduction to Bootstrap Methods: Examples and Ideas," in J. Fox and J. S. Long, eds., *Modern Methods of Data Analysis* (Newbury Park. Calif.: Sage Publications, 1990), pp. 325–73; and Bradley Effron, "The Jackknife, the Bootstrap and Other Resampling Plans" (Philadelphia, Pa.: Society for Industrial and Applied Mathematics, 1982).

a. Weighted two-stage least squares regressions performed; treatment status used as instrument. All models control for baseline test scores and lottery indicators. Impacts expressed in terms of national percentile rankings. In New York City, 2.8 percent of the African American control group in the year two models attended a private school for one of two years; in Dayton, 2.0 percent of the African American control group in the year two models attended a private school in the second but not the first year; and in Washington, D.C., 3.7 percent of the African American control group in the year two models attended a private school in the second year but not the first year. When using boot-strapped standard errors, the year two math score in New York is not statistically significant; the significance levels of all other estimates remain the same when significance levels are estimated using the bootstrap technique.

city. Washington, D.C., logged the largest differences between African American students who switched from public to private schools and those in the control group. In this city, black students attending private schools for two years scored 9.0 percentile points higher than students in the control group. The smallest differences after two years were observed in New York City, where African American students attending private schools scored 4.3 percentile points higher. In Dayton, the difference was 6.5 percentile points, nearly at the midpoint between the differences observed in the other two cities.

The trend over time also varies from one city to the next. In New York City, substantial test-score differences between African American students in private and public schools appear at the end of the first year but then attenuate slightly in the second year. The combined score difference after two years is 4.3 percentile points, which is slightly but not significantly (in statistical terms) less than the 5.8 percentile points observed after one year. In New York, one may reasonably conclude that the initial gains from the school voucher program for African Americans are preserved but do not increase between year one and year two.

In Dayton, there seems to be a steady upward trend in the combined test-score performance of African Americans. African American students who switched from public to private school performed 3.3 percentile points higher on the combined test in year one and 6.5 percentile points higher in year two.[27]

In some ways the most striking results concern African Americans in Washington, D.C. After one year, no significant differences were observed for African Americans as a whole. Significant differences, however, were observed for older and younger students.[28] While younger students may have benefited slightly from the voucher program after one year, older students did not. The older students who switched to private schools scored significantly lower than their public school peers.[29] By the end of the second year, however, these students seem to have overcome initial adjustment problems, as both younger and older African American students who switched from a public to a private school posted positive and significant gains. Younger students in private schools performed on the combined test 9.3 percentile points higher than those remaining in public schools. Older African American students in private school scored 10.3 percentile points higher.[30]

Controlling for Family Background Characteristics

Most research on the impact of private schools attempts to control for differences in family background characteristics among students attending public and private schools. When a randomized field trial is conducted, however, such statistical adjustments are generally unnecessary, given that the two groups being compared are virtually identical to one another. While including explicit controls for family background characteristics in the regression may increase the precision of the estimates, they should not affect the point estimates.

Upon the initial release of our study, a number of commentators nonetheless objected to the apparent absence of controls for family background characteristics. Bruce Fuller and his colleagues, for instance, argued that "the experimental group may have been biased as some of the most disadvantaged voucher winners did not switch to a private school, and therefore were excluded from the group (possibly boosting mean achievement levels artificially)."[31] An interest group made much the same criticism: "The . . . study's key finding improperly compares two dramatically different groups and may well reflect private school screening out of the most at-risk students."[32]

In the three cities, roughly half the students took the voucher that was offered to them (the takers) and about half did not (the decliners). Takers and decliners differed in a number of respects. Takers, for instance, had higher family incomes in New York and Washington, D.C., but lower incomes in Dayton. The New York and D.C. findings are not surprising, given that the voucher awards did not cover all the costs of a private education. These additional costs were the reason most frequently given by families for not using the voucher. Presumably, take-up rates would rise if the monetary value of vouchers were increased.

To estimate the impact of switching from a public to a private school, we do not simply compare takers and members of the control group, as Fuller and his colleagues contend. All members of the control and treatment groups were invited to follow-up testing sessions, and every one of these families who participated is included in the analysis. We use the fact that the vouchers were awarded randomly to generate an instrumental variable that produces a consistent estimate of the effect of switching to a private school that draws upon the evidence from all of our respondents, including students who declined to use a voucher.

Because vouchers were randomly offered at baseline to test and control groups, results are unlikely to vary materially when one controls for family background characteristics. Still, though, given the availability of baseline information, we can easily do so. In table 8-4, we reestimate the models, except this time we include explicit controls for mother's education, mother's employment status, family size, and whether or not the family received welfare.

Table 8-4. *Estimated Effects of Switching from a Public to a Private School on African Americans' Combined Test Scores after Two Years*[a]

City	Controls for initial test scores	Controls for initial test scores and family background
Three-city average impact	6.3**	6.3**
New York City	4.3*	4.2*
Dayton, Ohio	6.5*	5.9
Washington, D.C.	9.0***	9.1***

*Significant at .10 level, two-tailed test.
**Significant at .05 level, two-tailed test.
***Significant at .01 level, two-tailed test.
a. Weighted two-stage least squares regressions performed; treatment status used as instrument. All models control for baseline test scores, mother's education, employment status, whether or not the family receives welfare, and family size (missing case values for demographic variables estimated by imputation); New York City model also includes lottery indicators. Impacts expressed in terms of national percentile rankings. Average three-city impact is based on effects observed in the three cities weighted by the inverse of the variances of the point estimates.

The estimated impacts of switching from a public to a private school on the test scores of African Americans in the three cities remain the same—6.3 NPR points, which is statistically significant. Minor differences are observed within each individual city. When analyzing the New York City data without controlling for family background characteristics, the estimated impact is 4.3 NPR points; when family background controls are added, the impact is 4.2 NPR points. In Dayton, when controls are introduced, the point estimate drops from 6.5 to 5.9 NPR points. And in Washington, D.C., the estimated impact increases from 9.0 to 9.1 NPR points. In two of the three cities, the estimated impacts, when controls for family background characteristics are introduced, remain statistically significant, and in the third, the impact just misses the standard threshold for statistical significance.

Testing the 'Sore Loser' Hypothesis

Some have hypothesized that applicants who are denied vouchers are sufficiently frustrated by the experience to no longer remain engaged in their children's education. *New York Times* columnist Richard Rothstein, for example, suggested that parents who lost the lottery were "sore losers."

Parents know if their children got vouchers and this knowledge can affect results. For example, volunteers for vouchers, already more dissatisfied with public schools than others, may have their hopes raised, then dashed when they were not selected for a voucher. Sorely disap-

Table 8-5. *Percentage of Control Group Parents Very Satisfied with Their Public School at Baseline and after One and Two Years, New York City*[a]
Percent

| | Control group parents very satisfied | | |
Aspect of school	Baseline	Year one	Year two
Teaching	14	23	10
School safety	13	21	9
Parental involvement	11	19	12
Class size	7	12	7
School facility	9	14	5
Student respect for teachers	18	21	11
Communication regarding student progress	18	23	19
Freedom to observe religious traditions	8	9	5
Location	25	34	28

a. Baseline satisfaction rates are for all families in the control group. Year one and year two figures are weighted to adjust for nonresponse.

pointed, they may then demand less of their children in public school.[33]

Perhaps observed test-score impacts stem not so much from higher quality private schools as from a deterioration in the levels of parental involvement of families who applied for, but did not receive, a voucher.

To test this claim, we assessed parental satisfaction rates in New York City at baseline, after one year, and after two years. (Comparable findings hold for Dayton and Washington, D.C.) On each of these occasions, we queried parents about the following aspects of their schools: teaching, school safety, parental involvement, class size, school facility, student respect for teachers, communication regarding student progress, freedom to observe religious traditions, and the school's location.

In all cases, those not receiving the voucher reported slightly higher levels of satisfaction one year after having been denied a scholarship than at baseline (see table 8-5). At the end of two years, control group satisfaction levels deteriorated somewhat. On five of nine items, parents in the control group expressed slightly but not significantly less satisfaction than at baseline. Overall, though, there is very little evidence that upon learning that they had not won a voucher, satisfaction rates among the control group bottomed out, accounting for the positive test-score impacts observed for the treatment group.

Table 8-6. *Parental Involvement in Child's Education after Two Years,*
New York City

	Average number of involvements in past month		
Type of involvement	Private school families	Members of the control group	Programmatic impact
Helped child with homework	11	12	0
Helped child with reading, math not related to homework	10	10	0
Talked with child about school	13	14	1
Attended school activity	5	5	0
Worked on school project	6	5	1

Parental responses to questions about their relationships with their children cast further doubt on the sore loser hypothesis. Parents were asked how often they helped their child with homework, talked with their child about school, attended school activities, and worked on school projects. In every case, after two years, the answers given by parents with children in private school resembled those of the control group (see table 8-6). Comparable findings were observed after one year.[34]

Discussion

Conditions specific to an individual city or minor fluctuations in testing conditions might skew results in one direction or another. But when similar results emerge from evaluations of school voucher programs in three very different cities, we can proceed with a fair measure of confidence that observed differences between treatment and control groups reflect actual programmatic impacts.

Surveying the three evaluations, one ethnic group appeared to benefit from school vouchers, while all others seem to have remained unaffected. After two years African Americans who switched from public to private schools in the three cities scored, on average, approximately 6.3 percentile points higher on the ITBS than comparable students who remained in public schools. We find no evidence, however, that vouchers significantly improved the test scores of any other ethnic group, most notably the reasonably large samples of Latinos in New York and whites in Dayton.

The observed effects for African Americans are moderately large. As can be seen in table 8-7, black students who switched to private schools scored, after one year, 0.17 standard deviations higher than the students in the con-

Table 8-7. *Size of the Effects of Switching to a Private School on African Americans' Overall Test Score Performances*[a]
Standard deviation

	Effect size	
Test score performance	Year one	Year two
Overall	0.17	0.33**
Math	0.29*	0.30*
Reading	0.07	0.26**

*Significant at .10 level, two-tailed test.
**Significant at .05 level, two-tailed test.
a. Figures represent the average impact of switching to a private school on test scores in New York City; Dayton, Ohio; and Washington, D.C. Individual point estimates are weighted by the inverse of their variances.

trol group. After two years, the effect size grows to 0.33 standard deviations, roughly one-third of the difference in test-score performances between blacks and whites nationally. Continuing evaluations of voucher programs may determine whether or not these gains can be consolidated and extended.

Another way of assessing the magnitude of these effects is to compare them with those reported in the RAND Corporation study entitled *Improving School Achievement* released in August 2000.[35] Identifying the most successful states, Texas and North Carolina, which have introduced rigorous accountability systems that involve statewide testing, the study finds "remarkable" one-year gains in math scores of "as much as 0.06 to 0.07 standard deviation[s] per year"—or 0.12 to 0.14 over two years. The two-year effects of the school voucher intervention on black students observed here are over twice as large. Similarly, the impacts of vouchers are comparable to those found in an evaluation of a class-size reduction intervention conducted in Tennessee, the only other major education reform to be studied with a randomized field trial. According to a recent reanalysis of data from Tennessee, the class-size reduction effect for African Americans after two years was, on average, 7–8 percentile points, only slightly larger than the 6-point gain associated with switching school sectors.[36]

Given the widespread concern about racial differences in academic performance, our research is particularly salient in that it suggests that school voucher programs may have the capacity to shrink the black-white test-score gap for participating students. At this point we are uncertain why these ethnic differences appear. We hope that continuing analysis of the data will yield additional insights.

One must qualify any generalizations from the results of these pilot programs to a large-scale voucher program that would involve all children in a large urban school system. Only a small fraction of low-income students in these three cities' schools were offered vouchers, and these students constituted only a small proportion of the students attending private schools in these cities. A much larger program could conceivably yield different outcomes. The only way to know for sure, however, is to introduce larger pilot programs and carefully study them for longer periods of time. Given that vouchers appear to hold some initial promise for African American children living in inner cities, ratcheting up the size and scope of these pilot programs appears warranted.

Notes

1. The authors wish to thank the principals, teachers, and staff at the private schools in Dayton, Ohio, Washington, D.C., and New York City who assisted in the administration of tests and questionnaires. We also wish to thank the School Choice Scholarships Foundation (SCSF), Parents Advancing Choice in Education (PACE), and Washington Scholarship Fund (WSF) for cooperating fully with these evaluations. Kristin Kearns Jordan, Tom Carroll, and other members of the SCSF staff assisted with data collection in New York City. John Blakeslee, Leslie Curry, Douglas Dewey, Laura Elliot, Heather Hamilton, Tracey Johnson, John McCardell, and Patrick Purtill of the WSF provided similar cooperation. T. J. Wallace and Mary Lynn Naughton, staff members of PACE, provided valuable assistance with the Dayton evaluation. Chester E. Finn, Bruno Manno, Gregg Vanourek, and Marci Kanstoroom of the Thomas B. Fordham Foundation, Edward P. St. John of Indiana University, and Thomas Lasley of the University of Dayton provided valuable suggestions throughout various stages of the research design and data collection. We wish to thank especially David Myers of Mathematica Policy Research, who is a principal investigator of the evaluation of the New York School Choice Scholarship Program; his work on the New York evaluation has influenced in many important ways the design of the Washington, D.C., and Dayton evaluations. We thank William McCready, Robin Bebel, Kirk Miller, and other members of the staff of the Public Opinion Laboratory at Northern Illinois University for their assistance with data collection, data processing, conduct of the lottery, and preparation of baseline and year one follow-up data. We are particularly grateful to Tina Elacqua and Matthew Charles for their key roles in coordinating data collection efforts.

We received helpful advice from Paul Hill, Christopher Jencks, Donald Rock, and Donald Rubin. Daniel Mayer and Julia Chou were instrumental in preparing the New York City survey and test-score data and in executing many of the analyses reported here. Additional research assistance was provided by Rachel Deyette, Jennifer Hill, and Martin West; Shelley Weiner, Lilia Halpern, and Micki Morris provided staff assistance.

These evaluations have been supported by grants from the following foundations: Achelis Foundation, Bodman Foundation, Lynde and Harry Bradley Foundation, William Donner Foundation, Thomas B. Fordham Foundation, Milton and Rose D. Friedman Foundation, John M. Olin Foundation, David and Lucile Packard Foundation, Smith-Richardson Foundation, Spencer Foundation, and Walton Family Foundation. The methodology, analyses of data, reported findings, and interpretations of findings are the sole responsibility of the authors and are not subject to the approval of SCSF, WSF, PACE, or of any foundation providing support for this research.

2. R. J. Bridge and J. Blackman, *A Study of Alternatives in American Education*, vol. 4: *Family Choice in Education* (Santa Monica, Calif.: RAND Corporation, 1978); and Richard Elmore, "Choice as an Instrument of Public Policy: Evidence from Education and Health Care," in W. Clune and J. Witte, eds., *Choice and Control in American Education*, vol. 1: *The Theory of Choice and Control in American Education* (New York: Falmer, 1990), pp. 285–318.

3. Disparate findings have emerged from these studies. For example, one analysis of the Milwaukee, Wisconsin, choice experiment found test-score gains in reading and math, particularly after students had been enrolled for three or more years, while another study found gains only in math, and a third found gains in neither subject. Jay P. Greene, Paul E. Peterson, and Jiangtao Du, "School Choice in Milwaukee: A Randomized Experiment," in Paul E. Peterson and Bryan C. Hassel, eds., *Learning from School Choice* (Brookings, 1998), pp. 335–56; Cecilia Rouse, "Private School Vouchers and Student Achievement: An Evaluation of the Milwaukee Parental Choice Program," *Quarterly Journal of Economics*, vol. 113 (1998), pp. 553–602; and John F. Witte, "Achievement Effects of the Milwaukee Voucher Program," paper presented at the annual meeting of the American Economics Association, 1997. On the Cleveland, Ohio, program, see Jay P. Greene, William G. Howell, and Paul E. Peterson, "Lessons from the Cleveland Scholarship Program," in Paul E. Peterson and Bryan C. Hassel, eds., *Learning from School Choice* (Brookings, 1998), pp. 357–92; and Kim K. Metcalf, William J. Boone, Frances K. Stage, Todd L. Chilton, Patty Muller, and Polly Tait, "A Comparative Evaluation of the Cleveland Scholarship and Tutoring Grant Program: Year One: 1996–97," Indiana University, School of Education, Smith Research Center, March 1998. Greene, Peterson, and Du, "School Choice in Milwaukee," report results from analyses of experimental data; the other studies are based upon analyses of nonexperimental data.

4. Results from the Dayton evaluation after one year are reported in William G. Howell and Paul E. Peterson, "School Choice in Dayton, Ohio: An Evaluation after One Year," paper prepared for the Conference on Charters, Vouchers, and Public Education, Harvard University, John F. Kennedy School of Government, Program on Education Policy and Governance. 2000, available at http://data.fas.harvard.edu/pepg/. First-year results for Washington are reported in Patrick J. Wolf, William G. Howell, and Paul E. Peterson, "School Choice in Washington, D.C.: An Evaluation

after One Year," paper prepared for the Conference on Charters, Vouchers, and Public Education, Harvard University, John F. Kennedy School of Government, Program on Education Policy and Governance, 2000, available at http://data.fas.harvard.edu/pepg/. First-year results from the New York City evaluation are reported in Paul E. Peterson, David E. Myers, William G. Howell, and Daniel P. Mayer, "The Effects of School Choice in New York City," in Susan B. Mayer and Paul E. Peterson, eds., *Earning and Learning: How Schools Matter* (Brookings, 1999), chapter 12.

5. Derek Neal, *The Effects of Catholic Secondary Schooling on Educational Achievement* (University of Chicago, Harris School of Public Policy and National Bureau for Economic Research, 1996), p. 26.

6. William N. Evans and Robert M. Schwab, "Who Benefits from Private Education?: Evidence from Quantile Regressions," University of Maryland, Department of Economics, 1993; and David Figlio and Joe Stone, *School Choice and Student Performance: Are Private Schools Really Better?* (University of Wisconsin, Institute for Research on Poverty, 1977).

7. John F. Witte, "School Choice and Student Performance," in Helen F. Ladd, ed., *Holding Schools Accountable: Performance-Based Reform in Education* (Brookings, 1996), p. 167.

8. Major studies finding positive educational benefits from attending private schools include James S. Coleman, Thomas Hoffer, and Sally Kilgore, *High School Achievement* (Basic Books, 1982); John E. Chubb and Terry M. Moe, *Politics, Markets, and America's Schools* (Brookings, 1990); and Neal, "The Effects of Catholic Secondary Schooling on Educational Achievement." Critiques of these studies have been prepared by Arthur S. Goldberger and Glen G. Cain, "The Causal Analysis of Cognitive Outcomes in the Coleman, Hoffer, and Kilgore Report," *Sociology of Education*, vol. 55 (April–July 1982), pp. 103–22; and Douglas J. Wilms, "Catholic School Effects on Academic Achievement: New Evidence from the High School and Beyond Follow-up Study," *Sociology of Education*, vol. 58 (1985), pp. 98–114.

9. Results from these evaluations are reported in Paul E. Peterson and Bryan C. Hassel, eds., *Learning from School Choice* (Brookings, 1998).

10. The maximum amount of tuition support for high school students was $2,200.

11. Baseline data from the Washington, D.C., and Dayton evaluations are reported in Paul E. Peterson, Jay P. Greene, William G. Howell, and William McCready, "Initial Findings from an Evaluation of School Choice Programs in Dayton, Ohio and Washington, D.C.," paper prepared under the auspices of Harvard University, Program on Education Policy and Governance for presentation before the annual meeting of the Association of Public Policy and Management, New York, N.Y., October 1998. Baseline data for New York City are reported in Paul E. Peterson, David Myers, Josh Haimson, and William G. Howell, "Initial Findings from the Evaluation of the New York School Choice Scholarships Program," Harvard University, John F. Kennedy School of Government, Taubman Center on State and Local Government, Program on Education Policy and Governance, 1997.

12. Students who were entering grades two through five in New York City and grades two through eight in Dayton (and other parts of Montgomery County, Ohio) and Washington, D.C., were included in the evaluations.

13. The assessment used in this study is Form M of the Iowa Tests of Basic Skills, Copyright © 1996 by The University of Iowa, published by The Riverside Publishing Company, 425 Spring Lake Drive, Itasca, Illinois 60143–2079. All rights reserved.

14. Howell and Peterson, "School Choice in Dayton, Ohio"; Wolf, Howell, and Peterson, "School Choice in Washington, D.C."; and Peterson and others, "The Effects of School Choice in New York City." For detailed results from the second-year evaluation of New York City's voucher program, see David Myers, Paul E. Peterson, Daniel Mayer, Julia Chou, and William G. Howell, "School Choice in New York City after Two Years: An Evaluation of the School Choice Scholarships Program," occasional paper, Harvard University, John F. Kennedy School of Government, Taubman Center on State and Local Government, Program on Education Policy and Governance, September 2000.

15. Exact procedures for the formation of the control group are described in Jennifer Hill, Donald B. Rubin, and Neal Thomas, "The Design of the New York School Choice Scholarship Program Evaluation," paper presented before the American Political Science Association annual meeting, Boston, Mass., August 31, 1998.

Because many more families applied for scholarships in New York City than originally had been anticipated, the evaluation team randomly selected families for vouchers through a two-stage procedure. As families applied for vouchers, they were formed into groups on the basis of their application date. During the early stages, all families were invited to eligibility assessment and data collection sessions. However, after it became clear that more families would be attending these sessions than could be accommodated, the evaluation team began randomly selecting applicants, inviting only those selected to attend the sessions. After the first stage was completed, families who attended these sessions and met the eligibility requirements were then randomly selected for the scholarship group or the control group. To ensure that all families from the different groups had the same chance of being selected for a voucher, the evaluation team adjusted the second-stage selection probabilities to reflect the differential chances of being invited to the verification sessions.

16. In New York, SCSF decided in advance to allocate 85 percent of the scholarships to applicants from public schools whose average test scores were less than the citywide median. Consequently, applicants from these schools, who represented about 70 percent of all applicants, were assigned a higher probability of winning a scholarship. In the information reported in the tables, results have been adjusted by weighting cases differentially so that they can be generalized to all eligible applicants who would have come to the verification sessions had they been invited, regardless of whether or not they attended a low-performing school.

17. For additional baseline information on Washington, D.C., and Dayton, Ohio, see Peterson and others, "Initial Findings from an Evaluation of School Choice Programs in Dayton, Ohio and Washington, D.C."; for New York City, see Peterson

and others, "Initial Findings from the Evaluation of the New York School Choice Scholarships Program."

18. Difficulties were encountered in the administration of the first-year test at the initial pilot session in Washington, D.C. Test booklets were not available at the testing site for scholarship students in grades three through eight. Copies of the test arrived eventually, but the amount of time available for testing may have been foreshortened. Significant effects on reading scores are not apparent, but significant effects on math performance are evident, probably because the math test was the last to be administered. Statistical adjustments in the test-score analysis take into account the special circumstances of the pilot session.

19. Myers and others, "School Choice in New York City after Two Years." Although the background characteristics of participants and nonparticipants in the second year follow-up, as observed in the baseline survey conducted in 1997, resembled one another in most respects, they differed significantly in some. As compared with nonparticipants, participants were more likely to be non–Puerto Rican Hispanic. Mothers were more likely to be born outside the United States, more likely to have lived in the same residence, less likely to be working, more likely to state their religious affiliation as Catholic, and less likely to use food stamps or welfare. They originally reported an average income of around $9,900, as compared with $8,500 for the nonparticipants. They were less likely to speak English at home.

Members of the control group who participated in the second-year follow-up were less likely than nonparticipants to be black and more likely to be non–Puerto Rican Hispanic. They were more likely to report that their child had received help for a disability. They were more likely to have a Catholic religious affiliation. They were more likely to be receiving supplemental security income. They were less likely to speak English at home.

20. The one exception here concerns the year-two evaluation in New York where the treatment group's response rate was seven points higher than the control group's.

21. The characteristics of participants and nonparticipants in the second-year follow-up sessions are reported in William G. Howell, Patrick J. Wolf, Paul E. Peterson, and David E. Campbell, "Test-Score Effects of School Vouchers in Dayton, Ohio, New York City, and Washington, D.C.: Evidence from Randomized Field Trials," Report No. 00–16, Harvard University, John F. Kennedy School of Government, Program on Education Policy and Governance, 2000, appendix.

22. The appendix to Howell and others, "Test-Score Effects of School Vouchers in Dayton, Ohio, New York City, and Washington, D.C.," compares the characteristics of participants and nonparticipants in the second-year follow-up sessions in Dayton and Washington, D.C. For a discussion of the weighting procedures used in these evaluations, see Howell and Peterson, "School Choice in Dayton, Ohio"; and Wolf, Howell, and Peterson, "School Choice in Washington, D.C." For New York City, see Myers and others, "School Choice in New York City after Two Years."

23. See, for example, Alan Krueger, "Experimental Estimates of Education Production Functions," *Quarterly Journal of Economics*, vol. 114 (1999), pp. 497–533.

24. The voucher offer meets both criteria for an instrumental variable to generate consistent estimates. It is highly correlated with attending a private school and completely uncorrelated with the error term in the regressions that include student test performance after one and two years. This procedure is discussed in Joshua D. Angrist, Guido W. Imbens, and Donald B. Rubin, "Identification of Causal Effects using Instrumental Variables," *Journal of the American Statistical Association*, vol. 91 (1996), pp. 444–62. For a fuller discussion of how this instrumental variable technique was employed in this particular study, see William Howell, Patrick Wolf, and David Campbell, "School Vouchers and Academic Performance: Results from Three Randomized Field Trials," University of Wisconsin, 2001.

25. This procedure was also employed in Krueger, "Experimental Estimates of Education Production Functions."

26. Similarly, when information is limited and the number of available cases relatively modest, one should not divide the data into increasingly small categories by comparing students in the treatment and control group by grade level—unless consistent differences are observed either in adjacent grades or across cities in any particular grade. After one year, we did notice sharp differences between younger and older students in the Washington, D.C., program that seemed substantively meaningful and these results are discussed below. Otherwise, observed impact across grade levels did not reveal any consistent underlying patterns.

Random fluctuations often occur when one breaks down a sample and examines data grade by grade. For this reason, the education statistician Anthony Bryk and his colleagues recommend that conclusions about school impacts not be drawn from "only single grade information. . . . Judging a school by looking at only selected grades can be misleading. We would be better off, from a statistical perspective, to average across adjacent grades to develop a more stable estimate of school productivity." Anthony Bryk, Yeow Meng Thum, John Q. Easton, and Stuart Luppeseu, "Academic Productivity of Chicago Public Elementary Schools: A Technical Report Sponsored by the Consortium on Chicago School Research," March 1998.

Bryk and his colleagues' admonition is particularly compelling when, as is the case in these cities, only fifty to seventy-five African American students are observed in the treatment and control groups at each grade level after two years. Under these circumstances, separate analyses run on individual grade levels in each city are unlikely to generate stable estimates of causal effects. Instead of focusing exclusively on inconsistencies between grade-specific findings in New York, one needs to consider the overall pattern of results obtained from the full range of evidence collected from all three cities.

27. If those whose scores jumped or dropped dramatically between baseline and year one are excluded from the analysis, then the gains in year one are larger than those reported here. See Howell and Peterson, "School Choice in Dayton, Ohio." Now that data are available for two years, we have chosen not to exclude these students from the analysis, because it is more difficult to justify such exclusions after two years than after just one. After all, students might make striking gains that are real—

or suffer genuinely serious losses—over a two-year time period. Changes of this magnitude over one year seem less plausible. Given our decision not to exclude cases with significant changes in year two, it was desirable, for the sake of consistency, to apply the same framework to the analysis of year one data.

28. The Washington, D.C., program provided the only opportunity to examine the effect on test scores of an offer of a school voucher to older students. While vouchers were offered to middle-school students in Dayton, there were not enough cases to justify a separate analysis.

29. Parent and student surveys corroborate these test-score findings. Black students in grades six through eight who attended private schools expressed less satisfaction and lower morale, and they reported a higher frequency of expulsions and fewer friends than students attending private schools in grade two through five. See Wolf, Howell, and Peterson, "School Choice in Washington, D.C."

30. This turnaround in the test-score performance of the older kids in Washington, D.C., apparently is not due to changes in the sample of students who tested each year. When we limited the analysis to the older students who tested both years, we still uncovered a significant drop in scores the first year for the students who switched to private schools, followed by a dramatic increase in performance the second year.

31. Bruce Fuller, Luis Huerta, and David Ruenzel, *A Costly Gamble or Serious Reform? California's School Voucher Initiative—Proposition 38*, Policy Analysis for California Education (University of California, Berkeley, and Stanford University, 2000), p. 10.

32. "Deception by the Numbers: Ten Reasons to Doubt the Latest Claims for Vouchers," People for the American Way Foundation website at www.pfaw.org/issues/education.

33. Richard Rothstein, "Judging Vouchers' Merits Proves to Be Difficult Task," *New York Times*, December 13, 2000, p. A25.

34. Peterson and others, "Initial Findings from the Evaluation of the New York School Choice Scholarships Program," table 13.

35. See also Ann Flanagan, Jennifer Kawata, and Stephanie Williamson, *Improving Student Achievement: What NAEP Test Scores Tell Us* (Santa Monica, Calif.: RAND Corporation, 2000), p. 59.

36. Krueger, "Experimental Estimates of Education Production Functions," p. 525.

PART 3

School Choice and Public Schools

9

Hints of the Pick-Axe: Competition and Public Schooling in Milwaukee

FREDERICK M. HESS

The debate over school choice has been marked by a curious lack of attention to the nature of schools and schooling.[1] This oversight is of particular concern in the nation's troubled urban school systems, where organizational and institutional constraints have helped create the problems that choice seeks to solve. Although school choice rests explicitly on market-based logic, this inattention has led to a lack of understanding about the nuances of markets or how competition might work in practice.

Perhaps the most commonly advanced argument for school choice is that markets will force public schools to become more efficient and effective. Because public schools will continue to serve the vast majority of students for the foreseeable future, this claim may be the most significant argument made by choice advocates.[2]

The presumption is that markets will reward firms that efficiently deliver the goods and services that consumers desire, encouraging innovation and constant improvement. Scholarly consideration of deregulation and privatization suggests that such straightforward accounts pay insufficient attention to the nature and historical circumstances of many public sector activities.[3] More generally, if competition does change public school system behavior, there are two, possibly complementary, visions of how change may occur. The implications of these two different mechanisms are significant for policymakers and educators. One vision is of a competitive bulldozer that steamrolls away ineffective schools and systemic inefficiencies. An alternative vision depicts competition as a pick-axe that will gradually chip away at the forces constraining urban school systems, allowing existing educators to do new things, permitting new schools to enter the arena, and gradually changing the local education environment.[4] The changes produced by this second approach will be much less dramatic and less systematic than those produced by bulldozer-style competition.

Given the fervor of the school choice debate, surprisingly little research has been conducted on how public school systems respond to competition. As Patrick J. McEwan concluded in 2001, in the most recent overview of research on the question, "Evidence on the effects of competition on public school efficiency is sparse."[5] The work that has been done has paid scant attention to the particular question of how competition may affect urban districts in the United States.[6]

Urban school systems are highly visible public agencies that are disproportionately charged with the delicate task of educating disadvantaged children. The sensitive political demands on organizational leaders are likely to have significant implications for their response to market pressures. Trying to assess market effects in isolation from these larger political and organizational considerations risks missing much of the story of school choice.

Given those constraints, what happens when school choice is introduced? What kinds of changes occur? Do educational markets work as desired in urban school systems? These questions are considered here for the case of Milwaukee, Wisconsin, which launched the nation's first public school voucher program in 1990. The object of this case study is to deepen thinking about market-based school reforms and to foster a more robust and nuanced understanding of educational markets.

How Markets Affect Schools

The market presumption is that competition will compel school leaders to compete for students, improving the efficiency and quality of schooling. Market-driven improvements hinge on educators striving to attract students. Currently, however, individual public school teachers receive no benefits for attracting students into their classes or schools, while the benefits of enrollment growth are diffused over the school or school system.[7]

Therefore, market effects depend on system policymakers driving changes through urban school bureaucracies and into the schools. This is a difficult task, suggesting that significant outcome changes may emerge only gradually, if at all. To avoid these difficulties while pursuing more immediate results, leaders may focus instead on adding new programs that augment existing practices.[8]

Generally speaking, market models presume that producers will continually improve their product or be replaced by competitors that do, ensuring that all producers run scared.[9] In the absence of a credible threat, likely effects hinge on producers' internal motivation or anticipatory concern. This highlights two key considerations in urban education markets. First, current proposals rarely envision enrolling more than a small percentage of students in charter or voucher schools. This produces a diluted threat. Second, the skills and entrepreneurial temperament necessary to drive an anticipatory response are different from those that generally attract individuals into education.[10]

The rewards of teaching tend to be emotional, immediate, and rooted in a commitment to the ideal of public education. This presents problems for a competitive market in which system leaders generally attempt to motivate and encourage employees—at least in part—through such devices as money, promotions, and recognition. Although the organization and management of the public schools rely heavily upon intrinsically motivated behavior, intrinsic rewards have proven themselves unable to drive ambitious changes in schooling among less-effective teachers and in less-effective schools.[11]

Given existing constraints on salary, working conditions, and promotion, school administrators have a limited ability to reward or sanction individual teachers for their efforts. Whereas teachers in high-performing systems may worry about finding an equally attractive position elsewhere, such concerns are less relevant in urban districts. Moreover, the high rate of teacher turnover ensures that a loss of students will not lead to a loss of jobs. For instance, in the late 1990s, Milwaukee was hiring between 400 and 900 teachers a year—roughly 10 to 20 percent of its teaching force. Veteran teachers had little reason to fear layoffs, or even being forced to change schools. In this environment, it is unclear whether system leaders—even those seeking to answer market competition—can drive meaningful change.

Visible systemwide leaders such as superintendents and school board members do have incentives to respond to market competition. They can reap positive publicity and attract community support for taking popular actions. Similarly, while individual teachers have little incentive to act, because their efforts would outweigh any rewards, the union leadership can use its visibility and united strength to win teachers significant reputational and material benefits by participating in popular reforms.[12] The question is what motivated school system leaders and union leaders actually do.

Methodology

I examine the effects of competition by focusing on how school choice altered the political, organizational, and educational behavior of the Milwaukee Public School (MPS) system from 1990 to 1999.[13] Behavioral changes of this type cannot alone reveal what effect competition has on teaching and learning, but it can offer valuable clues. Moreover, if competition does not affect policymaking or administrative behavior, it is highly unlikely to have a significant effect on classrooms.[14]

Milwaukee is a natural site to study the effects of market competition because it has been home to the nation's largest and longest-running public voucher program since 1990 and because Wisconsin charter legislation sought to promote charter schooling in the city during the late 1990s.

The research reported here, conducted between September 1998 and September 1999, involved more than ninety interviews with educational participants and observers in Milwaukee, visits to nearly two dozen public and private schools, thorough archival searches of newspaper coverage, and extensive review of school system documents and private papers.

The Story of Competition in Milwaukee

As it entered the 1990s, the Milwaukee Public School system was a troubled urban system characterized by racial inequities, a long series of unsuccessful reform efforts, and dissatisfaction with the status quo.

In 1985 the state legislature enacted the Children at Risk program, allowing MPS to contract with certain nonpublic schools to educate a limited number of at-risk high school students. Along with an interdistrict busing program, which allowed MPS students to enroll in nearby suburban districts and suburban students to enroll in MPS, the "contract schools" provided a backdrop of choice in MPS.

Observers describe the MPS administration—both then and now—as an unwieldy bureaucracy. Administrators are tenured into their position after three years, producing a system of entrenched administrators who are not invested in the superintendent's agenda. Notes one longtime administrator, "[The MPS system] doesn't directly fire many principals and assistant principals. . . . What they do is . . . assign them to central office, and bury them."

Aside from the MPS administration, the other key educational player in the MPS system was historically the Milwaukee Teachers' Education Association (MTEA). Enrolling about 95 percent of MPS teachers, the MTEA protected faculty through a lengthy and detailed contract. The restrictions imposed by the contract substantially curtailed the freedom of action of system administrators. As in other districts, teacher salaries in MPS are solely a function of experience, degrees, and credit hours. The district and MTEA also bargained into the contract particularly rigid language on seniority, teacher discipline, and teacher termination. The degree of contractual constraint is illustrated by the fact that not one MPS teacher—out of 6,000—was fired for poor teaching between 1985 and 1995, and not one teacher hired between 1985 and 1990 was denied tenure.[15]

Choice Emerges

In the fall of 1985, a gubernatorial study committee issued a series of scathing reports on the status of MPS. The reports stoked African American anger, inspiring in 1988 a call for a separate, nearly all-black school district in northern Milwaukee. The proposal failed, but its failure, along with concern about the viability of Milwaukee's inner-city private schools, prompted Democratic state legislator Polly Williams to propose in 1989 that Wisconsin issue vouchers to a number of low-income MPS students for use at private schools. Williams, a black single mother, allied with Republican governor Tommy G. Thompson to push the Milwaukee Parental Choice Program (MPCP). Williams's role helped blunt criticism that MPCP was a conservative attack on Milwaukee.[16] The initial program offered vouchers to no more than 1 percent of MPS students (approximately 1,000 low-income children).[17]

The vouchers would be funded by state aid diverted from MPS, but enrollment-driven changes in Wisconsin state aid are phased in incrementally over three years, reducing the immediate impact of enrollment changes. Choice schools were required to adopt choice applicants by lottery, were not permitted to accept more than 49 percent of their total enrollment through MPCP, and had to meet performance criteria to be eligible.[18]

From the beginning, the choice program was bedeviled by court challenges that dramatically lessened the threat it posed. These courtroom travails made MPCP a highly imperfect test of the "pure" competition hypothesis but are a component of the institutional milieu in which vouchers operate. Immediately upon the passage of MPCP, in May 1990, the Wisconsin Education Association Council (WEAC) and other parties filed suit to stop MPCP. In a series of decisions, MPCP was first upheld, and then struck down in a stayed decision, and then, in March 1992, finally declared constitutional in a 4-3 ruling by a sharply divided Wisconsin Supreme Court. This ruling, however, would not end the challenges to MPCP.

The choice assault opened on a second front in 1992, when Partners Advancing Values in Education (PAVE) was launched. PAVE offered 50 percent scholarships for use at any private school—including religious ones. PAVE sought to stabilize enrollment in the troubled secular schools and to cultivate a constituency for vouchers. Because PAVE utilized Milwaukee's large network of religious schools, its enrollment rapidly outstripped that of the poorly publicized MPCP.

Crucial to the voucher coalition were the resources of the deep-pocketed, conservative Bradley Foundation. Bradley provided extensive support for the researchers, activists, and consultants making the case for school choice. One influential voucher advocate argued that the foundation provided "the financial footing for the voucher coalition."

A unified MPS board had hired respected reformer Robert Peterkin as superintendent in fall 1988. Peterkin decentralized the system and introduced parental choice of public schools. The timing of Peterkin's push for public school choice, implemented as the Milwaukee Three-School Selection Process in 1991–92, may suggest a response to MPCP. However, key participants from that time dismiss that notion. As a former Peterkin deputy recalled, "['Three-choice'] was something that Bob and I brought from Cambridge . . . in 1988."

In November 1990, Peterkin announced that he would be leaving in June 1991 for a job at Harvard University. In May 1991 the board named Howard Fuller superintendent. The board knew, recalled a former board member, that Fuller "was going to generate sparks." Many MPS critics thought that if anyone could significantly change the MPS system, it was going to be the credible and hard-charging Fuller. When Fuller's efforts bogged down amidst administrative recalcitrance, board temporizing, and union opposition, these critics took it as evidence that the MPS system could not be reformed by traditional means.

Fuller's aggressive 1991–95 superintendency coincided with the beginnings of MPCP, but observers agreed that neither Fuller's initiatives nor responses to those initiatives were caused by the voucher program. Fuller, an architect of MPCP, remembers, "The voucher program was a little too small to have had any effect [during my superintendency]. . . . Realistically, to be blunt, a thousand poor kids leaving at $2,900 [each] meant squat."

Between 1990 and 1995, MPCP drew a great deal of notice, but the nature of the program meant that competition had no substantive effects on MPS. First, MPCP's small scope ensured that its effects were minimal. During the 1991–95 period, the capacity of participating MPCP schools never equaled 1 percent of MPS enrollment (see table 9-1). The handful of MPCP schools were generally located in old, cramped facilities, limiting opportunities for expansion. Further, there was little indication that new private

Table 9-1. *Milwaukee Parental Choice Program (MPCP) Statistics, 1990–91 to 1998–99*

Program characteristic	1990–91	1991–92	1992–93	1993–94	1994–95	1995–96	1996–97	1997–98	1998–99
Value of vouchers ($)	2,446	2,634	2,745	2,985	3,209	3,667	4,373	4,696	4,894
September enrollment	337	504	591	718	786	1,320	1,606	1,501	5,830
Number of schools	7	6	11	12	12	17	20	23	88[a]
Total aid paid to MPCP ($ millions)[b]	0.74	1.35	1.63	2.10	2.46	4.61	7.07	7.03	28.41[c]
School operations fund in Milwaukee Public School budget ($ millions)	536.5	563.7	585.6	612.2	646.8	674.0	704.1	735.1	776.0
State and federal categorical aid estimated ($ millions)	48.0	31.5	59.1	61.2	76.9	82.8	90.9	104.8	97.5
Total educational spending ($ millions)[d]	584.5	595.2	644.7	673.4	723.7	756.8	795	839.9	873.5
MPCP aid as a percent of total education expenditures	0.09	0.23	0.25	0.31	0.34	0.61	0.89	0.84	3.25

a. There are three schools within one organization: Seed of Health.
b. This number does not equal September enrollment times voucher value, because the money paid to the MPCP is based on per pupil enrollment each month.
c. Estimate.
d. Excluding construction and recreational programs.

Table 9-2. *Milwaukee Public School (MPS) System*
Enrollment Statistics, 1990–98

Year	Enrollment (N)	African American (percent)	White (percent)
1990	92,789	55.1	30.8
1991	93,519	56.2	29.1
1992	94,301	57.1	27.5
1993	95,271	58.1	25.9
1994	96,773	58.9	24.2
1995	98,380	59.8	22.3
1996	101,110	60.6	20.7
1997	101,963	61.1	19.6
1998	100,525	61.4	18.5

Source: Numbers obtained from MPS system's third Friday in September enrollment count.

schools were planning to open. Second, any bite that choice did have was dramatically reduced because MPS enrollment continued to grow. One MPS principal recalled that MPCP "wasn't all bad. . . .We were—and are—hurting for space as it is." In 1990–91, MPS housed 92,789 students. By 1994–95, despite MPCP and PAVE, that figure increased to 98,380 (see table 9-2). Third, the schools participating in the program were accepted community schools with long track records and long-standing ties. This did not silence hostility to the voucher program, but it did blunt the perceived threat. Remembered one system administrator, "The thing to realize about the first version of choice was that these were schools we knew, people we had worked with." Finally, by excluding religious schools from MPCP, the legislation ensured that the threat posed by choice would be minimal. Religious schools made up 80 percent or more of Milwaukee's private schools. A 1993–94 count found 108 private schools in Milwaukee, of which 85 were religious.

The Fuller Years

As in 1991, the 1993 MPS board elections were a quiet affair. Three of the four candidates won with more than 80 percent of the vote; all three were endorsed by the MTEA. The MTEA continued to exert substantial influence on the nine-member board.

Fuller's reign was marked by tension. Frustrated by the early response to his efforts to significantly alter system behavior and the terms of the MPS-MTEA contract, he started talking to private vendors about having them take over the management of some MPS. Starting in February 1993, after

Fuller's massive $366 million building referendum lost by a 3-1 margin, Fuller entered into discussions with the for-profit firms Education Alternatives Inc. (EAI) and the Edison Project. In fall 1993, the MPS board declined to hire either firm, but it did enact board member Sandra Small's proposal to create "innovative schools" in the MPS system.

Innovative schools would be created in partnership with the MTEA, which agreed to negotiate memorandums of understanding (MOUs) to free the schools from particular elements of the collective bargaining agreement— especially the provision requiring that all MPS use the same seniority-based hiring approach. In May 1994, the board approved a radically decentralized governance model for the Hi-Mount Community School, and in June a formal policy on innovative schools was adopted. The first innovative school was approved in December.

The Hi-Mount proposal created a faculty-governed school with a community focus and an emphasis on technology. Responding to the persistent demands of principal Spence Korte, regarded within the system as a highly effective maverick, the board gave Hi-Mount hands-on control of 85 percent of the per pupil allocation for each student. The deal was a product of the contracting threat. Korte recalls, "As radical as people think I am, we were actually the safe alternative. The board was really getting a lot of pressure . . . so we . . . said, 'Look, if you're going to make a deal with for-profit organizations to take schools, we want to run our own school. We'll take the same financial deal, only . . . we'll take what would've been the profit and plough it back into instruction.' " Korte got his deal not because he was beloved by the MPS hierarchy, but because he had a plan of action. Korte recalls, "There were a lot of [employees] in central administration who would disappear into doorways when they'd see me coming down the hallway. They didn't want to have to deal with me."

The union contract limited the ability of administrators to force changes through the system, so most change was initiated by entrepreneurs who obtained waivers to create new programs. Despite Fuller's push to get tough with teachers, between 1990 and November 1995 no teacher was fired for incompetence and only seven for misconduct.[19] In the end, Fuller won some small victories that helped entrepreneurial leaders crawl through the administrative cracks, but he produced a powerful MTEA-led political backlash that cost him his position.

In the spring of 1995 board elections, the MTEA, motivated by its distaste for Fuller, mounted an unusually aggressive effort. MTEA-backed candidates won four of the five elections, prompting Fuller to tender his resignation. Fuller departed in July 1995 and was replaced by his deputy, Bob Jasna.

MTEA-backed candidates had spent $132,897 in the five races, while their opponents spent $58,331. The union lost only one race—but it would prove to be a major loss. In the election for the symbolically important citywide seat, outspoken choice advocate John Gardner defeated his MTEA-backed opponent.

Fuller's frustrations, the MTEA's 1995 victories, and the emergence of Gardner prompted a new wave of organization, particularly in Milwaukee's influential business community. One prominent official of the Metropolitan Milwaukee Association of Commerce (MMAC) remembered that Fuller's travails caused the MMAC to reevaluate its efforts to aid the MPS system and to begin actively supporting vouchers.

MPCP Expansion

During the 1995 legislative session, at the urging of Governor Thompson, the tiny MPCP got a radical facelift when its enrollment cap was raised to 7 percent of MPS enrollment (or about 7,000) students for 1995–96 and to 15 percent (roughly 15,000 students) thereafter.[20] The expansion allowed religious schools to participate in MPCP, dramatically increasing the number of available seats. As a consequence, in spring 1995 MPCP was set to balloon from an insignificant program to a significant threat that could soon drain tens of millions of dollars from the MPS system. However, court challenges ensured that the threat was not concrete until the June 1998 Wisconsin Supreme Court ruling on behalf of the expanded MPCP.

Through this time, the choice and charter debates were distant abstractions for school personnel and had little evident impact. Observed one veteran system insider, "I haven't noticed any evidence at the school level that things have changed due to choice." When asked, principals uniformly explained that choice had no impact on the daily business of schooling. Said one, "You've got to understand, in just trying to run a good school I've already got a full plate. There's not a lot of time to worry about things like vouchers."

The effects of the voucher program were blunted by continued MPS enrollment growth, as enrollment continued to increase between 1995 and 1997. The system enrolled 101,110 students in 1996, exceeding MPS projections by nearly 2,000 students. In 1997–98, system enrollment grew to 101,963, again exceeding MPS projections.

While choice did not have a systemic impact on MPS, the size and drama of the expansion did affect the school board and the MTEA. Recalled one board member who supported vouchers, "When it became pretty clear that [expansion] was going to pass . . . board candidates supported by the MTEA, and the MTEA itself, suddenly made noises about all the reforms they were going to do and, probably more significantly, the reforms they were not going to oppose. . . . Choice brought external pressures so the MTEA Executive Committee and the system's not-terribly-entrepreneurial administration began . . . saying, 'Okay, we'll let you do it to show that we're doing something.' "

The impact of MPCP expansion can be examined by looking at the period between the passage of expansion in spring 1995 and the February 1996 Wisconsin Supreme Court decision to leave in place the injunction excluding religious schools from MPCP, defanging expansion. The record shows a clear publicity-oriented response by the school board and the MTEA. The response created opportunities for entrepreneurial educators, but efforts bogged down amid administrative and contractual constraints once the threat receded.

First, the expansion pushed the MPS system to increase its offerings, particularly through an explosion of schools approved under the innovative schools program. The board's interest in approving the proposals and the MTEA's willingness to issue MOUs relaxing the collective bargaining agreement were evident only once choice expansion seemed imminent.

In December 1994 the board had approved the first innovative school, the Grand Avenue Secondary School. The board authorized no more schools until it rapidly approved four additional innovative schools in February and March 1995 while expansion was debated in Madison. Then, in October 1995, the board approved four more schools for 1996–97. The explosion of innovative schools was a case of energetic educators popping through cracks, not conscious central action. A gaggle of self-motivated leaders, who stood to reap no material benefits, spent unpaid weekends and evenings pulling together plans to launch their own schools.

The importance of the threat posed by Fuller and the MPCP expansion was illustrated when the innovative schools process ground to a halt in 1996 once Fuller was gone and expansion was under injunction. Remembered one MTEA-backed board member, "It was choice and vouchers that encouraged the board to pull together with the union to create innovative schools. . . . They were protecting their own butts. Once the takeover threat was no longer there and choice was pretty much a done deal they went back to their old ways." After the spring of 1996, the MTEA did not approve another MOU allowing innovative schools to waive the seniority process.

The MPS system had long faced demands for increased Montessori programs but had moved slowly to address them. In the fall of 1995, the board approved expansions of both existing Montessori schools and in January 1996 it decided to open a third school in the fall of 1996. In early 1996, the system also took steps to add hundreds more early childhood seats. In June 1996, the MPS board approved Highland Montessori to be the district's first charter school. However, no additional charters were launched, as the MTEA filed suit to stop the district and the board chose not to press the issue.

Second, the effort to decentralize money to the schools, which had been pursued intermittently since 1988, made some progress in late 1995. During the period of September to December 1995, the board pushed the administration to proceed with the pilot decentralization of funding at nine MPS schools. The system trumpeted the change as a major shift, although administrators and the evidence on central administration suggest little or no concrete effects. Proposals in 1997 and 1998 to cut central spending were either rebuffed by the board or simply not implemented by the administration.

Third, system graduation requirements were visibly strengthened post-expansion. In September 1995, the board passed a resolution directing the administration to consider higher standards for graduation and in February 1996 it enacted significantly toughened standards. Concerns that had been voiced in opposition to Fuller's efforts to raise standards and require algebra of all students were barely evident post-expansion.

Fourth, the MPS report card accountability measures were dramatically toughened and made more visible, clear, and comprehensive. Before 1996–97, the MPS "report cards" were unimpressive and somewhat sporadic. After exploring the issue during 1994–95, the board in June 1995 approved a more comprehensive report and also ensured that more schools would be rated positively by loosening the definitions for "improving" and "high-achieving." The move was part of the MPS system's effort to enhance its reputation.

Fifth, the most visible response was the sudden proliferation of public slogans promoting the system's commitment to parental choices and high standards. Orange and black banners proclaiming "High Standards Start Here" were displayed on MPS and other property. Similarly, in the spring of 1995, a banner proclaiming "MPS, Milwaukee's First Schools of Choice" was hung behind MPS board members' seats. In 1995 the board made a commitment to public choice by making "First Choice Within MPS" the system's planning priority for 1995–96, though, in practice, administrators involved in running the program questioned the commitment and resources devoted to it.

Some voucher advocates suggest that the district, in 1995, for the first time felt compelled to bargain more toughly with the MTEA. However, little evidence exists of significant union concessions as the union maintained its aggressive legal campaign against MPCP, charter schooling, and reconstitution. The MTEA claimed to be receptive to reform during the negotiations of the 1995–97 contract, but it refused to contemplate changing seniority rules, closing of schools, and evaluation provisions.[21] While the union agreed to MOUs at individual schools in 1995 and early 1996 that it would previously have rejected, it fiercely resisted contractual reforms. Noted a former board president, "[The union] always do[es] MOUs but they never put those MOUs into the contract. In other words they never make it practice, which means that they're always playing the gatekeeper."

The union's incremental acceptance of reform provisions was partially the consequence of an internal conflict between the dominant, traditionalist wing and an outgunned "progressive" faction. Executive director Sam Carmen tried to bridge this divide with symbolic gestures. For instance, at a September 1995 meeting, in the midst of the post-expansion furor, Carmen told MTEA members that the union needed to "change the way we operate" even as he and the executive board proposed a two-year ban on further contract concessions modifying the seniority system.[22] After a protracted negotiation, the MPS system and the MTEA settled the 1995–97 contract in August 1996. The union made a small concession in agreeing to a new peer evaluation process but held firm on other concerns.[23]

By fall 1996, the MTEA had filed suit to block choice expansion, the district from "reconstituting" schools and moving teachers out of targeted schools without regard to seniority, Highland Community from becoming a charter school, and the MPS system from contracting with partnership schools to educate at-risk students. The union offensive prompted board president Mary Bills to fume in August 1996, "The MTEA makes the Teamsters look enlightened."[24]

During 1995 to 1997, PAVE played a critical role in maintaining the momentum of choice. When the courts held up the MPCP expansion to religious schools in fall 1995, and then again in fall 1996, PAVE raised millions for an emergency fund to help the students who were going to enroll in religious schools and were left in a bind. PAVE raised roughly half of the two-year total of $6 million from the Bradley Foundation.[25]

In 1995–96, MPCP enrollment rose to 1,115 students, and more than 4,000 students were enrolled in religious schools through PAVE. By 1996–97, MPCP enrollment had more than doubled and 2,500 students were using vouchers worth $4,300 to attend private schools. Meanwhile, another 4,300 students were in religious schools through PAVE scholarships (see table 9-3).

Two clear political camps took shape between 1995 and 1997. In the fall of 1995, former state delegate Warren Braun, a Catholic church official and supporter of vouchers, defeated the MTEA-backed candidate in a special board election. In 1997 Bruce Thompson, Gardner's 1995 campaign man-

Table 9-3. *Partners Advancing Values in Education (PAVE) Statistics, 1992–93 to 1998–99*

Program characteristic	1992–93	1993–94	1994–95	1995–96	1996–97	1997–98	1998–99
Number of scholarships awarded	2,089	2,450	2,654	4,303	4,201	4,371	846
Number of schools participating	86	102	103	106	106	109	112
Number of students wait-listed	0	1,093	1,036	0	0	0	0
Total value of scholarships ($)	1,278,932	1,704,007	1,954,257	Not known	Not known	4,100,000	1,052,000
Number of schools participating	86	102	103	106	106	109	112
Total funds contributed ($ millions)	2.4	1.5	2.0	2.2	3.7	4.2	Not available
Number of private foundations contributing	10	18	21	49	65	77	Not available

ager, defeated an MTEA-backed opponent, while MTEA-backed candidate Charlene Hardin managed the exceedingly rare feat of defeating an incumbent board member. The board now broke cleanly into two camps: the six MTEA allies and the three choice sympathizers. Whereas urban board elections are generally amorphous, MPS board politics was evolving into a two-party system.

In 1997 the legislature made significant modifications to the Wisconsin charter school law, giving the city of Milwaukee, the University of Wisconsin at Milwaukee (UWM), and the Milwaukee Area Technical College (MATC) the power to approve charter schools. Because charter school students did not have be low income and because they received a much more generous per pupil allocation than did MPCP schools, interest in opening new schools rapidly grew.

In 1997–98 the city moved to launch charter schools, UWM launched a planning process, and the MATC exhibited no interest in using its charter authority. Prodded by Mayor John Norquist, who appointed Howard Fuller chair of the city's Charter School Review Committee, the Common Council approved the city's first charter schools during 1997–98 and launched the city's first three schools, with a combined enrollment of 300, in fall 1998. A fourth school, Bruce Guadalupe Community School with nearly 500 students, declined a city charter.

Meanwhile, in January 1997 Superintendent Bob Jasna announced his resignation. After numerous stops and starts, the board voted 5-4 in September 1997 to hire career educator and Waukegan, Illinois, superintendent Alan Brown as the new superintendent. All five Brown votes came from MTEA-backed board members. The confusion of the divisive Brown search had paralyzed the district, smothering any coordinated response to competition. In January 1998 the whole issue of vouchers was again pushed aside for five months when Governor Thompson called for a state takeover of the MPS system. The African American community led a successful fight to reject the proposal, which faded out after spring 1998.

MPCP Expansion Endorsed by Courts

The competitive environment changed radically in June 1998 when the Wisconsin Supreme Court ruled 4-2 that the MPCP expansion was constitutional. In October 1998, the U.S. Supreme Court let the ruling stand. Once the future of MPCP was secure, the interest expressed in choice by potential school operators increased rapidly.

The new threats posed by charter schools and expansion triggered another wave of peak-level responses, as in 1995. Early in the spring of 1998, after

Norquist had launched the city's charter school push, Brown and a few key lieutenants sat down with partnership school leaders to hear their concerns and asked them to stay with the MPS system. The most common complaint voiced was that the schools wanted contracts that offered more stability than the one-year agreements the MPS system offered. Several meeting participants reported being disappointed by the overall effort and the lack of follow-up.

A second major event was the MPS system's aggressive courtship of Bruce Guadalupe after the city had offered the school a charter. Seeking to retain market share, the district brought a new school model within the system without altering current practice elsewhere in MPS. As a charter, the school would receive $6,100 per pupil. However, Director Walter Sava was concerned about legal confusion regarding Bruce Guadalupe's obligations to provide potentially costly services for disabled students and therefore accepted Brown's contract of $5,000 per pupil and the assurance that the MPS system would not require Guadalupe to enroll such students. After overcoming last-minute MTEA snags, Guadalupe signed a one-year deal with the city.

The effects of MPCP struck home for the first time in September 1998. From 1,501 students in 1997–98, before the state Supreme Court ruling, MPCP nearly quadrupled in size to 5,830. The number of participating schools grew from 23 in 1997–98 to 88 in 1998–99. The vast expansion was possible only because the religious schools that made up roughly 80 percent of Milwaukee's private schools were now part of the voucher program. In 1998–99, for the first time in the 1990s, MPS enrollment fell. It dropped from 101,963 in 1997–98 to 100,525. MPS system's forecast—known for its consistent accuracy—had projected an increase of 629 students. An administrator involved in enrollment management termed the numbers a "shock" and said that the drop forced the district to trim dozens of elementary teaching slots and to "hedge its bets on everything." For the first time MPS lost significant state aid because of MPCP—about $28 million from a school operations budget of $874 million.

However, because MPS had to hire more than 600 new teachers for 1998–99 and anticipated needing about 900 in 1999–2000, the loss of even hundreds of teaching slots would have had no direct impact on school personnel. Explained MTEA director Sam Carmen in fall 1999, "All in all, [the voucher issue] has not [affected the teachers]. . . . Enrollments have gone up each year until this year . . . [and] this year we still hired over seven hundred new teachers. . . . The existence of vouchers and choice and charter schools . . . hasn't [been] a hold on the work force, so thus far it hasn't adversely affected us." Not one interviewee recalled a teacher being forced out of a school owing to enrollment changes. Finally, because MPS have no system to track why students leave a school, because of the high rate of student mobility, and because MPS budgeting practices meant losing a student had a minimal impact on a school's resources, no one knew which schools were losing dissatisfied students or why.

The system took two visible actions in response to the enrollment drop. First, in December 1998, shortly before the annual "three-choice" school selection process, Brown announced a "reading guarantee" program with much fanfare. Any second-grade student who had attended MPS system K–2 and had a 90 percent attendance record but was reading below grade level would receive extra tutoring at the MPS system's expense. Second, during the winter of 1998–99, after the MTEA agreed to allow non-MTEA staffing and to waive several contract provisions, the MPS system agreed to share governance at a new Milwaukee Tech with a consortium of local organizations. MPS and MTEA concessions were driven by the threat of a local philanthropist to otherwise contribute the promised $25 million to fund the tech as a city-run charter school. Both programs involved adding new services, but did not significantly disrupt existing routines.

In January 1999, the MTEA leadership made several concessions it had long rejected. In September 1998, the MPS system and the MTEA had settled a long-running contract fight in what was widely characterized as a massive union victory. By December 1998, however, the U.S. Supreme Court's nondecision on MPCP, growing interest in charter schooling, and the burgeoning voucher coalition campaign for the school board had changed the negotiating context.

Paulette Copeland, a leader of the reform faction opposed to the traditional MTEA leadership, had narrowly won the union's presidency in 1997 in a 3,221-2,710 vote. The new environment, as well as public voucher coalition attacks on the September 1998 contract agreement, enabled the reformers to argue that the union had to appear cooperative. In January 1999, the MPS system and MTEA settled the 1999–2001 contract before the previous agreement had expired, the first time that had occurred in three decades of collective bargaining.

Most significant, the MTEA yielded on teacher seniority rules, making it easier for MPS to hire teachers of its choosing. Essentially, this put in the contract a version of the language that the union had agreed to on a case-by-case basis for innovative schools. The agreement freed MPS from the obligation to accept incoming teachers based on seniority if the schools elected to participate in one of several specified programs. The union and MPS also compromised and agreed to settle the union's long-running lawsuits against measures such as increased contracting and charter schools.

In December 1998, the City's Charter School Review Committee approved four applications for charter school status. UWM initially approved two charter schools for fall 1999, both to be managed by the for-profit Edison Project. However, the Edison role infuriated teachers and local opponents of for-profit education and prompted UWM to delay the opening of the schools. Meanwhile, the emergence of a radicalized MPS board in spring 1999 shifted the locus of action to the MPS system, which approved two charter schools for fall 1999.

There also emerged renewed interest in expanding existing schools or opening new ones. The need for PAVE scholarships largely evaporated with the approval of the full MPCP expansion; PAVE's enrollment plunged from 4,371 in 1997–98 to 846 in 1998–99. PAVE responded by shifting its focus to helping to launch new schools and facilitate the development of existing ones, spearheading foundation and business support for such endeavors. Previously, school supply had grown very slowly, largely as a result of the small size of the Catholic schools, which made up close to half of Milwaukee's private school system.[26]

A Political Revolution

By late 1998, a rough approximation of a two-party system had emerged around the MPS system. In place of the eclectic campaigns that had characterized MPS board elections before 1995, a unifying campaign theme emerged. The MTEA and the opponents of school vouchers mobilized behind one slate; the choice coalition behind a second.

Drawing on professional assistance, local choice networks, and the MMAC, Gardner coordinated a careful campaign. Gardner alone spent $190,000, more than tripling the previous record for a board campaign, while sources estimate the MMAC spent tens of thousands more supporting the coalition slate. Meanwhile, independent observers estimated the MTEA spent as much as $400,000 on the election. In the end, each side spent at least $250,000, shattering all previous records in a board election of unprecedented scope and policy coherence. Shockingly, the voucher slate swept the April elections as it unseated three MTEA-backed incumbents. Only three incumbents had been defeated in the previous twenty years. The bloc of choice sympathizers now numbered seven.

Bruce Thompson was quickly named the new board president. At the urging of the four board freshmen, the board bought out Superintendent Brown's contract and then hired maverick Hi-Mount principal Spence Korte to take the job. Korte immediately pushed an agenda of aggressive decentralization.

The new board took a number of aggressive and symbolic steps on its own, rapidly authorizing a structure for creating charter schools, approving an administration plan to increase contracting, considering a Gardner proposal to radically revise district accounting to permit significant decentralization, and signing off on the MPS system's second and third charter schools.

Ironically, just as leadership able to drive systemic response came to power, MPS won a victory in Madison that dramatically lessened the competitive pressure that MPCP and charter schooling posed, by reducing the amount of state funding that would follow students into these programs.

It is difficult to explain how little this turmoil had affected the great swath of MPS classrooms by the end of 1998–99. When asked about how competition had affected their schools, typical teacher comments were, "You need to understand, many teachers are unaware of this," or, "Teachers are so stressed out keeping their heads above water. . . . They have [no time] to worry about vouchers and charters." Through 1999, teachers were confused about choice and charters, suggested that they felt ill-equipped to do anything in answer to competition, and saw the notion of competing for students as alien and somewhat unsavory. Many teachers, and even some principals, were so confused about MPCP and charter schooling that it is not clear they understood how they might respond productively.

The only school-level activity respondents consistently mentioned was a spate of school advertising that broke out in 1997 and 1998, particularly after the June 1998 Wisconsin Supreme Court decision. A few schools aired radio and newspaper advertisements to attract students, while others took modest steps such as adding parent information nights or increasing the distribution of fliers or t-shirts. Advertising efforts seemed to die out rapidly, were made only in a handful of schools, and appeared to be as much a response to "three-choice" as to MPCP. In general, observed one pro-voucher board member in 1999, "[MPS employees] are just not marketers. For instance, parents of four-year-olds are always telling me that they haven't heard anything from the schools. I suggested the schools ought to buy a mailing list of these families [but] they just don't think that way. Partly it's ideological. They think, 'We're the schools, you're lucky that we're here to provide this service.'"

Similarly, in the bowels of MPS administration, little change was evident by fall 1999. In 1997 and 1998, the central administration continued to resist proposed decentralization and budget cutting, sometimes simply refusing to implement board directives.

Markets are driven by entrepreneurs. In Milwaukee, as in most places, the pool of educational entrepreneurs is relatively small. The complexity and uncertainty of the environment shrink it further. No more than a handful of people in Milwaukee understood the implications of the legal conflicts; statutory and judicial mandates; the financial implications of being a choice, charter, or partnership school; the funding restrictions; and the impact of enrollment changes on MPS. Most of those were voucher advocates, not educators. Amidst such confusion, subtle incentives may not have the intended effects and potential entrepreneurs may not emerge. As more individuals become more knowledgeable, as the rules stabilize, and as resources emerge to help address the confusion, the amount of entrepreneurial activity is likely to increase.

Also significant is the MPS system's ignorance regarding which schools students are leaving or where they are going. The MPS system is very good at counting the heads of students in school but has no mechanism for tracking students across schools or sectors. Similarly, despite a decade of commitment to decentralization, the system has yet to develop the ability to break out costs on a unit basis. Until such systems are in place, MPS cannot hold school personnel responsible for efficiency, student retention, or outlays.

Conclusions

As of fall 1999, competition had not significantly affected teaching and learning in Milwaukee public schools and classrooms. The 1990–98 MPS experience featured a small, contested voucher program that posed little systemic threat. Most proposed voucher programs are small in scope, however, even as advocates make outsized claims for their likely competitive effects. The real impact of such programs must be recognized. Through 1999, limited competition did not refocus teachers or principals or change how they did their jobs. It did produce some board-driven efforts to raise standards, increase choices, and open new schools. Choice and charters have provoked—at times of potential threat—largely symbolic reactions from MPS and MTEA leaders. This outcome is not unexpected. Because it is difficult for them to control classroom-level teaching and learning, system leaders in urban districts have incentives to focus on visible, easily launched measures rather than changes in classroom practice.[27] The irony is that these responses can have substantive effects—in particular they can create the potential for change by permitting new schools and programs to break through the many existing constraints.

While market forces did not bulldoze away inefficiencies, competition did chip at the barriers stifling entrepreneurial energy in the MPS system and prompt erratic, sporadic change. Choice brought change by allowing entrepreneurs to seize political openings to create new programs on the fringes of the MPS system to translate their personal visions into practice. Reformers used their new leverage to obtain resources and freedom from an administration that turned to them because its leadership felt compelled to react to competition but was not sure how to do so. This dynamic may produce substantial change, if enough cracks are created and enough weeds grow, but it depends on the supply of entrepreneurial leaders. The resulting changes may strengthen or weaken schooling, depending on the schools that emerge and their systemic consequences.

During 1999, observers generally agreed that there were probably no more than 20 entrepreneurial principals among the 150+ in MPS. One principal who serves in the leadership of the administrators union estimated "there are no more than five real tigers in MPS." Most of these "tigers" were previously regarded as oddballs, marked as suspect by their entrepreneurial energy. They desired neither money nor prestige and often received nothing but new, uncompensated responsibilities for their efforts. However, they were driven by a missionary commitment to public schooling. Because these entrepreneurs were motivated by an emotional attachment to education, it is unclear just what policymakers might do to lure new members into their ranks. Also problematic was that these leaders generally expressed little interest in running multiple school sites, as they bask in hands-on management of "their" school. Key unanswered questions are how to summon forth more of these leaders, how to leverage their influence, and how their schools will fare under new leaders.

While the most significant effects produced by vouchers were the political pressures that led to changes in system behavior, these pressures may not last. The emergent two-party system focuses debate, makes it easier to hold board members accountable, and promotes a governing bloc able to provide consistent direction. However, participation in MPS elections remains low, and other cities have had antiunion coalitions rise and then fade away.[28] Further, coalition members have voiced frustration at the difficulty of replicating the broad Milwaukee coalition in other cities. It may be that the roots of choice in Milwaukee, the role of African American and Democratic leaders, and the resources of the Bradley Foundation created a unique dynamic. Moreover, the voucher coalition suffered significant setbacks in the spring 2001 board elections, including the defeat of Bruce Thompson, raising questions as to its viability even in Milwaukee.

The consequences of competition will be particularly shaped by three elements. One is the extent of the threat. As the number of private or charter schools grows, as the choice or charter funding level is increased, or as the link between public enrollment and school funding grows tighter, the threat posed by choice grows. The state's 1999 decision to increase funding for MPSs and reduce the losses caused by lost enrollment promised to greatly reduce the threat posed by choice and charter programs. A second is the sensitivity of educational leaders to market pressures and the sanctions and incentives these leaders are able to wield. A third is the temperament and skills of educators. If educators enter the profession for more market-oriented reasons, are socialized in different ways, or expect to derive different kinds of rewards, then the constraints imposed by the schoolhouse culture may soften.

Features of public schooling that have stymied earlier reforms and fed the call for school choice are also likely to structure the effects of competition. The pivotal point is this: Except when considering choice proposals that abolish public school systems altogether, debates about school choice must be integrated into the larger educational conversation.

Finally, two caveats are in order. First, whether schools should be more responsive to markets is a question that I have left unaddressed here. Second, even those who judge educational competition desirable may shy away from the changes necessary to make schools more responsive. Both of these questions will require careful consideration in the years to come.

Notes

1. The author wishes to gratefully acknowledge the support that the Spencer Foundation, the WKBJ Foundation, and the Olin Foundation have provided for this research and to thank Dana Brower, Michele Davis, and Michelle Tolbert for their research assistance.

2. For instance, Jeanne Allen, president of Center for Education Reform, predicted that Florida's 1999 voucher program would prompt "a dramatic improvement of the public schools." See Kenneth J. Cooper and Sue Anne Pressley, "Florida House Approves School Vouchers; Senate Votes Today," *Washington Post*, April 29, 1999. Allen's statement echoed Milton Friedman's 1962 contention that competition would stimulate the "improvement of all schools." For the discussion, see Milton Friedman, *Capitalism and Freedom* (University of Chicago Press, 1962), p. 93.

3. See John J. DiIulio, ed., *Deregulating the Public Service: Can Government Be Improved?* (Brookings, 1994), for a thoughtful discussion of these issues.

4. This school of thought derives from Joseph A. Schumpeter's notion of "creative destruction" as the means by which free markets operate. For discussion, see Joseph A. Schumpeter, *Capitalism, Socialism, and Democracy* (Harper and Brothers, 1947).

5. Patrick J. McEwan, "The Potential Impact of Large-Scale Voucher Programs," Review of Educational Research 70 (2001), pp. 103–50; quote is on p. 136.

6. For examples of the more interesting work that has been done on the effects of educational competition in the American context, see David J. Armor and Brett M.

Peiser, *Competition in Education: A Case Study of Interdistrict Choice* (Boston: Pioneer Institute, 1997); Bryan C. Hassel, *The Charter School Challenge: Avoiding the Pitfalls, Fulfilling the Promise* (Brookings, 1999); Caroline M. Hoxby, "Does Competition among Public Schools Benefit Students and Taxpayers?" *American Economic Review,* vol. 90 (2000), pp. 1209–38; Caroline M. Hoxby, "School Choice and School Productivity (Or, Could School Choice Be a Tide That Lifts All Boats?)," presented at the National Bureau of Economic Research Conference on the Economics of School Choice, Islamorada, Florida, February 22–24, 2001; and Eric Rofes, *How Are School Districts Responding to Charter Laws and Charter Schools?* (Policy Analysis for California Education, 1998).

7. Mancur Olson has provided perhaps the most elegant discussion of this collective action problem, in *The Logic of Collective Action* (Harvard University Press, 1970). Individuals who will reap collective benefits if everyone undertakes an action, but who incur costs if they themselves act, are unlikely to act unless a mechanism exists to compel them to do so.

8. For discussions of this point, see Frederick M. Hess, *Spinning Wheels: The Politics of Urban School Reform* (Brookings, 1999), chapter 2; and James Q. Wilson, *Bureaucracy: What Government Agencies Do and Why They Do It* (Basic Books, 1988), chapter 12.

9. For a lucid statement of this premise, see Friedman, *Capitalism and Freedom.*

10. See Larry Cuban, *The Managerial Imperative and the Practice of Leadership in Schools* (Albany, N.Y.: SUNY Press, 1988).

11. For the classic discussion of the schoolhouse culture, see Dan C. Lortie, *Schoolteacher: A Sociological Study* (University of Chicago Press, 1975). For a more recent discussion of the culture of schooling, see Joel Westheimer, *Among School Teachers: Community Autonomy and Ideology in Teachers' Work* (New York: Teachers College, 1998). For consideration of how the nature and culture of schooling interacts with efforts to use rewards and sanctions in promoting school improvement, see David K. Cohen, "Rewarding Teachers for Student Performance," in Susan H. Fuhrman and Jennifer A. O'Day, eds., *Rewards and Reform: Creating Educational Incentives That Work* (San Francisco: Jossey-Bass, 1996), pp. 60–112; and Linda Darling-Hammond, "Restructuring Schools for High Performance," in Susan H. Fuhrman and Jennifer A. O'Day, eds., *Rewards and Reform: Creating Educational Incentives That Work* (San Francisco: Jossey-Bass, 1996), pp. 144–92. For an excellent discussion of the difficulties in relying upon intrinsic incentives to get most teachers and school communities to embrace educational change, see Richard F. Elmore, "Getting to Scale with Good Educational Practice," *Harvard Educational Review,* vol. 66 (1996), pp. 1–26.

12. The union leadership will take such action when political pressure becomes sufficiently intense that the leadership feels it can better serve its members by appearing flexible than by safeguarding the status quo.

13. In focusing on the response to choice, I have explicitly chosen not to look at test scores or other outcome data. Because competition was an indirect mechanism being piloted on a small scale, any outcome effects might not be apparent in the

short term. More broadly, competition may have significant systemic effects without producing visible changes in student performance. Finally, at least for periods of less than five to ten years, outcome data can prove misleading in understanding the effects of educational change. For a discussion of this last point, see Anthony S. Bryk, David Kerbow, and Sharon Rollow, "Chicago School Reform," in Diane Ravitch and Joseph P. Viteritti, eds., *New Schools for a New Century: The Redesign of Urban Education* (Yale University Press, 1997), pp. 164–200.

14. The churning of policies and reforms that characterizes urban school districts can make it difficult to clearly determine the nature or source of any particular change, but this account tries to use multiple sources and the documentary record to minimize confusion.

15. For an outstanding discussion of the contract and how it evolved over time, see Howard L. Fuller, George A. Mitchell, and Michael E. Hartmann, *The Milwaukee Public Schools' Teacher Union Contract: Its History, Content, and Impact on Education* (Marquette University, Institute for the Transformation of Learning, Marquette University, 1997). For the statistics on Milwaukee Public School (MPS) firing and tenure between 1985 and 1990, see John H. Fund, "Can Competition Save America's Failing School Systems?" *San Diego Union-Tribune,* September 9, 1990, p. 1. For the statistics on MPS firing of teachers between 1990 and 1995, see Steve Shultze and Mary Zahn, "Kids Take 2nd Place in Discipline System; Problem Teachers a Poison," *Milwaukee Journal-Sentinel,* November 20, 1995, p. 1.

16. Later, during the course of 1995–98, Polly Williams would break with Gov. Tommy G. Thompson and the other leaders of the Milwaukee voucher coalition, arguing that they were not focused on her mission of helping poor inner-city children.

17. To be eligible for the Milwaukee Parental Choice Program (MPCP), a student's family income could not exceed 175 percent of the federal poverty level and the student could not have attended private school or a public school outside the MPS system the previous year.

18. Governor Thompson was able to push through a bill that slightly boosted the cap on MPCP enrollment from 1 percent of MPS enrollment to 1.5 percent for the 1994–95 school year. That increased the number of eligible students to about 1,450. The change also permitted voucher schools to enroll up to 65 percent of their students—up from 49 percent—through MPCP. The change had no significant impact on the MPS system, as the program continued to be regarded as a distraction.

19. See Shultze and Zahn, "Kids Take 2nd Place in Discipline System."

20. During the session, the legislature also expanded charter schooling, permitted the MPS superintendent to "reconstitute" failing schools, and expanded the ability of the MPS system to contract with partnership schools.

21. See John Stanford, "MTEA, School Board Must Put Kids First," *Milwaukee Journal-Sentinel,* November 26, 1995, p. 6. As Mike Casserly, the executive director of Council of Great City Schools, has observed, "A school district's inability to get rid of incompetent teachers is a major hindrance to reform," in Danyel Hooker, "MPS Restructurings: Closings' Help Staff, Some Say; Restructuring Schools Could Shift

Teachers to a Better Environment," *Milwaukee Journal-Sentinel*, December 30, 1995, p. 7.

22. In Curtis Lawrence, "Union Vows Change But Clings to Old Ways," *Milwaukee Journal-Sentinel*, November 21, 1995, p. 1.

23. See Danyel L. Hooker, "MPS, Union Reach Agreement; Tentative Deal Includes Raises, Health Savings," *Milwaukee Journal-Sentinel*, August 14, 1996, p. 1.

24. See Danyel L. Hooker, "Suit Seeks to Block Charter School; Teachers Union Wants Injunction to Prevent MPS Program Set to Begin This Fall," *Milwaukee Journal Sentinel*, August 7, 1996, p. 1.

25. See Jay Purnick, "Metro Matters; In Milwaukee, School Choice with Caution," *New York Times*, October 24, 1996, p. B1.

26. As of December 1998, just six of the thirty-five Catholic K–8 schools in Milwaukee enrolled as many as 300 students.

27. See Hess, *Spinning Wheels*; John Meyer and Brian Rowan, "Institutionalized Organizations: Formal Structure as Myth and Ceremony," in Walter W. Powell and Paul J. DiMaggio, eds., *The New Institutionalism in Organizational Analysis* (University of Chicago Press, 1991); and David B. Tyack and William Tobin, "The Grammar of Schooling: Why Has It Been So Hard to Change?" *American Educational Research Journal*, vol. 31 (1994), pp. 453–79.

28. See Milwaukee Public Schools, *Special Report: School Board Elections and Election Districts* (Milwaukee, Wis.: Milwaukee Public Schools Office of Board Governance, 1998).

10

Can Charter Schools Change Traditional Public Schools?

PAUL TESKE, MARK SCHNEIDER,
JACK BUCKLEY, AND SARA CLARK

O f the many school choice initiatives spreading throughout the country, charter schools are by far the most common.[1] Despite the rapid growth of charter schools (and other forms of choice), however, nearly 90 percent of American children continue to be enrolled in "traditional" or "regular" public schools. Given that this distribution of students across sectors is likely to change only modestly in the near future, we believe that one of the most important issues facing education reformers is the extent to which charter schools affect the behavior of traditional public schools by competing with them for students.

Only a few scholars have examined this question. Eric Rofes interviewed leaders in twenty-five school districts around the country and found that while some districts reacted to competition from charter schools, many did not.[2] Given that his fieldwork took place in 1997 when the charter movement was in its early stages, Rofes's research may have come too early to detect major effects. However, more recent research has also been unable to find large effects. For example, Frederick M. Hess found little influence on the Milwaukee Public School system from the competition from various forms of school choice available in that city.[3] Using 1998 data, Robert Maranto and others compared Arizona districts, where charters hold a fairly large market share, with Nevada, which had no charter schools.[4] Based on teacher responses, these researchers found some evidence that loss of market share led to certain kinds of reforms in some districts; however, the relationships were inconsistent and often weak. In addition, the charter school system in Arizona is extensive compared with those in place in the rest of the country, and consequently these results might represent an "extreme" case. All in all, the effect of competition from charter schools on the existing traditional school system has yet to be clearly demonstrated.

Why Might School Districts Respond?

From our review of the literature on how competition can affect the behavior of organizations, we identify two theories explaining how the presence of charter schools can affect the behavior of traditional public schools. The first theory is based on the diffusion of innovation; the second, on the financial effects of losing students.

New Ideas Can Leverage Change

Many proponents argue that, because of their greater freedom and fewer bureaucratic rules, charter schools can be laboratories for change and experimentation. By designing original curricula and programs, by experimenting with new models of school organization, and by developing new methods to encourage parental involvement, according to their supporters, charter schools will provide examples for the traditional public schools to follow.[5] For this to work, however, at least two assumptions must hold. First, charter schools must develop and implement innovative models. Second, a flow of information and communications must exist between the two sectors. Both of these assumptions are open to question in the field.

Financial Pressure Can Force Change

The second theory is that if there are financial penalties for any loss of students to charter schools, competition will force the traditional public schools to respond. Such financial incentives could also support the flow of information concerning successful education programs and techniques between charter and traditional schools. If traditional schools face a loss of budget resulting from declining market share, their incentives to adopt programs that have been proven successful elsewhere should increase.

Charter school laws around the country have effectively codified this argument by mandating that some percentage of per pupil educational expenses follow the child to the charter school, leaving less money in the traditional public school district (although also leaving fewer children to educate). Some analysts, such as Richard Rothstein, have questioned whether insulated urban school districts, often run by large bureaucracies, can be pressured to change by these incentives.[6]

The broader literature on the effects of competition on public organizations shows that responses can be more complex than the above arguments indicate. Responses from traditional public sector organizations can range from outright hostility and resistance, to various degrees of realistic adaptation, including the use of competition to achieve other organizational goals, through attempts to co-opt the competitive process to the advantage of the organization or its sponsors.[7] The school districts we studied have responded to the increased competition from charter schools in ways that span the spectrum of responses cited in the literature.

Case Selection and Methodology

Given the early state of research into the question of cross-sector effects, we chose to undertake relatively detailed case studies in a small number of school districts instead of trying to construct a large national database. We study five urban districts facing growing competition from charter schools: Springfield, Massachusetts; Worcester, Massachusetts; Jersey City, New Jersey; Trenton, New Jersey; and the District of Columbia (D.C.). In each of these districts, we interviewed the district superintendent, school board leaders, charter school heads, teachers union leaders, and other district leaders (such as parental placement center heads and school principals).

We had several criteria in mind in choosing these cities. First, we chose to focus on urban districts because they experience so many of the problems common to the public education system and charter schools are emerging in larger numbers in urban areas.[8] Second, we chose to focus on midsize urban districts because they were more accessible than the largest cities for the type of exploratory study we conducted. Third, we chose not to study cities in the states in which the spread of charters is most advanced (for example, Arizona, Michigan), because these locations are already receiving scholarly attention. Conversely, we avoided states that only recently passed charter legislation (for example, New York), as the impact of charters on the traditional schools is likely to be small and too early to detect. However, we wanted to ensure that the cities selected for study would be representative of the widely varied strengths of charter legislation throughout the country. The laws in Massa-

Table 10-1. *Summary of Conditions in the School Districts Studied*

Condition	Jersey City, N.J.	Springfield, Mass.	Trenton, N.J.	Washington, D.C.	Worcester, Mass.
1990 enrollment	27,612	23,454	11,850	67,313	22,084
1998 enrollment	32,902	25,649	13,106	~76,000	25,552
Number of public schools	33	42	23	~150	45
Number of charter schools	9	3	7	29	2
Charter school enrollment as percent of total enrollment	4.5	4.1	7.5	9	4.7
Percent black	39	31	70	85	10
Percent Hispanic	39	41	24	9	28
Percent limited English proficient	11	12	6	10	7
Percent free lunch	75	71	75	62	50

chusetts and D.C. have been ranked among the most favorable to charters, while New Jersey's law is ranked in the middle of the thirty-seven states studied by the Pacific Research Institute.[9] Finally, to hold constant some of the situational context in which cities are attempting to meet the challenges of education reform, we chose two cities in each of two states. Table 10-1 illustrates important demographic characteristics of each of these districts.

Though we lack the space to provide complete histories, a few important elements should be noted about the backgrounds of each district. In Springfield, about ten years ago, a reform coalition of business leaders and politicians decided to improve the schools, and they hired Peter Negroni, a reform-oriented superintendent. When he arrived, the district was under a court order to desegregate. With Negroni's support, Springfield has used controlled interdistrict choice as a means of voluntary desegregation. While Springfield faces competition from three charter schools, the largest and most visible is the Sabis International School.

In Worcester, the public schools have generally performed better than those in the other districts we are studying, partly because the student body is not as low-income as in the other cities. In recent years, as the high-technology development around Boston has pushed out further, Worcester's public schools have received good press. As a result of this sense of success, leadership has been fairly stable in Worcester. Three years ago, the elected school board appointed as superintendent James Caradonio, who had formerly been the deputy superintendent of the district for several years before his appointment. There are two charter schools in the Worcester area, Seven Hills, which is associated with the Edison Project, and the Abby Kelley Foster school, which is run by Advantage Schools.

In Trenton, for the past decade, the schools have performed at the very lowest level in the state. Under the previous chief school administrator (the equivalent of superintendent), the Trenton schools were clearly failing and the district's efforts at reforming operations were lagging. As a consequence, in 1998 the mayor and the appointed school board hired James "Torch" Lytle, who was known as a reformer and a supporter of charter schools from his experience in Philadelphia. There are seven charter schools in the Trenton area, of which the Granville School, associated with the Edison Project, is by far the largest.

Jersey City schools also performed poorly and were taken over by the state ten years ago, partly because there was corruption related to the elected school board, which was using the schools as a source of patronage. The current superintendent, Richard DiPatri, was a state education official appointed three years ago to head the Jersey City schools. There are nine charter schools in the Jersey City area.

The public school system in the District of Columbia has long been regarded as one of the worst in the country, despite funding that is 26 percent higher than the national average. In 1996, using a military crisis approach, the board hired three-star Army General Julius W. Becton Jr. as superintendent, who was replaced in 1998 by Arlene Ackerman. Charter schools have grown rapidly in D.C., with twenty-nine schools that serve one out of every eleven public school students.

To get a more complete picture of these districts, in addition to our interviews of school district leaders, we searched various newspapers and databases about local politics, population trends, and issues surrounding the public and charter schools in these districts. We examined the written materials and websites prepared by state education departments and the school districts. We combined these interview and other data with district-level objective data on enrollment trends, demographics, and test scores. In addition to this district-level information, we surveyed school principals by mail, e-mail, and telephone. The response we received to the survey of principals depended greatly on the degree of support we received from the district superintendent in carrying out the survey, which varied across districts, as shown in table 10-2.

Table 10-2. *Principal Response Rates Vary Widely across Districts*

District	Number of responses	Response rate (percent)
Jersey City, N.J.	9	25
Springfield, Mass.	17	37
Trenton, N.J.	20	87
Washington, D.C.	12	8
Worcester, Mass.	30	61

Factors Limiting the Competitive Effects of Charter Schools

Although our districts were neither chosen as a random sample nor selected to increase the variance on the dependent variable, we found a wide range of district-level responses to charter schools.

In Springfield, district officials are so supportive of charter schools that Superintendent Negroni, a member of the elected city School Board, and the mayor all sit on the Board of Directors of the Sabis International Charter School. Further, Negroni considers charter schools as part of a "toolbox" of techniques available to him to leverage reform in his district, and he argues that "beating Sabis" has now become a mantra in the district, energizing the public schools to perform better.[10]

In Trenton, district leaders also support charter schools as a form of competition they can use to leverage further reform activity by their own principals. Chief School Administrator Lytle notes, "I believe in competition. We intend to be in the forefront of urban education reform. We welcome this competition and believe we'll all be better for this."[11]

Jersey City has a fairly neutral response to charter school competition. Public school officials report cooperating with charter schools, which they do not see as strongly positive or negative influences on their actions, as they continue to implement their own reforms. According to Superintendent DiPatri, "We cooperate with the charter schools, but our business, and our state mandate, is to improve the whole Jersey City public school system."

Leaders in the two other districts, Worcester and Washington, D.C., are negative toward charters and have actively worked against them. Worcester officials, including the superintendent, are leading a lobby of municipalities in Massachusetts to change state rules governing charters. They have many concerns, among the most basic is the claim that parental choice of charter schools is motivated by racial concerns instead of by academic or programmatic considerations. In addition, most of the Worcester officials we interviewed argued that the charter schools do not "add value" to the education of their students and that the charters represented an unnecessary drain on the resources of a district that they argue is performing well. Moreover, several officials we interviewed argued that the charter schools, despite laws to the contrary, were screening students and either not admitting or "counseling out" high cost students, such as students in need of special education.

In D.C., although official statements from the office of Superintendent Arlene Ackerman reflected a neutral attitude toward the charter schools, the system demonstrates opposition by increasing the level of difficulty charter school organizers face in locating suitable facilities. Despite the congressional mandate to give District charter schools priority in obtaining vacant public school buildings, new charters continue to face great difficulty in exercising this priority. Jeffrey Henig and his colleagues cite several examples of "puzzling" occurrences surrounding the sudden unavailability of previously available and occasionally already promised school facilities.[12] For example, the Hyde Park charter school negotiated for fifteen months with D.C. school officials to lease a vacant school building, but when the plan was submitted to the Board of Trustees for approval, the lease process was halted without explanation. Council member Kevin Chavous told the *Washington Post*, "It sounds like [school officials] reneged on a deal."[13] In another example, the Kwame Nkrumah charter school was told that the board had approved a charter, and it prepared to open. But, just days before the school year, the board voted against a charter in a closed meeting and sent security officials to tell students that their school was not authorized.[14] These actions are not surprising given that Superintendent Ackerman and other district leaders have expressed concerns about loss of financing to charter school competition and argue that such competition is not fair.

Our original hypothesis was that as the market share of charters increased the resulting loss of market share for traditional schools would lead district school officials to respond. Figure 10-1 shows that the attitude of school district leadership to charter schools is not a direct function of the loss of market share.

Two main reasons exist for this lack of relationship. First, districts and their individual schools have to date been shielded from most of the costs of losing students to charter schools. Second, the attitude of the district superintendent and, through the superintendent, the attitudes of other high-level administrators seem to be more a function of their individual beliefs than a function of the current level of charter school enrollment in their district.

Districts Shielded from Financial Impacts

Theoretically, the loss of students in the traditional public schools to charter schools should be accompanied by a corresponding loss of resources. When

Figure 10-1. *Relationship between Level of Support and Percent of Students Enrolled in Charter Schools*[a]

Percent of students
in charter schools

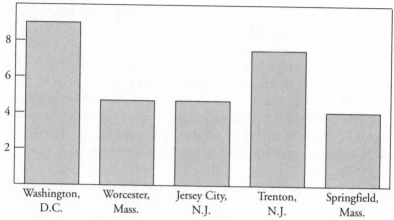

a. Order of cities reflects amount of public school district support for charter schools: lowest is Washington and highest is Springfield.

districts start to lose a significant share of students, they are likely to feel the financial shortfalls. This could then lead to the restructuring of failing public schools to attract students back and, in the extreme, a district-level decision to close (the equivalent of bankruptcy) those schools that cannot or do not respond.

We found, however, that in every district we studied a variety of financial and policy mechanisms have shielded the districts from most financial losses and, at the state or district level, compensatory financial mechanisms have been put in place to soften the impact of the growth of charters. For example, in our Massachusetts fieldwork, we found almost universal agreement among district leaders and principals that the financial impacts of growing charter school enrollment were negligible. This is partly because a Massachusetts law enacted in 1995 and amended in 1999 created a sliding scale of state reimbursement for financial losses resulting from charter school enrollment.[15] The amount reimbursed decreases over four years after the new school opens its doors (from 100 percent to 60 percent to 40 percent to 0 percent). This slow adoption of full financial penalty for loss of students, along with additional state aid to the schools through other channels, has thus far prevented the traditional schools in Massachusetts from experiencing the true effects of competition from the charter schools.[16]

The schools in the two New Jersey districts have also been spared the full financial losses that should flow from growing charter enrollments. As a consequence of *Abbott* v. *Burke,* the latest N.J. Supreme Court decision in a twenty-five-year-long educational funding legal saga, the thirty poorest districts in New Jersey, which include Trenton and Jersey City, are entitled to a large share of financial resources from the state.[17] These extra funds will support new pre–K programs, reduce class size, and fund a variety of other compensatory programs. To make sure that these funds are well spent, the court has mandated a set of reforms known as Whole School Reform (WSR). Thus Trenton and Jersey City are receiving new funds to implement WSR far in excess of the amounts they have lost to the charter schools. Most notably, Trenton received more than $10 million for WSR. In addition, the state of New Jersey is expected to provide substantial funding for new school construction and school modernization, which are critical issues in Trenton and Jersey City.

In D.C., budgets of both traditional and charter schools are supposed to be determined by a uniform per student formula that includes a base allotment of $5,500 per pupil, with extra monies available for various add-ons and facilities allowances. However, federal legislation permits block appropriation of funds to the public schools for special needs, thereby allowing individual school budgets to be enlarged or held constant despite drops in enrollment and, at least so far, preventing the district from experiencing an overall budget decrease. Henig and his colleagues observe, "With enrollment levels in public charter schools expected to grow, it is unclear how schools will be able to meet their financial responsibilities without sacrificing their educational missions. Luckily for both DCPS [D.C. public schools] and public charter schools, the size of the elementary and secondary education budget has grown substantially in recent years, easing, at least for the time being, the potential for intense competition between the two types of schools."[18] In the near future, this may change. As the *Washington Post* recently reported, "City officials have been warning [Superintendent Ackerman] that the school system could wind up with millions of dollars less than expected for the 1999–2000 school year, in part because of the growing popularity of new D.C. public charter schools—which are drawing public funds away from traditional schools."[19] Thus while in the future the financial costs of losing students to charter schools may force a response, to date, these costs have not yet been fully imposed.

Individual Schools Held Harmless

Just as no district has yet been held fully accountable for losses to charter schools, no district has yet held individual schools fully accountable for their losses of students to charter schools. For most districts, in the long run, money will have to have some reasonable relationship to enrollment in particular schools. In some of these districts, at least a portion of school-level budgets is tied to the number of pupils served—but probably not yet enough to force reforms. And this budgeting trend often comes into conflict with a much more traditional response: School boards and superintendents often redistribute money to failing schools to try to prop them up.

In some districts the resolution of these two forces may be changing in favor of holding individual schools more responsible. For example, only a few principals in Trenton reported feeling budget constraints in 2000 associated with loss of students, but many more expected to feel a large budget pinch in 2001 as a result of choice. This is not surprising, because Chief School Administrator Lytle plans to implement a flexible (50–60 percent "cash-based") school-based budget process that will allocate funding on a per pupil basis, with decisions made by a team of administrators, teachers, and parents. With this kind of budget process in place, school-level losses of students will translate into financial cuts.

In the other districts, however, we did not hear much about any efforts to apportion cuts to specific schools. This is not because districts are ignoring school-level activities. In several of these districts, superintendents are holding principals more accountable. In Springfield, Negroni has replaced more than a dozen of his forty-two principals. Caradonio in Worcester has not replaced large numbers of principals, because he believes that he and his predecessor put a strong cadre in place. He has nonetheless developed an elaborate school-level accountability tracking system. DiPatri made principal accountability a centerpiece of his reform in Jersey City, appointing a new supervisor of principals. But in general, while district superintendents must ultimately care about how individual schools are being run, so far, they are not explicitly punishing schools for losing students to charter schools.

Population Trends Blunting the Impact of Charter Schools

Despite the general decline in inner-city populations over the past few decades, as a result of both the "echo baby boom" and recent immigration all of our districts have experienced increases in total enrollment. This has acted to relieve the traditional schools of some of the competitive threat from charter schools as new students quickly fill seats vacated by those opting for a charter school. Thus, even if enrollment in charter schools increases, the traditional public schools do not necessarily experience a net decline in the number of students in attendance. For example, even with the 9 percent loss to charter schools in the District of Columbia, the total number of students

Figure 10-2. *Enrollments in Traditional Schools and Charter Schools, Washington, D.C.*

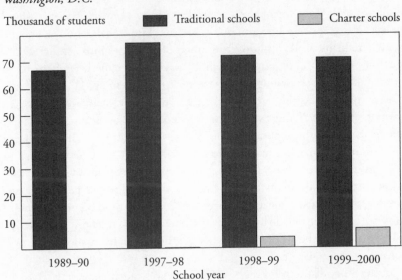

Thousands of students   ■ Traditional schools   ☐ Charter schools

School year

in all public schools has increased over the last decade. As figure 10-2 illustrates, the growing number of charter school students is taking an increasing proportion of total enrollment, but even then, total public school enrollment is higher at the end of the decade than it was at the beginning.

While D.C. has surplus buildings, none of the New Jersey or Massachusetts districts has excess space to accommodate growing enrollments. Trenton, for example, is already sending its special education children to other districts because it lacks space to house them. In Jersey City and Springfield, school district leaders explicitly regarded charter schools as one way of avoiding large capital outlays to house an expanding student population.

In short, urban districts currently experiencing growth may view charter schools, at least in the short run, as an effective way to deal with space problems. The fact that many schools are not seeing fewer students, even as charter schools are created, blunts the competitive pressure they feel from expanding charter schools.

Factors Affecting How Traditional Public Schools Respond

The role of school and school district leadership is critical to how the traditional public schools respond. This corresponds with the most important findings from the effective schools literature and other studies of high-performing schools showing the importance of leadership.[20] We found that district leaders and principals who are entrepreneurial and reform-oriented are using charter schools as a tool to increase their leverage over their schools and force them to institute new programs and improve performance. We also found that the predisposition of superintendents toward competition seems to precede the growth of charters.[21]

Of all the district leaders we interviewed, Springfield superintendent Negroni was the most vocal supporter of charter schools. Given his background working with Anthony Alvarado, one of New York City's most successful advocates of choice, Negroni not surprisingly regards charters as "a spark plug to accelerate change in the system." And he has borrowed ideas developed in local charter schools: Springfield's traditional public schools will soon include a Montessori-type school and a school based around laptop computers, a key element of the Edison Project's approach. Perhaps most important, Negroni believes that his principals have the power and the flexibility necessary to improve the quality of services their schools provide—and that charters are forcing them to use that authority to make beneficial changes.

Similarly, in Trenton, Lytle had an explicit mandate to reform the public schools and he came to Trenton having already written an application to create a charter school. Lytle appreciates the increasingly competitive environment in which public schools are operating. In his first speech to Trenton principals, Lytle pointed out that he could, in effect, "sell" the whole system to the Edison Project, which could operate it more cheaply and perhaps better than it was being run. Lytle was explicitly using the threat of market competition to support his push for reform.

In contrast, Worcester superintendent Caradonio took over a relatively stable school district after serving for over ten years as the deputy superintendent. He simply does not see the need for wholesale reform and views the resources and attention given to charter schools as harming his progress toward incremental improvements.

Although DiPatri had been involved with charter school legislation as a state official, he felt that his state mandate in Jersey City was to clean up the previous mess and to do so with a centralizing approach, emphasizing top-down accountability. For example, he has implemented a principal mentoring program and an academy for the preparation of principals. While not at all hostile to charters, he views them as largely irrelevant to his central reform agenda.

Finally, in D.C., Superintendent Ackerman has been working hard to reform, and to improve the image of, the traditional public schools. But she has been criticized for putting more resources into attempting to improve the worst schools, at the expense of maintaining the good ones. And, some principals feel that she has increased their bureaucratic burdens, while not forming strong and useful relationships with them.[22]

Principals Respond to Pressure

While superintendents clearly set the tone for their school districts, we found evidence from our survey of principals that the sound of parent footsteps heading to charter schools is being heard at the school level. As frontline managers, principals recognize that the funding of their schools and even their job tenure will increasingly be tied to enrollment trends, so perhaps this is not surprising—and occurs even as some superintendents say that a response is not necessary.

Part of the school-level response is to compete with charter schools that seem to be both popular and performing well. For example, the Center for School Change at the University of Minnesota reports that when the Sabis school in Springfield was converted from a regular public school, in 1995, only 38 percent of students performed at or above grade level, making it one of the lowest-performing schools in Springfield.[23] At the end of the second year, with essentially the same student body, about 62 percent of Sabis students performed at or above grade level. This success of Sabis forced the traditional public schools to put much more emphasis on testing their students more often, according to Peter Levanos, head of Springfield's interdistrict choice program. Several schools also started up Saturday programs, to match the Saturday programs at Sabis. Levanos noted that this competition has led to ten of Springfield's twenty elementary schools now outscoring Sabis, five of which were previously scoring at those levels, with the other five stepping up to "beat Sabis."

We found several broader patterns in our surveys that suggest that the growth in charter school enrollments is affecting how principals behave. In figure 10-3 we report data from our survey of seventy-six principals in the four districts with reasonable response rates (we exclude D.C. because of the low response rate).

As the data in figure 10-3 illustrate, a relationship exists between the principal's expectation of loss of students to charter schools and other forms of competition in the near future and the number of recent reforms introduced or expanded in a school.[24] Similarly, as expected losses to competitors increase, principals report spending more of their time on improving the efficiency of their schools (see figure 10-4). And figure 10-5 shows that principals who fear the loss of students to competitors are also more likely to feel

Figure 10-3. *Relationship between Competitive Pressure and Number of Innovations by Principals*

Number of innovations

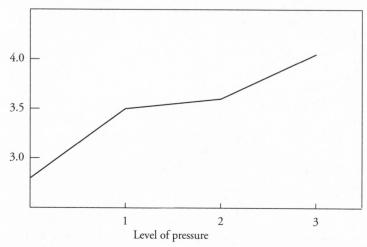

Level of pressure

Figure 10-4. *Relationship between Competitive Pressure and Principals Spending Time Increasing Efficiency*

Percent of principals

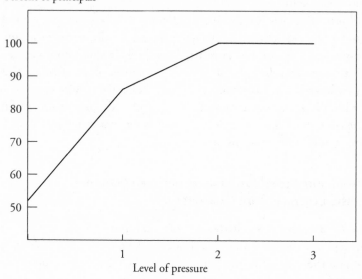

Level of pressure

Figure 10-5. *Relationship between Competitive Pressure and Autonomy of Principals*

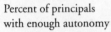

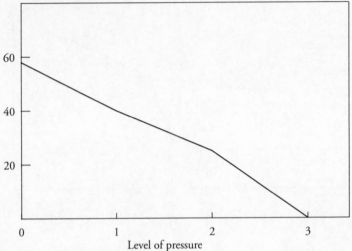

that they do not have enough autonomy to implement the kinds of changes and policies that they see as necessary to make their schools perform better and more competitively.

In short, principals feeling competition are trying to act more entrepreneurially: enhancing efficiency, changing the mix of their school's programs, and expressing frustration over restrictions on their ability to do more. So, principals may be feeling the effects of competition more strongly and, in turn, may be trying to react more quickly, than are district officials.

In addition to these district and school-level leadership issues, we found that the concept of charter schools as "models for innovation and imitation" is running into some problems in these cities.

Perceived and Actual Differences between Schools Limit the Leverage from Charters

The literature supporting charter schools often portrays them as venues in which new teaching techniques and new packages of services will be pioneered and then spread to the traditional public schools. For some charter proponents, this diffusion of innovation is as important as any theory of market competition.

We found, however, a sharp divide between leaders in the traditional public schools and the charter schools that has so far muted any diffusion effects of charter school reforms. At the most fundamental level, many leaders in the traditional public schools feel that the environment in which charter schools operate is not the same one they face and that the charter schools are not doing anything new or innovative that they wish to emulate.

Hostility Limits Spillovers from Charter Schools

A fundamental hostility is often found between the traditional public schools and the charter schools. Even in districts where the level of hostility is low, we noted little evidence that schools in either sector have reached out to one another. Each side feels that the other side has great advantages that make for an uneven playing field and limit the lessons that can be learned across sectors.

Not surprisingly, district officials in Worcester were not interested in what the charters are doing. Superintendent Caradonio does not believe that charters are real laboratory schools introducing real innovations. In addition, district and union leaders share the view that charters are union busters. Mark Brophy, the president of the Worcester teachers union, called them "a conspiracy to implode public education."

While these actors may have a vested interest in dismissing the role of charter schools, the Rosenblum Brigham report on Massachusetts charter schools supports many of their contentions.[25] It found that "there is no significant sharing or dissemination of practices from charter schools to district schools at this time. The reasons range from the practical (a lack of mechanisms for sharing) to the philosophical (there is a sense of competition and even hostility toward the charter school system that precludes sharing)."

In D.C., a high-ranking public school official echoed this, arguing that "there is no incentive for charters to convey information back to traditional public schools about what is and isn't working for them. Administrators, faculty, and staff at charters either have too much to do to have time to do this, or they have consciously left the traditional system so they don't want to communicate with DCPS regarding successful and/or failed programs."

One fundamental source of the suspicion that leaders of traditional public schools show for charter schools is that, despite the laws and empirical evidence to the contrary, many public school officials believe that charter schools educate a different population than the traditional schools do. For example, officials in Jersey City argued that charter schools can effectively force or counsel out problem students, who then return to the responsibility of the traditional public schools. Similarly, in a front-page *Education Week* article, Caradonio pointed out that Abby Kelley Foster has no limited English proficiency (LEP) students (compared with 7 percent in Worcester public schools) and only half the proportion of students eligible for the federal free lunch program as the traditional Worcester public schools.[26]

While hostility is common, there are some examples of cooperation. The best example we found was in Springfield. In that district, which uses controlled choice to achieve court-ordered desegregation, the charter schools are part of the system. While charter students are selected by lottery, the charter schools agreed to be part of the controlled choice system to achieve racial balance. This may not be surprising given the positive view of charters held by district leaders and the institutional links between schools in the two sectors.

Public School Officials: Charter Schools Are Not Innovative

Particularly in terms of curricula, many public school officials do not believe that charter schools are doing anything fundamentally different or better. Thus, even if lines of communication between the sectors were more open, in reality there may not be much new information flowing.

We found that charter schools are clearly doing some good things that parents like, but many of their innovations are based on a return to basics and a rejection of progressive education that may be more popular in some regular public schools. Even in Trenton, where Lytle embraces competition, he argues that charter schools are not particularly innovative in curriculum, emphasizing instead basic education and parental involvement.

In Worcester, Superintendent Caradonio, teachers union president Brophy, and the district research director all stated that the charters in their district have not introduced any new educational ideas. According to Caradonio, while they do offer extended day programs that parents want, the rest of their package is the recycling of old, unproven ideas and "selling snake oil." In Springfield, where Superintendent Negroni and several members of the elected school board are positive about charters, none of them points out any particular innovations, apart from before- and after-school programs. The 1998 Rosenblum Brigham report concluded that the most prevalent innovations in Massachusetts charter schools are "attention to the development of character, citizenship, respect for self and others, and positive school climate."

We did find some exceptions to this general lack of curricular innovation or diffusion. In Trenton, the Granville charter school introduced laptops for all students and their parents. In response, the district is now examining the development of "net-schools," which would give parents laptops that could be easily connected to a mainframe controlled by the school. But examples like this are rare. For the most part, charter schools are not striving to become laboratories of innovation; they mostly want to please parents.

Steven Wilson, chief executive officer of Advantage Schools, argues that his schools, like Worcester's Abby Kelley Foster, are responsive to their "customer base." "These parents," he states, "crave a school setting that is orderly and safe and focused and on task. And that's the brand we endeavor to provide them with."[27] The fact that the implementation of these ideas in practice is new and that parents enroll their children in these schools is itself a significant indicator of what many parents find lacking in their district public schools.

Charter Schools and Traditional Public Schools Differ in Patterns of Innovations

The differences in outlook lead to significantly different emphases on which innovations each sector adopts. In our survey, we presented principals with a list of common innovations that schools are implementing and we asked which of these reforms they have introduced or expanded in the last year. In a separate set of interviews, we presented the charter school principals in D.C. with the same list and asked them the same questions. In figure 10-6, we compare the pattern of innovation across the schools in these two sectors.

Figure 10-6. *Range of Innovations by Traditional Public Schools and Charter Schools*

Percent of schools adopting

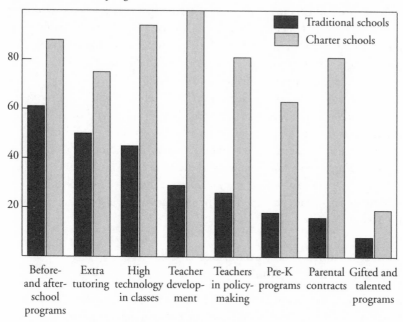

The traditional public schools are much less likely to have implemented or expanded any of the reforms in our battery than are charter schools.[28] The innovation most likely to be adopted by the traditional public schools is the creation or expansion of programs that take place before or after the traditional school day. In our fieldwork, the expanded school day was the aspect of charter school programs that was most frequently mentioned by traditional public school leaders as attractive to parents and is the clearest case of charter schools leveraging change.

In addition, while charters often adopt many of these innovations as part of their school culture and mission, traditional public schools usually adopt reforms in a piecemeal fashion without changing their standard operating procedures. Some innovations, such as parental involvement, are more difficult for traditional schools to implement, as they cannot negotiate the kinds of parent involvement contracts that are common to charter schools. Because increasing parental involvement may be particularly important in creating a viable school community, the limits on the ability of traditional public schools to use such parental contracts may handicap them.[29]

Traditional Public Schools Have Limited Responses to Competition

While we believe that public school officials often exaggerate the constraints they face, traditional public schools are more constrained by state rules and union contracts in their ability to enact reforms. The parental involvement contract is one illustration. The issue of teacher pay and teacher assignments is another critical element. For example, Worcester superintendent Caradonio admitted that charters offer the before- and after-school programs that parents want and that his principals are trying to do the same but are hampered by the requirements of the union wage scale.

Traditionally, one limiting factor on reform in public schools has been the inability of superintendents to replace failing principals who, as frontline managers, are key to the success of schools. However, in several of the districts we studied, superintendents have replaced a significant number of principals, helping to expand the number of entrepreneurial leaders in the district and helping to create a management team more interested in reform. In some districts, charter school competition helps provide the justification for such turnover.

Charter Schools Treat Parents Better Than Do Traditional Public Schools

Parents as consumers exercising choice can be a major force for change, and many parents are clearly voting with their feet in favor of charter schools.

Other parents and public officials see these decisions. Peter Levanos, who advises parents in Springfield, notes that many parents know of the Sabis School's reputation for improved test scores. Officials in Jersey City believe that parents like the newer buildings and the smaller schools that characterize charter schools there.

But even parents who do not enroll their child in a charter school may gain more leverage from the presence of such schools. There is a relationship between exit and voice—as parental exit options increase, schools are forced to pay more attention to the preferences (voice) of parents. For example, in Trenton, Lytle notes that in neighborhoods most affected by the new charter schools two elementary schools chose to expand their grades from K–6 to K–8, because parents expressed concern about the level of safety in the regular public middle schools.

This additional leverage from parental voice may ultimately pressure all public schools to become more consumer-friendly. But, at present, there is a large gap between charter schools and traditional public schools, at least in D.C.

Consumer-Friendly D.C. Charter Schools

To assess the level of consumer friendliness of schools, we contracted D.C. Parents for School Choice, a nonprofit group, to train parents to assess a sample of D.C. charter and traditional public schools. We asked them to report on the condition of the schools, how well they were treated, and how responsive the school staff was to their requests for information about programs and performance. The parents told the schools that they were thinking about enrolling their children and were trained to ask for information pertinent to that enrollment decision. Because all of the parents selected had recently enrolled their own children in new schools, they were already familiar with District procedures.

We prepared a checklist for each parent to fill out reporting on the observed conditions in the schools they visited and reporting on what they experienced during their visit. Parents were asked to evaluate the physical condition of the school and its neighborhood and, more subjectively, the "feel" of the school. They also asked school personnel for information about the programs that the schools offer and for materials about programs and performance.

Substantial differences emerged in the physical conditions of the D.C. public schools and the charter schools (see figure 10-7). On all four dimensions measuring the physical environment, the public schools are in worse condition than the charter schools. For example, our site visitors found slightly more than 10 percent of the public schools had broken windows and

Figure 10-7. *Physical Environment in Public Schools and Charter Schools,*
Washington, D.C.

Percent of schools

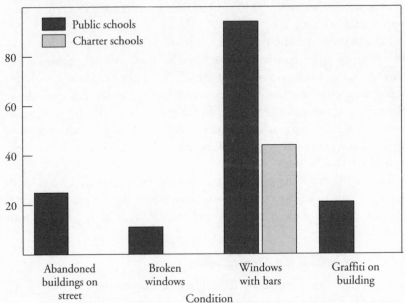

more than 20 percent were marked by graffiti. In contrast none of the parents visiting the D.C. charter schools found these conditions. A body of
research links these conditions to feelings of safety, actual levels of safety, and
performance.[30] Our visual evidence points to the fact that the charter schools
provide a better environment than the public schools.

Because schools may not have complete control over these conditions, we
also asked parents to evaluate a set of physical conditions that are more under
the control of the school. As demonstrated in figure 10-8, we again find a
consistent set of results indicating better performance by the charter
schools—their facilities were more likely to be judged in good working order;
they felt cleaner, safer, and more exciting.

Parents entered the schools and asked staff about the schools' programs
and performance. We asked our parents to evaluate how well the staff treated
them. As evident in figure 10-9, parents evaluated charter school staff as
more responsive and more courteous than the staff of the D.C. public
schools visited.

In addition, we asked parents to evaluate how responsive staff was to a
series of requests for information about school programs. As shown in figure

Figure 10-8. *Other Conditions in Public Schools and Charter Schools, Washington, D.C.*

Average score

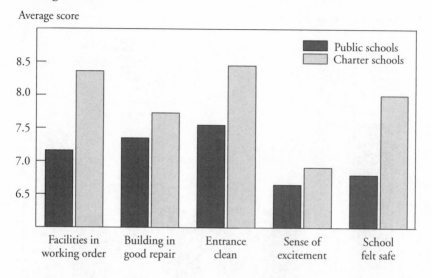

Figure 10-9. *Staff Treatment of Parents in Washington, D.C., Schools*

Average score

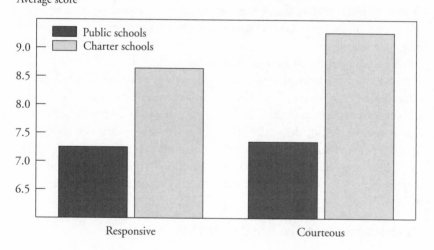

Figure 10-10. *Other Indicators of Parent Treatment in Washington, D.C., Schools*

Percent of parents reporting yes

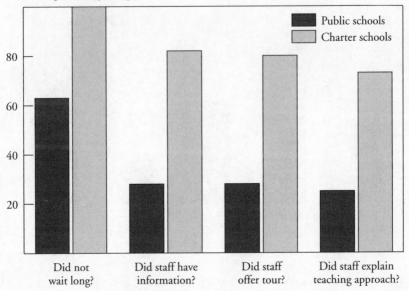

10-10, on each measure that we report, the charter schools were by far more responsive to the legitimate requests of parents for information essential to judging a school.

Our findings are based on small numbers (although our parents did visit almost half of the charter schools and 15 percent of the traditional public schools that were open at the time of this research). Because the charter schools are relatively new, they may be more likely to be in newer facilities in better locations. And, their relatively smaller size may enable charter staff to be more parent-friendly. Nonetheless, the patterns here are consistent. At this time, both the "hardware" of the charter schools (the buildings and their facilities) and the "software" (the staff) are consistently more appealing and open to parents.

An Unanticipated Consequence of Parental Preferences

As parents often prefer charter schools to public schools, we found an interesting emerging relationship between charter schools and private schools in this study. Some parents seem to perceive charter schools as "free" private schools, in part because, like many private schools, they are small, safe, and often have thematic emphases. Many charter school pupils are coming from parochial schools, particularly in Trenton, where the local Catholic diocese is closing several schools, as it claims to have lost 15 percent of its enrollment since charter schools opened.[31] Superintendent Lytle estimates that as many as 30 percent of the charter school students are former private school students. Similarly, in Jersey City, about 20 percent of charter school students have come from private schools.[32]

This student flow in New Jersey suggests that charter schools are creating a larger market for schools, expanding the choice set of parents who might otherwise have left the public school sector entirely for sectarian schools. For some observers, this is a positive development, as the retention of students (and their parents, who are clearly motivated to make active choices) in the public school system has many positive benefits. For others, such movement suggests that charter schools are subsidized private schools for parents who would otherwise not cause any financial expense to the public system.

Conclusions

While competitive effects from charter schools are not yet as extensive as many advocates had hoped, our research has uncovered some reasons that this may be so: resistance from officials who do not like charter schools; policies that shield districts and schools from feeling the financial consequences of failing to attract students; increasing enrollments because of demographic changes; and a belief among traditional public school leaders that charters are not doing innovative things that are worthy of imitation.

Our research also uncovered evidence that traditional public schools are reacting to charter school competition when they have reason to feel threatened. Principals report they change educational and administrative procedures when they feel competitive pressure, and districts adopt new programs when they can clearly see that parents want those programs. Those who believe traditional public schools can be driven to improve efficiency and achievement from competition can take heart from these findings.

States wishing to see more competitive effects ought to consider changing many policies that currently shield public schools from feeling the effects of competition and hinder their ability to respond when they do feel pressured. These changes would include:

—Enacting and implementing statewide school finance policies that subtract money from school districts on a per pupil basis when students enroll in charter or other nondistrict schools;

—Resisting the temptation to replace any financial losses caused by these policies through increases in other funding sources for affected districts;

—Encouraging districts to enact and implement similar per pupil financing policies for individual schools;

—Providing principals with more autonomy to effect administrative and educational changes at the school level; and

—Encouraging districts to work with teachers and other unions to foster experimentation and flexibility in educational and administrative practices.

States that embark on such reforms will provide the conditions for a purer test of the effects of market-style competition on schools and school systems, enabling parents and policymakers to determine whether such competition does improve student achievement or produce other measurable improvements in the quality and efficiency of the educational experience.

Notes

1. We would like to thank the Manhattan Institute and the Smith Richardson Foundation for their financial support of this research.

2. Eric Rofes, *How Are School Districts Responding to Charter Laws and Charter Schools?* Policy Analysis for California Schools (Berkeley, Calif.: University of California, School of Education, 1998).

3. Frederick M. Hess, *Hints of the Pick-Axe: The Impact of Competition on Public Schooling in Milwaukee* (Washington, D.C.: Association for Public Policy Analysis and Management, 1999).

4. Robert Maranto, Scott Milliman, Frederick Hess, and April Gresham, eds., *School Choice in the Real World: Lessons from Arizona Charter Schools* (Boulder, Colo.: Westview Press, 1999).

5. Ted Kolderie, *Beyond Choice to New Public Schools: Withdrawing the Exclusive Franchise in Public Education* (Washington, D.C.: Progressive Policy Institute, 1990); and Joe Nathan, *Charter Schools: Creating Hope and Opportunity for American Education* (San Francisco: Jossey-Bass, 1996).

6. Richard Rothstein, "Charter Conundrum," *American Prospect* (1998), pp. 46–60.

7. The classic discussion of adaptive public sector organizations with a customer orientation is David Osborne and Ted Gaebler, *Reinventing Government: How the Entrepreneurial Spirit Is Transforming the Public Sector* (Reading, Mass.: Addison-Wesley, 1992). See also Michael Barzelay and Babak J. Armajani, *Breaking Through Bureaucracy: A New Vision for Managing in Government* (Berkeley, Calif.: University of California Press, 1992).

8. While schools in rural areas often have severe problems, their relatively sparse populations limit the number of competitive schools that can be supported. And while some suburban schools are failing, most produce a relatively satisfactory education for their students.

9. K. Lloyd Billingsley and Pamela Riley, *Expanding the Charter Idea: A Template for Legislative and Policy Reform* (San Francisco: Pacific Research Institute for Public Policy, 1999).

10. Unless otherwise cited, all quotes are taken from our interviews with the person quoted.

11. Crissa Shoemaker, "Expectations Are Great for Charter School," *Times of Trenton*, November 3, 1998, p. A2.

12. Jeffrey Henig, Michele Moser, Thomas T. Holyoke, and Natalie Lacireno-Paquet, *Making a Choice, Making a Difference?: An Evaluation of Charter Schools in the District of Columbia* (George Washington University, Center for Washington Area Studies, 1999).

13. Debbi Wilgoren, "Chavous Proposes New Office to Supervise Charter Schools," *Washington Post,* December 18, 1998, p. C4.

14. Valerie Strauss, "Parents Seek to Save School; D.C. Officials Order Chartless Kwame Nkrumah to Close Today," *Washington Post,* September 30, 1999, p. B2.

15. Massachusetts General Law, chapter 71, section 89.

16. This is likely to change as the scheduled reductions take place. According to Worcester, Massachusetts, superintendent James Caradonio, his district, with 1,100 charter pupils, could lose up to $5 million in three years when the reductions begin to more fully reflect the recent growth in charter school enrollment.

17. 153 N.J. 480.

18. Henig and others, "Making a Choice, Marking a Difference?" p. 38.

19. Valerie Strauss, "A Leader's Pass-Fail Test," *Washington Post,* January 10, 2000, p. B1. Our finding of blunted financial losses is not limited to our case districts. Hess, *Hints of the Pick-Axe,* found that the Milwaukee public schools received increased funding to make up for the financial losses from students choosing private schools with vouchers.

20. See, for example, Paul Teske and Mark Schneider, *Principals as Leaders,* Endowment Report (Arlington, Va.: PricewaterhouseCoopers, 1999); John E. Chubb and Terry M. Moe, *Politics, Markets, and Schools* (Brookings, 1990); Frederick M. Hess, *Spinning Wheels* (Brookings, 1999); and Stewart Purkey and Marshall Smith, "Effective Schools: A Review," *Elementary School Journal,* vol. 83 (1983), pp. 427–54.

21. District superintendents do not hire themselves. We recognize that their appointments and some of their success are related to their relationships with the school board and local politicians. Nevertheless, superintendents have a great deal of freedom in the operation of their school systems and in how they respond to charter school competition.

22. For a detailed recent profile of Washington, D.C., superintendent Arlene Ackerman's leadership style, see Strauss, "A Leader's Pass-Fail Test."

23. Stella Cheung, Mary Ellen Murphy, and Joe Nathan. *Making a Difference?: Charter Schools, Evaluation and Student Performance* (Minneapolis, Minn.: Center for School Change, 1998).

24. The "pressure" variable is a count of the number of competitive sources an individual principal expects to lose students to in the near future, including charter schools, private schools, and intradistrict movement of students to other public schools.

25. Rosenblum Brigham Associates, *Innovation and Massachusetts Charter Schools* (Boston: Massachusetts Department of Education, 1998).

26. Lynn Schnaiberg, "Seeking a Competitive Advantage," *Education Week*, December 8, 1999, p. 1.

27. Schnaiberg, "Seeking a Competitive Advantage."

28. We note two limitations on these data. First, we are comparing traditional public schools in districts other than D.C. with charter schools in D.C. Second, there is the baseline problem; that is, some innovations may not be adopted or expanded in some schools because they have already been in place for some time. In our analysis, we tried to minimize this problem by dropping from consideration reforms that were already in place in most traditional public schools and that could not be expanded. For example, we dropped all day kindergarten from figure 10-6 because most public schools in our survey already had them and it is a binary condition—either you have it or you do not have it—and, thus, asking principals if they expanded the program makes no sense. In contrast, we believe that the innovations that do appear in figure 10-6 can be expanded or else were in place in relatively small numbers of traditional public schools.

29. See, for example, Mark Schneider, Paul Teske, and Melissa Marschall, *Choosing Schools: Consumer Choice and the Quality of American Schools* (Princeton University Press, 2000).

30. See, for example, Mark Schneider, Melissa Marschall, Christine Roch, and Paul Teske, "Heuristics, Low Information Rationality, and Choosing Public Goods: Broken Windows as Shortcuts to Information about School Performance," *Urban Affairs Review*, vol. 34 (1999), pp. 729–41.

31. Ron Southwick, "Blessed Sacrament School to Close in Trenton," *Times of Trenton*, March 3, 1999, p. A3.

32. Nancy Parello, "Charter Schools Stealing Catholic School Students," *Times of Trenton*, March 20, 1999, p. B5.

11

Responding to Competition: School Leaders and School Culture

FREDERICK M. HESS, ROBERT MARANTO,
AND SCOTT MILLIMAN

A dvocates of choice-based school reform have long claimed that school choice will not only provide new and superior educational alternatives to families, but also enhance the performance of traditional public schools.[1] Researchers investigating these claims usually have paid a great deal of attention to the argument that schools of choice will outperform their public counterparts.[2]

The argument that market competition will promote more effective education in the traditional public schools has received far less attention. This "market hypothesis" assumes that school districts will respond to competition by improving the efficiency and quality of the education they offer.[3] We examine the market rationale in this chapter, by investigating one key dimension of how competition affects public schools. Conventional wisdom holds that a key to improving a school is administration direction, so one crucial question of market competition is how it affects school-level leadership.[4] We examine that question in this chapter, hoping in the process to cast some light on the larger validity of the market hypothesis.

This subject is of great significance because, for good or ill, the vast majority of American children will continue to attend traditional public schools in the coming decade. As a result, the largest potential effects of market-based reform, at least in the short term, may come from competition-induced change in public schooling.

If hoped-for competitive effects are to materialize, school administrators will play a pivotal role. Educational scholarship suggests that efforts to improve schooling hinge on the commitment and energy of faculty.[5] Motivating, supporting, and monitoring this kind of effort on a schoolwide basis demand active leadership. Quite simply, classroom teachers have neither the time nor resources to undertake significant changes on their own in response to competition. Because any individual teacher can do little to alter overall school performance, little incentive exists for an individual teacher to react in the face of competition unless that teacher knows that his or her colleagues will be making an effort. Such facultywide cooperation requires the active involvement of the school principal.

In the case of public schools, given their amorphous structure, lack of hierarchy, and lack of firm accountability structures, leadership is particularly important. Principals do not have the tools to force their will upon teachers who find it easy to retreat behind closed doors. Instead, administrators must lead informally, inspiring teachers and encouraging the school community to establish high standards and professional norms. A key question for choice-based reforms is whether markets are capable of encouraging this kind of behavior on the part of school leaders.

Determining whether leaders will respond to competition requires an understanding of the costs and benefits of such a response. The benefits are the resources that otherwise will be lost if a school did not respond to competition. Those schools most at risk of losing resources will have the most to gain through efforts that reassure families and attract new families (these efforts might include measures such as curricular reform, improved parental outreach, or enhanced teaching). However, principals may be unable or unwilling to pursue those benefits if the cost of responding is also high. We suggest that a key cost for school principals is the organizational disruption produced by the effort to respond to competition and that the culture of a school—the extent to which the principal and staff had a prior cooperative relationship—plays a vital role in determining the size of this cost. Therefore, how school leaders respond to competition is likely to be a function of both the resources the school stands to lose through inaction and the nature of the school organization and culture.

Much consideration of choice-induced competition has treated competitive pressure in stark terms. Discussion tends to be simply about whether competition will or will not appear and about whether its effects will be good or bad. In reality, competitive effects are likely to be much more complex, and they therefore require more sophisticated analysis. Consequently, while examining the general responsiveness of school leadership to competition, we also operationalize and analyze the impact of four contextual factors likely to play crucial roles in determining how schools respond to competition. First, we distinguish between actual and potential competition. Second, we consider the extent of the competition that schools face. Third, we consider how organizational culture may influence the response to competition. Finally, we examine which kinds of leadership behavior change in response to competition and which do not.

Three caveats are in order. First, some uncertainty exists as to what constitutes effective leadership at the school level. For instance, some educators suggest that quality education requires a free-flowing constructivist approach, while others maintain that education requires discipline and order.[6] Fortunately, it is not necessary for us to resolve these disputes here. Instead, we will assess how competition affects traditional public school leadership and report the nature of those impacts. In the conclusion, we offer some general comments on the potential value of observed changes, but we must leave it to future scholars to study the desirability of the observed effects.

Second, because our data come from teacher surveys, we are able to assess only those leadership behaviors that teachers observe.

Third, some may think the only useful approach to testing the market hypothesis is studying the change in school system outputs (such as test scores) induced by competition. We do not utilize such an approach. Instead, we focus on how competition may affect one key element of effective schooling. We agree that researching output effects is important. However, test scores or other output changes induced by competition, if they occur, may take many years to materialize. Moreover, for the hoped-for effects of competition to come about, it is first imperative that school administrators demand improvement and that classroom teaching change in response.

Arizona as a Test Case

To assess the impact of competition on principal effectiveness, a study should examine schools subject to a substantial and potentially threatening school choice system but should encompass schools with significant variation in the degree of competition. Arizona fits the bill. First, the Arizona charter school law is widely regarded as the nation's most far-reaching. During the 1999–2000 school year, 359 charter schools operated in Arizona; this comprised 20 percent of the nation's charter schools. In that year, approximately 6 percent of all Arizona public schoolchildren attended charter schools.

Meanwhile, during the 1997–98 school year—when our data were collected—extensive variation existed in the distribution of the charter school population. In a few Arizona school districts the charter school market share was over 10 percent; in many others it was zero. This variation provided an ideal laboratory, one made even more useful given that ethnicity, income, and several other factors were otherwise similar across low- and high-competition districts.

Charter schools expanded rapidly across Arizona during the 1995–2000 period, creating a real sense of competition and growing threat. This context is particularly relevant because other forms of competition, such as school vouchers, were hampered almost everywhere by political and judicial conflict and expanded much more slowly throughout this period. Hence, assessing the validity of the market hypothesis by looking at charter school competition in Arizona is an especially useful test and has particular relevance for the national educational policy debate.

Competition in Theory: Two Viewpoints

Two competing schools of thought exist on the validity of the market hypothesis. The first school, which encompasses many free-market economists, stresses research that concludes that competition has improved the performance of many formerly regulated U.S. industries in the last twenty-five years.[7] The expectation is that U.S. public schools will be no different.

The second school, composed of many organization scholars, is more skeptical of the efficacy of competition, especially for public sector industries. These scholars argue that various institutional constraints can greatly limit the ability of public agencies—such as schools—to respond to competition. First, organizational leaders are not able to fully consider and assess their situation; instead they rely on proxies and easy cues.[8] Second, when leaders have difficulty providing the public with the good it demands, they often turn to symbolic responses and gestures.[9] Third, leaders will tend to rely upon routines that they already know how to do when confronted with new or threatening situations.[10] The reasoning here is that established routines can be increased at relatively low cost—in terms of persuasion and monitoring activities—because employees are already familiar with them. Finally, as a rule, public sector leaders are constrained by external scrutiny, divided and uncertain authority, and internal regulations, making it particularly difficult to develop and implement coherent change strategies.[11]

In the case of education, scholars have argued that organizational and cultural constraints significantly hamper leaders. Because principals are highly dependent upon largely autonomous teachers to execute changes in teaching, curriculum, and evaluation, communication and cooperation are central to effective school improvement.[12] Because administrators lack many of the tools that their private sector counterparts possess (such as the ability to readily fire employees or to wield monetary incentives), it is particularly important that they utilize moral leadership and cultivate employee commitment.[13] Such cultural transformation takes time to implement. Accordingly, in their analysis of Chicago's school reform efforts during the 1988–95 period, Anthony S. Bryk and his colleagues found that preexisting school practices strongly influenced the manner in which schools implemented reform.[14] They observed that principals had great difficulty bringing about short-term change, although principals who enjoyed faculty respect and cooperation were better able to implement change. Some strong principals were able to alter their organizational cultures over time.

When building our conceptual model of school leadership and competition, we will draw on both schools of thought. In particular, the supporters of the market hypothesis often stress the high benefits associated with responding to competition when asserting that this response will be sizable. In contrast, organizational scholars, when suggesting that this response will be either modest or nonexistent, stress the institutional constraints placed on traditional public schools and thus the potentially high costs associated with responding to competition. Both positions have merit—they are the flip sides of the same coin—and so will be incorporated into our analytic model.

Previous Research

Only modest empirical research makes the case that the competition produced by choice will significantly change traditional public schooling. In a 2001 overview of research on the question, Patrick J. McEwan concluded, "Evidence on the effects of competition on public school efficiency is sparse."[15] Anecdotal evidence exists that competition can produce potentially positive changes in local school systems. For instance, Eric Rofes conducted case studies of twenty-five districts in eight states and Washington, D.C., in 1997 and found that nearly half reported either strong or moderate district-level responses to competition from charter schools.[16] Similarly, David J. Armor and Brett M. Peiser reported that school districts losing large numbers of students through interdistrict choice programs behaved in a manner consistent with market principles, by changing programs and policies to regain all or part of the lost student population.[17] Other scholars have provided similar accounts of possible responses.[18]

In the most extensive econometric analysis into the effect of competition between public school systems, Caroline M. Hoxby has concluded that schools and school districts subjected to competition become more effective and more productive.[19] Hoxby's conclusions are consistent with the analyses of some other scholars, such as Thomas S. Dee, who found that greater private school enrollment prompted higher graduation rates in nearby district high schools.[20] Other economists, such as Christopher Jepsen, have challenged the conclusion that educational markets boost productivity.[21] The greatest limitation in this body of econometric work is that, even if one is inclined to accept the findings of positive effects, this work cannot explain how these changes occur. This chapter seeks to tackle that question, without taking a side in the larger debate regarding the effects of competition on public school student performance.

Some critics of choice systems doubt that charter or voucher plans can improve existing public schools, because they argue there is little evidence that parents make enrollment decisions based on school quality. For instance, research using data on Florida counties conducted by Kevin B. Smith and Kenneth J. Meier and on Texas counties conducted by Robert Wrinkle and his colleagues found no evidence that private school enrollment drives educational improvement in nearby public schools.[22] These findings suggest that families make enrollment decisions based on religious preference and race-based considerations. They also imply that enhancing school choice will increase religious and ethnic segregation but will not motivate public schools to improve. After all, if families are not choosing schools based on performance, there is little competitive incentive for public school personnel to pursue more effective performance. Other critics question whether school system leaders are capable of responding to competitive threats by imposing change on the "street-level bureaucrats" in individual schools.[23]

Competition will not necessarily bring out the best in schools and school systems. Anecdotal evidence suggests that schools sometimes respond to competition in unproductive ways. Districts threatened with losing money to charter competition have sometimes sought to galvanize support among local parents by announcing that they would cut or reduce popular school programs such as art, Advanced Placement courses, sports, and tutoring. Other observed behaviors included the harassment of charter school personnel, efforts to undermine the ability of charter schools to find suitable facilities, and refusing to provide necessary student records to charter schools.[24]

A Simple Model of School Leadership Change

The simple model we will construct assumes that an important goal of school leaders is to maximize the school's resources over time and that they weigh both the benefits and costs of achieving this objective.[25] Given this assumption, the charter school threat becomes clear. The threat is that students will abandon the district schools to attend charter schools, reducing district school funding as state funding follows the students to their new schools. Lost enrollment equals lost money because Arizona law stipulates that the state's per pupil maintenance and operations subsidy, which provides most operating revenues for most of the state's school districts, moves with the student after a lag of a year or less. An additional risk is that families who abandon the district schools will cease to support local educational expenditures, will cease to contribute to the schools, and may cease to be interested in local education.

Given the risks associated with lost student enrollment, the question is what district schools do to answer the potential or realized competitive threat. Our focus here is on what school principals do, and particularly what steps they take that may enhance school performance or make the school work environment more attractive to teachers. Either activity would presumably help schools provide educational programs that will attract students, although it does not necessarily hold that such changes will lead to improved student learning or outcomes. School-level activity will probably be approved, and perhaps even instigated, by the district leadership. However, the costs of making any changes are generally determined by the culture of the individual school. Hence the school itself is our unit of analysis.

The Costs of School Leadership Change

The ability of principals to foster cooperative efforts at teaching and learning is largely determined by the extent to which they enjoy generally cooperative relations with their staff. Where a cooperative culture exists, the principal is already accustomed to working with teachers and teachers are receptive to such efforts. A relationship of established trust and teamwork makes it much easier and less costly, in terms of time and resources, for principals to implement changes in policy and governance. Changing the roles and expectations of teachers inevitably requires the principal to invest time and energy. The harder the principal must work to persuade teachers to accept the changes and then monitor them to see that they act as directed, the more costly change will prove.

Principals in schools with hostile or uncooperative principal-faculty relationships will find promoting change difficult. Principals in these situations will have less success convincing teachers to invest themselves in change, will have teachers who are less accustomed to their principal making such efforts, and will lack established routines for fostering collaborative efforts. Such a situation will increase the time and energy principals must invest in convincing teachers to commit themselves to new directives and to ensuring that teachers act as instructed. In particular, while districts may be able to move or fire a principal, tenure guidelines and the culture of education make it far more difficult to fire teachers or alter the make-up of a school's faculty. Hence, at least in the short run, principals seeking to overcome faculty resistance must seek to do so without being able to bring in large numbers of new, more receptive employees.

The Benefits of School Leadership Change

Although school routines may help a school either by improving its performance, thus reducing student exiting and the associated revenue loss, or by keeping entrepreneurial-minded district teachers happy so that they will not attempt to launch competing schools.[26] As they consider efforts along these two lines, school leaders will find that the benefits of their actions depend greatly upon the kind of competitive threat they face. Broadly speaking, two potential kinds of competition require consideration.

First, after the passage of charter legislation, all Arizona districts immediately faced an entry threat. A charter could now open in any Arizona district, creating the possibility of future losses. Future losses have a discounted value—because they may not materialize and because there are always more pressing immediate concerns—and they may be difficult to predict. These characteristics weaken the competitive impact of potential entry. Moreover, the entry threat is not constant across districts but varies with the district's reliance on state aid. Districts that stand to lose more money with each lost student will reap greater benefits by forestalling potential charter entry than will districts that will lose less money per pupil. We measure the extent of entry threat by determining what percentage of maintenance and operations (M&O) funds a district receives from state authorities. Essentially, we are measuring how much each lost pupil costs a district. Responding to a potential threat is problematic for schools and districts, however, because the costs of change are visible while the attendant benefits are amorphous.

The second type of competition is "actual entry." This refers to how many students a district or a school is losing to charter schools. When students in a district are physically enrolled in charter schools, the revenue losses become clear and immediate. In addition, the possibility of lost future support—as a result of reduced community political support and a shrinking base of supportive parents—becomes more concrete. When money is lost, the benefits produced by leadership changes that make the school more appealing are immediate and visible. The charter school market share of school district enrollment is used to measure the existing competition faced by a school.

A final point is that persuading teachers to cooperate with changes and then monitoring their behavior will be easier in small schools than in large schools. Therefore, other things being equal, we hypothesize that both potential and actual competition are more likely to prompt changes in leadership behavior in small schools.

Methods

Given that we opted to examine changes in school-level leadership, rather than attempting to measure changes in output, we surveyed teachers to obtain systematic data on principal activities and behavior they observed on a daily basis. In March 1998, we mailed surveys to more than 1,300 targeted Arizona teachers in ninety-eight schools. The teachers were asked to report on several dimensions of principal behavior for both 1997–98 and 1994–95 (the latter based on recall), using agree-disagree items.[27] In each school, the survey responses from the teachers were averaged together to generate a composite response. The result is that the mean observation represents the aggregate judgment of roughly eleven teachers.

The key quantity of interest is principal leadership and how it was affected by competition, so the dependent variables examined are reported changes in principal behavior at each school between 1994–95 and 1997–98.[28] Focusing on principal behavioral changes from 1994–95 to 1997–98 has several advantages. First, this measures effects that probably occurred as competitive responses, given that 1994–95 was the last school year before the start of charter schooling in Arizona. This short time period also reduces the chance that economic or demographic changes drove leadership changes. It also minimizes simultaneity between our dependent and independent variables, as it seems unlikely that changes in principal behavior induced by competition could have had a significant impact on local charter school market share in this relatively short three-year period. By analyzing one state, we also eliminate many other potential sources of state-induced variance.

We only examine the behavior of principals in elementary schools (grades K–8), because this is where competition for typical Arizona students was most intense. Arizona educators explain that charter school operators can afford to provide competitive elementary programs but lack funds for more expensive high school infrastructure, such as stadiums or science labs, that families demand. Consequently, most Arizona charter high schools target at-risk populations (students that district schools are often happy to lose) and are not perceived as a threat by district high schools.

Table 11-1. *Selected Demographic Characteristics for the High-Competition and Low-Competition Districts*

Demographic	Low-competition districts (N = 21)	High-competition districts (N = 24)
Percent white	57.8	64.8
Percent Hispanic	31.9	24.3
Percent Native American	9.5	7.5
Percent African American	2.5	2.3
Mean children below poverty line	23.0	24.0
Mean district enrollment	6,191	7,527
Mean school size	614	617
Elementary market share in charter schools (percent)	0.5	9.0
Percent of maintenance and operation funds provided by the state	61.6	51.2

Sampling

Sampling was structured to ensure that the sample would include schools from both high-competition and low-competition districts. Arizona has 204 school districts with elementary schools. Of these, 45 had charter schools within their borders in 1997–98. We selected sample schools in 24 of the 25 school districts where charter schools accounted for 30 percent or more of the public elementary schools, and in 19 of the 159 districts with no charters. Because the no-charter districts tended to be smaller than the high-competition districts, we also included in the low-competition group schools from two very large districts that each had just a handful of charter schools. In selecting the sample, an effort was made to pair up districts from each half of the sample and to match them as closely as possible on district enrollment, poverty, and racial composition. This process yielded high- and low-competition districts of similar size and demographics (see table 11-1). Save for charter school market share, t-tests find no differences between the groups that were significant at p < .10. In the forty-five sample districts, ninety-eight schools were randomly selected for study.

We sampled one school from school districts with fewer than five elementary schools, two from districts with five to eleven elementary schools, and four from districts with twelve or more schools.[29] In each school, eighteen teachers who had taught at the school for three years or longer were surveyed. If fewer than eighteen teachers met the criterion, all were surveyed. Respondents were paid $5 for participating, and 79.1 percent of respondents returned their survey. There were 1,065 respondents, of whom 75 (7.0 percent) indicated that they had not been at their present school in 1994–95. These teachers were dropped from the analysis because they could not provide 1994–95 ratings. Eliminating schools with fewer than five respondents left eighty-seven schools with 959 teachers (a mean of 11.02 per school).

Dependent Variables

We use six measures of changing principal behavior, examining the extent to which the principal reportedly changed in terms of (1) encouraging experimentation in teaching; (2) shielding teachers from outside pressure; (3) consulting with staff; (4) promoting the use of technology; (5) following up on initiatives; and (6) facilitating the upgrading of the school's curriculum. Most of these behaviors require principals to either work more closely with (or else delegate more responsibilities to) the staff. Survey questions inquiring about these behaviors were generally taken from the U.S. Department of Education School and Staffing Surveys.

Cooperative and Uncooperative School Cultures

Given the expectation that the nature of school culture will influence how principals respond to competition, we examine competitive effects separately in two groups of schools. The first group includes schools in which teachers reported the existence of a cooperative culture in 1994–95 (just before charter school competition); the second, those schools in which they reported relatively uncooperative cultures. The determination for each school was based upon the reported amount of faculty influence over the school's curriculum in 1994–95. Curriculum is a universal and central aspect of school design, making the faculty role in this area a useful and simple proxy with which to measure the real influence the principal accords to the faculty.[30]

Independent Variables

The extent of competitive threat is measured using local charter market share, which is the total K–8 charter school population in a district divided by the district's total district school and charter school K–8 population.[31]

The latent (or potential) charter school threat is measured using the percentage of district maintenance and operations subsidies supplied by the state. School districts with a low subsidy level may be less concerned about a charter entry threat, while the opposite is true for districts with a high level. Of the forty-five sample districts, eight received less than one-third of their M&O budget from the state, while thirteen received over two-thirds. This variable was stable for 1995–98, changing by less than 5 percent for two-thirds of the districts and by less than 10 percent for nine out of ten.

To assess possible synergistic effects produced by the double-barreled effect of a large potential threat and a large actual threat, we include an interaction term that is equal to market share times subsidy. The hypothesis is that principals in districts that are losing students and where each lost student represents a significant hit may be especially likely to take action.

Finally, we also control for school enrollment to see whether principals with smaller staffs are more inclined or more able to respond to competition.

Omitted Variables

Omitted variables might influence both principal behavior and charter school market share, rendering spurious the seeming impacts of charter competition on teacher empowerment. For example, highly motivated parents in a school district could be influencing both principal behavior and charter schooling. This seems unlikely, however, because the dependent variables measure the reported changes in principal behavior from 1994–95 to 1997–98, a constricted time period. Community effects ought to already be accounted for in the 1994–95 baseline, eliminating fears of bias. Moreover, Arizona educators suggest that charter formation is often driven by the perceived unresponsiveness of districts to parental and teacher concerns. Administrators in such districts are not rushing to change current arrangements.

Another possible concern is that teachers who reported high 1994–95 empowerment levels are more optimistic and so will overstate any principal behavior changes after 1994–95. If this is true (and we have no reason to suspect that it is—if anything, veteran teachers are often cynical about school reform), then reported principal behavior should be assessed positively across all decentralized schools. Consequently, the competition variables would have no significant effects. Similarly, it might be wondered whether school decentralization efforts, which may be likelier to occur in schools with already empowered faculties, might be responsible for any principal behavior changes observed in these schools. Again, if this dynamic were driving behavior changes in the decentralized schools, then these changes should occur uniformly across these schools and would therefore be unaffected by competition.

Still another concern is the possibility that personal characteristics may influence how teachers evaluate leadership changes and be nonrandomly distributed across schools in a fashion that correlates with one or more independent variables. For example, more experienced teachers may be less likely to observe changes in principal behavior than their less experienced counterparts, and they may disproportionately be employed in low-competition environments. However, a more complex regression procedure designed to account for such a possibility yields findings almost identical to the reported results, so we report only the more easily interpreted results.[32]

A final issue is whether the analysis suffers from "regression to the mean," the tendency for those organizations whose behavior is significantly different from the norm to converge on it over time. However, this phenomenon would bias results only if it were significantly correlated with the independent variables. Otherwise it would simply wash out across the sample and add random noise to the findings. In any event, the findings are the reverse of those that would suggest regression to the mean. Over time, it appears that those schools furthest above the norm continue to move further from the mean.

Results

We examine the effects of competition, of school culture, and of school size on changes in principal leadership between 1994–95 and 1997–98. Results from the analysis are presented in table 11-2.

Schools with relatively uncooperative cultures in 1994–94 had no significant changes ($p < .05$) in leadership behavior produced by competition. This held true for each of the six kinds of leadership behavior. Market forces appear to have had no impact on schools where persuading teachers to change and then monitoring those changes was costly.

In marked contrast, market competition had a consistent effect on behavior in schools with relatively cooperative cultures. Competition produced significant leadership change in four of the six behaviors studied. Actual charter penetration produced significant changes in four of the behaviors ($p < .01$), while potential competition (measured by the state subsidy percentage) significantly affected two ($p < .05$).

Little evidence exists that school size had any significant impact on changes in leadership behavior.

The four behaviors with strong reported competitive effects were principals encouraging experimentation in teaching, principals shielding teachers from outside pressure, principals consulting with staff, and principals facilitating the upgrading of the school's curriculum. Note that all four require either administrator-teacher cooperation or administrator confidence that teachers will use enhanced autonomy in a productive fashion. These effects, not surprisingly, are only observed in schools where teacher involvement in decisionmaking is an established element of the culture. In the case of these four behaviors, the two competition variables explained a significant percent-

Table 11-2. Impact of Competition on Principal Behavior for the Initially Noncooperative and Cooperative Schools, 1994–95

Leadership dimension	Constant	Percent state-provided funds	Charter market share	Interaction term	School size	Adjusted R squared	Number of observations
Principal encourages experimentation in teaching							
Noncooperative schools	-1.824	.0204	15.773	-.179	.0007	-.073	34
	(1.926)	(.024)	(22.710)	(.343)	(.001)		
Cooperative schools	-.827**	.0169***	17.978***	-.287***	-.0004	.433	34
	(.339)	(.005)	(3.616)	(.073)	(.000)		
Principal effectively buffers outside pressures that affect teaching							
Noncooperative schools	-1.577	.0167	7.491	.090	-.0002	.100	34
	(2.122)	(.027)	(25.013)	(.377)	(.001)		
Cooperative schools	-.026	.0103	15.873***	-.247***	-.0008*	.351	34
	(.397)	(.006)	(4.237)	(.086)	(.000)		
Principal consults with staff							
Noncooperative schools	-2.619	.0204	4.263	.093	.0017**	.229	34
	(1.617)	(.020)	(19.068)	(.288)	(.001)		
Cooperative schools	-.691	.0216***	20.740***	-.358***	-.0008	.328	34
	(.460)	(.007)	(4.902)	(.0099)	(.001)		

Principal increases staff access to technology

Noncooperative schools	−1.144 (1.859)	.0154 (.023)	15.810 (21.914)	−.157 (.331)	.0003 (.001)	−.060	34
Cooperative schools	−.0202 (.410)	.0052 (.006)	3.300 (4.370)	−.0329 (.088)	−.0001 (.000)	−.074	34

Principal follows through on new initiatives and programs

Noncooperative schools	−.630 (1.918)	.0084 (.024)	10.227 (22.617)	−.0461 (.341)	.0001 (.001)	−.018	34
Cooperative schools	−.420 (.630)	.0138 (.010)	13.134* (6.717)	−.225 (.136)	−.0004 (.001)	.006	34

Principal supports teacher efforts to upgrade curriculum

Noncooperative schools	−2.171 (1.587)	.0256 (.020)	15.219 (18.709)	−.104 (.282)	.0005 (.001)	.048	34
Cooperative schools	−.633 (.382)	.0139** (.006)	15.911*** (4.069)	−.273*** (.082)	−.0003 (.000)	.275	34

*p < .10; **p < .05; ***p < .01.

age (25 percent to 45 percent) of changes in leadership behavior in the cooperative schools.

Market competition had no significant impact (at $p < .05$), regardless of school culture, on the degree to which principals promoted the use of technology or followed through on new initiatives. The technology finding may suggest that, regardless of the "soft" organizational resources available to principals in cooperative environments, these are not sufficient to overcome material resource limitations. Technology can be expensive and difficult to procure, which may make alterations in the use of technology too costly to pursue. Similarly, it is not clear that competition will cause administrators to increase follow-through on initiatives—the pressures of competition could prompt administrators to try more initiatives, causing them to devote less energy to following through on each individual effort.[33]

One complication for the analysis is that the data in table 11-2 show that the interaction term (measuring the multiplied effect of charter market share and state subsidy percentage) has a significant negative effect in schools with cooperative cultures. This means that when cooperative schools face a relatively high level of both forms of competition, leaders gradually cease changing their behavior in response to competition.

The effect of this interaction term means that we cannot simply infer the effects of actual or potential competition from the results in table 11-2. Instead, determining the net effects of competition requires us to account for both the individual variable effects and the interaction variable effect. We do this by inserting representative values for state subsidy and market share into the regressions and then estimating the effects. We could use the extreme low and high values for state subsidy (0.6 percent and 94.1 percent) and for market share (0.0 percent and 32.5 percent), but these values are not representative of the typical Arizona district. Instead, we determine the school with the top value of the lowest quintile and the school with the lowest value of the top quintile for each competition variable. We then insert those values to calculate the effects of a change in competitive threat on leadership behavior. The three-quintile change produces a market share range of 0.0 percent to 7.74 percent and a state subsidy range of 36.6 percent to 75.2 percent.

Table 11-3 reports the results when these values are used to assess the effects of competitive pressure on leadership behavior in cooperative schools. Table 11-3 only includes results for the four regressions where at least one competition variable was statistically significant ($p < .05$). The results demonstrate that the net effect of competition in all cases is to increase the frequency of the reported behavior, but that the size of this impact depends on the nature of competition.

Table 11-3. *Principal Behavior Changes from 1994–95 to 1997–98 Induced by Various Forms of Competition, Cooperative Schools*[a]

Principal behavior	Subsidy change only	Market share change only	Subsidy and market share change
Encourages teaching experiment	.65	.58	.37
Buffers outside pressures	.40	.53	.19
Consults with staff	.83	.59	.35
Supports curriculum upgrade	.54	.46	.18

a. Effects calculated based on a three-quintile change in subsidy or market share. Effect sizes represent the degree of change calculated in terms of the one-to-six scale on which the dependent variables are measured.

The measured three-quintile change in latent threat (state subsidy percentage) spurs a change of 0.40 (8.0 percent) to 0.83 (16.6 percent) in the four dependent variables examined. Surprisingly, the effect of a three-quintile change in actual threat is somewhat weaker, varying from 0.38 (7.6 percent) to 0.59 (11.8 percent). Finally, the combined impact of a three-quintile change in both subsidy and market share produce an increase of between 0.18 (3.6 percent) and 0.37 (7.4 percent) for the behaviors examined.

In other words, the presence of either kind of competition individually produces a stronger reaction than the presence of both kinds of competition. That is, when the state subsidy percentage in a school district is already relatively high, an increased charter market share appears to dampen the extent of leadership response. This could be true for several reasons. First, a high charter market share means that a district is losing money and school leaders may lack the resources to promote change. Second, a high market share may induce the district to undertake many changes, so the amount of change observed on any one dimension—such as school leadership—may be less noticeable. Regardless of the explanation, in the short run, there appears to be a ceiling effect on changes in leadership behavior. Determining the cause and significance of this effect must await future research.

Overall, in cooperative schools that faced relatively competitive environments, principals were reported to be about 5 percent to 15 percent more likely to have increased the incidence of these four behaviors than were cooperative school principals in relatively noncompetitive environments. No such changes emerged in those schools characterized by low initial levels of competition. These contrasting results are consistent with the hypothesis that school culture is important in determining the effects of choice-based competition in schooling.

Conclusions

When faced with charter school competition and in an organizational setting conducive to active leadership, Arizona principals do respond to market pressures. Competition does not affect all schools equally, however. We find that the effect of competition depends critically on school culture. On the one hand, when schools with cooperative school cultures faced competitive pressures, principals were reported to have increased by about 5 percent to 15 percent their efforts to support, involve, consult, and protect teachers. On the other hand, principals in uncooperative schools did not significantly alter any of the examined behaviors in response to competition. These results offer some broad support for the market hypothesis that schools will respond to competition but suggest that—at least in the short term—such effects emerge in some schools but not others.

The evidence suggests that principals were more likely to change those behaviors that were less costly to change. Principals appear to have pursued change when the organizational and resource costs of action were low, but either high organizational costs or high resource costs (as in the case of technology or the need to follow through on initiatives) were sufficient to halt such efforts.

The observed effects are generally modest in size. Moreover, in the short run, a ceiling effect exists; beyond a certain point, school leaders cease to respond to competitive pressure. This suggests that competition does not have a dramatic impact on the traditional public schools in the short term. That said, several caveats are in order. First, although Arizona had the nation's most developed charter school system in 1998, competition was still modest in size and early in its development. Further, rapid population growth throughout the 1990s meant that many Arizona districts were struggling to cope with expanding enrollment. This alleviated some concern about students lost to charter schools. Given these caveats, the institutional rigidities that characterize public schooling, and the lack of success characterizing conventional educational reform efforts, the modest changes induced by charter school competition in their initial years ought not to be dismissed too readily.

The key question for many will be whether the evidence suggests that competition is good for public schools. This is a difficult and complex question, and one that requires data much more extensive than that examined here. However, we will note that the observed changes—increased principal support for teaching experimentation, increased principal efforts to buffer outside pressures, increased principal consultation with staff, and increased principal support for upgrading the curriculum—appear to be generally beneficial and to reflect conventional thinking about the kinds of action that will improve public schooling. We cannot here determine whether these efforts are effective, or whether principals are pursuing them effectively, but they do appear potentially promising. Nonetheless, these behavioral changes cannot readily be deemed evidence of school improvement, and it cannot be assured that they are necessarily positive changes.

Furthermore, we examined only selected dimensions of principal behavior. The dependent variables examined focus on leadership activity that is generally deemed positive. We do not know what effect competition may have had on other forms of principal behavior. More generally, this analysis is confined to studying the impact of competition on school leadership. The impact of competition on other dimensions of school organization and culture needs to be examined.

If, for a moment, one does presume that the observed changes are generally promising, a potentially troubling equity issue arises. Because only cooperative schools change in response to competition, there may be a "rich get richer" dynamic. There is reason to believe that schools with cooperative cultures will tend to be the more effective schools, suggesting that more effective schools may prosper and improve in the face of competition while other schools do not. This state of affairs appears very possible, at least in the short term and under moderate levels of competition. A longer time frame or more insistent competitive pressure might erode this gap in responsiveness. However, if the "rich get richer" dynamic does hold in the long run and if it does have significant implications for school performance, it will raise difficult issues about the ability of markets to foster school improvement in an equitable fashion.

The findings suggest that the impact of competition will depend in significant part on financial incentives, such as state-level maintenance and operations subsidies. From a policy perspective, increasing the percentage of funds that follow the student appears likely to increase short-term district responses. This is not to argue that financial incentives are the only factor driving school change, or that such incentives are necessarily desirable, but to note that the financial impact of competition is a lever that may drive changes in school and district behavior. The analysis also suggests that the extent of charter market share does matter, so the development of a full-throated charter school system may produce competitive results substantially different from those produced by the presence of only a handful of charter schools.

The results cast significant light on the short-run relationship between competition and school leadership, but additional research is needed to better understand competitive effects in both the short and the long run. Educational competition, even where widespread as in Arizona, is still so new that it is not possible to examine long-term effects. Our results, in short, are applicable only to the near term. At this point, we can envision two plausible long-term scenarios consistent with the results. First, the changes we find could be precursors to more significant long-term changes in schools that boast cultures conducive to leadership change. Schools with cultures initially less conducive to change might also become more proactive with time. Alternatively, the observed changes in leadership may be primarily symbolic and may reflect the full extent of the changes that school leaders make in response to competition. In that case, long-term changes resulting from competition are likely to be slight.

Finally, our results suggest that the real-world impact of competition on school leadership lies somewhere between the effects claimed by the proponents and opponents of school choice. In the near term, despite the rhetoric of some proponents, we do not find competition radically changing traditional public schools. However, contrary to the claims of some choice opponents, we do not see evidence that competition adversely affected school leadership. Instead, competition appears to have spurred principals in a subset of schools—those with already cooperative cultures—to encourage teacher autonomy and professionalism. Traditionally, professional educators have suggested that such change is desirable. While these results are instructive, future research must continue to assess the extent and implications of competitive effects to explore how these effects evolve over time.

Notes

1. The authors wish to gratefully acknowledge the support provided for this project by the Bodman Foundation and the Spencer Foundation.

2. See, for instance, John E. Chubb and Terry M. Moe, *Politics, Markets, and America's Schools* (Brookings, 1990); Jay P. Greene, William G. Howell, and Paul E. Peterson, "Lessons from the Cleveland Scholarship Program," in Paul E. Peterson and Bryan C. Hassel, eds., *Learning from School Choice* (Brookings, 1998), pp. 357–92; Jay P. Greene, Paul E. Peterson, and Jiangtao Du, "Effectiveness of School Choice: The Milwaukee Experiment," *Education and Urban Society*, vol. 31 (1999), pp. 190–213; Cecilia Elena Rouse, "Private School Vouchers and Student Achievement: An Evaluation of the Milwaukee Parental Choice Program," *Quarterly Journal of Economics*, vol. 113 (1998), pp. 553–602; and John F. Witte, *The Market Approach to Education: An Analysis of America's First Voucher Program* (Princeton University Press, 2000).

3. See Milton Friedman, *Capitalism and Freedom* (University of Chicago Press, 1982), p. 93.

4. For classic discussions of this point, see Roland S. Barth, *Run School Run* (Harvard University Press, 1980); Larry Cuban, *The Managerial Imperative and the Practice of Leadership in Schools* (Albany, N.Y.: SUNY Press, 1988); and Sara L. Lightfoot, *The Good High School: Portraits of Character and Culture* (Basic Books, 1983). For more recent, more applied discussions, see Samuel C. Carter, *No Excuses: Lessons from 21 High-Performing, High-Poverty Schools* (Washington, D.C.: Heritage Foundation, 2000); and Paul E. Teske and Mark Schneider, *The Importance of Leadership: The Role of School Principals* (Arlington, Va.: PricewaterhouseCoopers Endowment for the Business of Government, 1999).

5. For insightful discussions, see Richard F. Elmore, "Getting to Scale with Good Educational Practice," *Harvard Educational Review*, vol. 66 (1996), pp. 1–26; Milbrey W. McLaughlin, "Learning from Past Experience: Lessons from Policy Implementation," in Allan Odden, ed., *Educational Policy Implementation* (Albany, N.Y.: SUNY Press, 1991); and Michael Fullan, *The New Meaning of Educational Change* (New York: Teachers College, 1991).

6. For instance, compare the different implications for effective educational leadership of Theodore Sizer's constructivist educational model and E. D. Hirsch's highly structured approach. See Theodore Sizer, *Horace's Hope: What Works for the American High School* (Houghton Mifflin, 1996); and E. D. Hirsch, *Cultural Literacy: What Every American Needs to Know* (Houghton Mifflin, 1987).

7. See, for instance, Murray Weidenbaum, *Progress in Federal Regulatory Policy, 1980–2000* (St. Louis, Mo.: Center for the Study of American Business, 2000); and Robert W. Crandall, Christopher DeMuth, Robert W. Hahn, Robert E. Litan, Pietro S. Nivola, and Paul R. Portney, *An Agenda for Federal Regulatory Reform* (American Enterprise Institute and Brookings, 1997).

8. For classic discussions of this topic, see James G. March, *Decisions and Organizations* (New York: Blackwell, 1988); James G. March and Johan Olsen, *Ambiguity and Choice in Organizations* (Oslo, Norway: Universitetsforlaget, 1987); and Herbert A. Simon, *Administrative Behavior: A Study of Decision-Making Processes in Administrative Organizations* (Free Press, 1997).

9. For discussion, see Frederick M. Hess, "A Political Explanation of Policy Selection: The Case of Urban School Reform," *Policy Studies Journal*, vol. 27 (1999), pp. 459–76; and John Meyer and Brian Rowan, "Institutionalized Organizations: Formal Structure as Myth and Ceremony," in Walter Powell and Paul DiMaggio, eds., *The New Institutionalism in Organizational Analysis* (University of Chicago Press, 1991), pp. 41–62.

10. For the classic work on this question, see Graham T. Allison, *Essence of Decision* (Little, Brown, 1971).

11. See, for instance, Graham T. Allison, "Public and Private Management: Are They Fundamentally Alike in All Unimportant Respects?" in Richard Stillman II, ed., *Public Administration: Concepts and Cases* (Houghton Mifflin, 1984); Alan A. Altshuler, "Bureaucratic Innovation, Democratic Accountability, and Political Incen-

tives," in Alan A. Altshuler and Robert D. Behn, eds., *Innovations in American Government* (Brookings, 1997), pp. 38–67; Alan A. Altshuler and Robert D. Behn, "The Dilemmas of Innovation in American Government," in Alan A. Altshuler and Robert Behn, eds., *Innovations in American Government* (Brookings. 1997), pp. 3–27; Jameson W. Doig and Erwin C. Hargrove, "'Leadership' and Political Analysis," in Jameson Doig and Erwin Hargrove, eds., *Leadership and Innovation* (Johns Hopkins University Press, 1990), pp. 1–23; and James Q. Wilson, *Bureaucracy* (Basic Books, 1989).

12. See Elmore, "Getting to Scale with Good Educational Practice"; Richard F. Elmore, Penelope Peterson, and Sarah McCarthy, *Restructuring in the Classroom: Teaching, Learning, and School Organization* (San Francisco: Jossey-Bass, 1996); Tony Wagner, *How Schools Change: Lessons from the Three Communities* (Boston: Beacon Press, 1994); and Wilson, *Bureaucracy.*

13. For thoughtful discussion, see Thomas J. Sergiovanni, *Moral Leadership: Getting to the Heart of School Improvement* (San Francisco: Jossey-Bass, 1992); and Teske and Schneider, *The Importance of Leadership.*

14. Anthony S. Bryk, David Kerbow, and Sharon Rollow, "Chicago School Reform," in Diane Ravitch and Joseph Viteritti, eds., *New Schools for a New Century: The Redesign of Urban Education* (Yale University Press, 1997), pp. 164–200.

15. Patrick J. McEwan, "The Potential Impact of Large-Scale Voucher Programs," *Review of Educational Research* 70 (2001), pp. 103–50, quote on p. 136.

16. Eric Rofes, "How Are School Districts Responding to Charter Laws and Charter Schools?" (Berkeley, Calif.: Policy Analysis for California Education, 1998).

17. David J. Armor and Brett M. Peiser, *Competition in Education: A Case Study of Interdistrict Choice* (Boston: Pioneer Institute for Public Policy, 1997).

18. Chester E. Finn Jr., Bruno V. Manno, and Gregg Vanourek, *Charter Schools in Action: Renewing Public Education* (Princeton University Press, 2000), pp. 192–219; and Bryan C. Hassel, *The Charter School Challenge* (Brookings, 1999), pp. 128–43.

19. Caroline M. Hoxby, "Analyzing School Choice Reforms That Use America's Traditional Forms of Parental Choice," in Paul E. Peterson and Bryan C. Hassel, eds., *Learning from School Choice* (Brookings, 1998), pp. 133–55; Caroline M. Hoxby, "Does Competition among Public Schools Benefit Students and Taxpayers?" *American Economic Review,* vol. 90 (2000), pp. 1209–38; and Caroline M. Hoxby, "School Choice and School Productivity (Or, Could School Choice Be a Tide That Lifts All Boats?)," presented at the National Bureau of Economic Research Conference on the Economics of School Choice, Islamorada, Florida, February 22–24, 2001.

20. Thomas S. Dee, "Competition and the Quality of Schools," *Economics of Education Review,* vol. 17 (1998), pp. 419–27.

21. Christopher Jepsen, "The Effects of Private School Competition on Student Achievement," Northwestern University, 1999.

22. See Kevin B. Smith and Kenneth J. Meier, *The Case against School Choice: Politics, Markets, and Fools* (Armonk, N.Y.: M. E. Sharpe, 1995), pp. 51–72; and Robert Wrinkle, Joseph Stewart Jr., and J. L. Polinard, "Public School Quality, Private

Schools, and Race," *American Journal of Political Science*, vol. 43 (1999), pp. 1248–53.

23. See Michael Lipsky, *Street Level Bureaucracy* (New York: Russell Sage Foundation, 1980).

24. See Hassel, *The Charter School Challenge*; Tom Loveless and Claudia Jasin, "Starting from Scratch: Political and Organizational Challenges Facing Charter Schools," *Educational Administration Quarterly*, vol. 34 (1998), pp. 9–30; and Robert Maranto and April Gresham, "The Wild West of Education Reform," in Robert Maranto, Scott Milliman, Frederick M. Hess, and April Gresham, eds., *School Choice in the Real World: Lessons from Arizona Charter Schools* (Boulder, Colo.: Westview, 1999), pp. 99–114.

25. For a critique of this assumption, see Andre Blais and S. Dion, *The Budget Maximizing Bureaucrat* (University of Pittsburgh Press, 1991). An alternative to the budget maximizing bureaucrat postulate is the assumption that school leaders seek to maximize district resources per student. In this case, if the marginal cost of educating an exiting student is high, and the associated loss in revenues is low, then the district may gain from losing the student. Unfortunately, we do not have any reasonable data on marginal cost and so revert to budget maximization as a fallback position.

26. See Maranto and Gresham, "The Wild West of Education Reform."

27. Survey respondents answered each question using a 1–6 scale in which the possible answers were labeled as follows: 1 = Strongly Disagree; 2 = Moderately Disagree; 3 = Slightly Disagree; 4 = Slightly Agree; 5 = Moderately Agree; 6 = Strongly Agree.

28. For example, if the school's mean rating of a principal behavior item in 1994–95 was 4.50 but increased to 5.15 in 1997–98, then the dependent variable is +.65. (Positive numbers indicate an increase in a specific behavior of the principal.)

29. In Mesa, which accounts for 9 percent of Arizona public school enrollment, we sampled fifteen schools.

30. To ensure a clean distinction between the groups of cooperative and uncooperative schools, and to avoid muddying the categories by including schools of middling cooperation in them, we excluded the middle 20 percent of the sample (sixteen schools) from the two categories.

31. This measure is imperfect because students may attend charter schools outside their districts (unfortunately, systematic data on the extent of this phenomenon are not currently collected). Still, the figure is likely to be reasonably accurate for elementary students, given that parents are generally loathe to send their children—especially elementary-age children—long distances to attend schools.

32. We employed a two-step regression technique to address these concerns. First, we regressed, at the individual teacher level within cooperative and then in uncooperative schools, principal behavior changes on individual teacher characteristics plus a series of dummy variables representing the individual schools. Separate regressions were run for each group to allow for the possibility that these characteristics might affect behavioral measurement differently across them. The nine characteristics exam-

ined were partisan affiliation, salary level, number of years in teaching, union membership status, type of undergraduate major (education versus noneducation), whether the teacher earned a graduate degree, race (white versus nonwhite), gender, and full-time versus part-time status. In these regressions, all variables proved statistically insignificant (at $p < .10$) for the teachers at the uncooperative schools and seven of nine were insignificant at this level for teachers at the cooperative schools. The resulting coefficients for the individual school dummy variables in each analysis represent the mean changes in principal behavior after accounting for the personal characteristics of teachers at that school. These coefficients were then analyzed in a second set of regressions that assessed the relationship between leadership changes and competition at the school level. The results from this second set of regressions match those reported in the main text almost exactly, enhancing our faith in the robustness of the findings.

33. At the district level, such a phenomenon is discussed in Frederick M. Hess, *Spinning Wheels: The Politics of Urban School Reform* (Brookings, 1999).

PART 4

*School Choice and
Civic Education*

12

Making Democratic
Education Work

DAVID E. CAMPBELL

E ducation is inextricably linked to America's democratic ideals.
At the core of virtually every battle over American education
policy is the assumption, stated or not, that education underpins
Americans' self-concept of democracy. Consider the words of
Chief Justice Earl Warren, when the eyes of the nation were centered on the Supreme Court as it issued the unequivocal decision
outlawing racially segregated schools in *Brown* v. *Board of Education*. As he articulated why segregated schools violate the Constitution, Chief Justice Warren explicitly invoked the integral role education plays in the American ideal of democracy.

> Today, education is perhaps the most important function of
> state and local governments. Compulsory school attendance
> laws and the great expenditures for education both demon-
> strate our recognition of the importance of education to our
> democratic society. It is required in the performance of our
> most basic public responsibilities, even service in the armed
> forces. It is the very foundation of good citizenship.[1]

Even in the clash over school vouchers, which is dominated by
shouting about the interpretation of both statistical and constitu-

tional tests, whispers of concern for the civic consequences of voucher programs can occasionally be heard. Consider two separate letters to the editor
written in November 1998, one in the *New York Times,* the other the *Boston
Globe,* both on the subject of Milwaukee, Wisconsin's, voucher program. In
the *Times,* Betty Phillips of Hillsdale, New York, wrote that with the spread
of vouchers, "communities will become badly fragmented, causing harm to
our democratic society." In the *Globe,* Peter Arlos of Berkshire County
defended vouchers by arguing that they will compel public schools to
improve and that "by becoming better, public schools . . . will produce better
citizens willing to vote to save their country from becoming an oligarchy
where fewer and fewer people exercise control."[2]

Is Betty Phillips or Peter Arlos right? Do private schools foster social divisiveness, as their critics often claim? Are there different civic consequences
from attending a religious private school instead of a secular one? The
answers to these questions are of particular relevance for contemporary
debate over school voucher programs. As highlighted in the aforementioned
letters to the editor, the civic consequences of school reform should be as
important as the academic consequences. While this paper only speaks to
students who are currently enrolled in private schools and not the effects of a
voucher program per se, it does provide a look at the civic environments of
the private schools that voucher recipients would attend.

Objectives of a Civic Education

"Producing better citizens" was the original justification for America's public
schools. In the 1800s, Horace Mann and others successfully argued that
immigrants to America's shores could be inculcated into the norms of American civic life through the public schools. Today, essentially the same objective
remains. In a 1996 Phi Delta Kappa/Gallup Poll, 86 percent of Americans
reported that they feel "preparing students to be responsible citizens" is a
"very important" purpose of the nation's schools, more than the 76 percent
who felt that it is equally important that schools should "help people become
economically self-sufficient."[3] However, while the schools have ostensibly the
same civic objective in the twenty-first century as in the nineteenth, the
norms of what constitutes good citizenship have changed. Then, being a
good citizen meant being a Protestant, which led the Catholic Church to
fund parochial schools that were (and are) independent of the publicly
financed school system. Now, while no agreement has been reached on all the
nuances of good citizenship, I propose that at least three objectives of civic
education enjoy broad consensus.

The first objective is to equip the nation's future voters with the capacity to be engaged in the political process. As only one example of the consensus that exists on this point, take a statement from the nation's governors in 1990. They met at the invitation of President George Bush and drafted a document detailing what the objectives of America's schools ought to be. Following the meeting, the National Governors' Association, without controversy, declared that "Americans must be prepared to . . . participate knowledgeably in our democracy and our democratic institutions."[4] It is difficult to imagine anyone arguing that schools should not prepare students for participation in the nation's politics. The civic objective of preparing soon-to-be voters to engage in political life is especially salient against a backdrop of declining rates of political activity, most notably among young people.

The second objective follows directly from the statement that citizens must not only participate in democratic institutions, but also do so knowledgeably. Students must be taught the history and politics of their own nation. In the 1996 Phi Delta Kappa/Gallup Poll, 86 percent of Americans reported that it is very or quite important for schools to "promote cultural unity among all Americans." Instruction in American political institutions and processes is an essential component of promoting such unity.

The third objective stems from political philosopher Amy Gutmann's argument that the defining characteristic of a democratic education is the "ability to deliberate" in a context of "mutual respect among persons." In other words, while the second civic objective of teaching particulars about the United States emphasizes *unum*, this third objective stresses *pluribus*. Gutmann reconciles this tension between the particular and the general with the rationalization that in emphasizing the history and politics of the United States, teachers can instruct students in the value of equality for all.[5] The general public would seem to agree. In a 1999 Phi Delta Kappa/Gallup Poll, 90 percent of Americans said that the schools should teach "patriotism and/or love of country." Virtually the same number, 93 percent, also reported that the schools should teach "acceptance of people of different races and ethnic backgrounds." Seventy-one percent stated that the schools should also teach "acceptance of people who hold unpopular or controversial political or social views."[6]

In summary, there are at least three civic objectives of America's schools:

(1) The capacity to be involved in the political process (civic engagement).

(2) An understanding of the nation's political system (political knowledge).

(3) Learning to respect the opinions of people different from one's self (commitment to civil liberties or political tolerance).

This paper follows in the wake of studies that examined how well different types of schools—most notably public versus private—provide general academic instruction.[7] But instead of academic output as it is usually defined, this analysis centers on the question of how well different types of schools provide these three objectives of a civic education.

Literature Review

A small but growing body of research exists on the subject of the civic effects of public versus private schools. Researchers have shown that Catholic schools are more racially integrated than public schools and that the only voucher program evaluated in this regard has not had an adverse effect on integration. Jay P. Greene, Joseph Giammo, and Nicole Mellow have also provided evidence that Hispanic adults who were educated in private schools are more likely to participate in politics than those who attended public schools. An analysis of the National Education Longitudinal Study further demonstrates that when compared with public school students, students in private schools are more likely to participate in community service. Similarly, when comparing administrators, those in private schools also more often rate their schools "as outstanding in promoting citizenship" than do their colleagues in public schools.[8]

In 1966, before school vouchers were on the nation's political agenda, Andrew M. Greeley and Peter H. Rossi used extensive survey data collected from American Catholics to argue that Catholic schools do not depress civic engagement or promote intolerance. More recently, Richard G. Niemi and Jane Junn have presented data that, at least briefly, compare the civic education of public and private school students. While not a central question in their research, Niemi and Junn note disparities in civics instruction across different types of schools but conclude (based on bivariate comparisons only) that there are only "relatively small, inconsistent differences." The 1998 civics report card by the National Assessment of Educational Progress (NAEP) states that students in private schools (both Catholic and non-Catholic) have higher average scores on the NAEP civics test than their peers in public schools. This conclusion is based on simple cross-tabulations without statistical controls for possible confounding factors such as parents' education. James S. Coleman and Thomas Hoffer, whose work I draw upon, did control for family background and found students in private schools, both Catholic and non-Catholic, to have higher scores on the High School and Beyond civics test than public school students, although the results were not statistically significant. Taken together, these findings suggest that there is little reason to suspect private schools do a worse job of providing a civic education than assigned public schools, and some reason to think they do a better job. But reasonable doubt remains.[9]

In addition to these studies of schools, Robert D. Putnam's research on civic participation more broadly provides reason to think that public and private schools should differ in their capacity to deliver civic education. Since the publication of Putnam's *Making Democracy Work*, the follow-up article "Bowling Alone: America's Declining Social Capital," and a similarly titled book, it has become increasingly common for political scientists to discuss civic participation by referring to social capital. As Putnam defines it, "social capital refers to features of social organization such as networks, norms, and social trust that facilitate coordination and cooperation for mutual benefit." While rarely mentioned in this literature, the concept of social capital provides a theoretical bridge between the literatures on academic instruction and civic engagement. Before Putnam employed the concept to explain differences in governmental performance between Northern and Southern Italy, Coleman and his colleagues developed it to theorize why students in Catholic schools excel academically when compared with students in public schools.[10]

The link between social capital as an explanation for both academic performance and civic engagement leads to the question of whether the varying effectiveness of civic education in different types of schools can be attributed to varying levels of social capital, either within a school or the community surrounding the school. The answer lies in understanding how Coleman and Putnam each use the term. Both agree that social capital consists of social networks that are able to enforce collective norms among their members. Coleman, however, makes an important distinction between two different types of communities in which social networks develop. In his framework, a value community consists of people who share a common belief system on at least one dimension and thus develop norms stemming from these beliefs. Almost by definition, private schools are value communities. Parents who have chosen to spend their money on private school tuition when a publicly funded education is available presumably share a commitment to the school's mission. They might value a particular type of instruction (for example, Montessori), strict discipline (for example, military schools), or religious beliefs. While value communities are necessary for social capital, they are not sufficient. Necessary also is a social network as a means to enforce the norms uniting the value community. That requires a functional community, by which Coleman means a group of people with whom one regularly interacts. Social capital, he argues, is found where value and functional communities overlap. Secular private schools are typically value communities with no functional component. In some settings, neighborhood public schools might be an extension of a functional community but often do not constitute a value community, as witnessed by the perennial debates in the United States over public school policies and curricula. Catholic schools consistently combine both.

While Putnam's application of social capital theory is consistent with how it was developed by Coleman, his focus is different. He centers on the particular norm of generalized reciprocity enforced within the social networks formed as people interact in voluntary associations and other social settings. Reciprocity means that people come to trust one another, and collaborative effort results. Social capital, therefore, leads to a virtuous circle of collective action. The more collective action, the more the norm of reciprocity is reinforced.

If Coleman is right and Catholic schools are flush with social capital, and Putnam is right that social capital facilitates collective action, then Catholic school students could be expected to be characterized by a greater degree of civic engagement than public school students. The same effect, however, should not be evident in secular private schools, given that they are value but not functional communities. For the same reason, there should not be much difference between assigned public and magnet public schools. This theoretically driven expectation is tempered somewhat though by the conclusion of Mark Schneider and his colleagues that school districts with public school choice increase social capital, at least among parents.[11] The expectation for religious but non-Catholic schools is equally ambiguous. Given the small fraction of students that attends these schools, little research has been done on them. Assuming that these non-Catholic schools embody a functional and value community similar to Catholic schools, then they might facilitate civic engagement. But because many of them are fundamentalist Christian schools, it could also be that they promote a sense of exclusion from the civic sphere, given that many fundamentalists seek to separate themselves from the wider society.[12]

Data

Because over 90 percent of American secondary school students attend public schools, a large sample size is needed to compare students in public and private schools. In addition, an analysis of students' civic attitudes requires comparable information from their parents, to account for the strong influence of the home environment on political socialization. The 1996 National

Household Education Survey (NHES) meets these criteria. Administered by the National Center for Education Statistics of the Department of Education, large, nationally representative samples of both parents and their children were administered telephone surveys. Some of this analysis draws upon questions asked of students (and their parents) in grades seven through twelve, for a total sample size of 7,983. Other questions were asked only of students in grades nine through twelve, yielding 4,213 respondents. It is rare that the sample size of a survey like this is large enough to create an analytically useful category for each type of school (by comparison, the typical national survey has around 1,500 respondents).[13] In each household, interviews were conducted with the parent or guardian "most knowledgeable" (as the interviewers worded it) about the child's education. The critical aspect of the NHES is that parents and their children were asked about the same aspects of civic involvement, meaning that in the analysis civic influences in the home can be statistically controlled for as the effect of the school is isolated.

Civic Engagement

The first objective of civic education is the capacity to be engaged in one's community. For this analysis, three different measures of civic engagement will be employed. One is a measure of what students are doing in the present—engaging in voluntary community service. The second is a measure of what students have learned to prepare them to be civically engaged in the future—acquiring "civic skills" in the classroom. The third extends from the second; it is a measure of whether students feel confident that they could use their civic skills outside of the classroom.

Community Service

While to most people volunteer work is undoubtedly commendable for its own sake, Putnam's research in Italy demonstrates that participation in voluntary associations has salutary consequences for the effectiveness of democratic governance. Turning to the United States, Putnam has expressed concern about the declining rate of Americans' participation in membership associations, a concern shared by many outside of academia.[14] For example, witness the high profile of the Voluntarism Summit hosted by General Colin Powell, the creation of AmeriCorps under President Bill Clinton, and increasing attention paid to service learning in high school. For those who are concerned about Americans' long-term rates of civic activity, social science suggests that initiatives among young people are well targeted. Past

Table 12-1. *School Type and Percentage of Students Participating in Community Service*
Percent

	Type of school				
Community service	Assigned public	Magnet public	Catholic	Religious, non-Catholic	Secular private
All students, without statistical controls	47	50	71**	64**	57**
Community service, not mandatory, without statistical controls	47	48	64**	61**	52
Community service, not mandatory, with statistical controls	48	49	59**	57	52
N	6,111/5,269	1,018/829	424/209	187/141	198/135

**p < .05.

studies have found civic activity while young to be a "pathway to participation" in adulthood.[15]

Table 12-1 displays the percentage of students in each type of school who have engaged in, as the questionnaire worded it, "any community service activity or volunteer work at your school or in your community." The asterisks indicate whether the percentage reported in that cell is, in statistical terms, significantly different from the percentage reported for students in assigned public schools (used as a comparison category because the vast majority of American students attend this type of school). The data in the table demonstrate that, statistically, no difference exists between assigned public schools and magnet public schools. However, students in all three types of private schools are more likely to engage in community service than are students in assigned public schools. Forty-seven percent of assigned public school students perform community service, compared with 57 percent of students in private secular schools, 64 percent of students in religious, non-Catholic schools, and 71 percent of students in Catholic schools.

A reasonable objection to the first row of table 12-1 is that the results are potentially misleading because many private and some public schools require their students to perform "voluntary" service. According to the NHES, 70 percent of students in Catholic schools report that their schools require community service in the ninth through twelfth grades. This compares with 16 percent of students in assigned public schools, 22 percent in magnet public schools, 28 percent in religious, non-Catholic schools, and 38 percent in secular private schools. It is not clear, however, what this variation in schools' service requirements means for the long-term impact of community service on individual students. Mandatory service may be less effective for promoting civic voluntarism than service that is initiated by the student, or it may not. On the one hand, students who are compelled to perform service may resent it and become disaffected with volunteering. But on the other hand, requiring service in the community would presumably mean introducing students to volunteer work who would not otherwise have had that experience. They might decide that they gain satisfaction from it and wish to continue even when they have fulfilled their school's requirement. The second row of table 12-1 is to assuage those who subscribe to the second point of view and feel that mandated service does not reflect a genuine sense of voluntarism. It includes only those students who reported that their school does not have a mandatory service requirement. The table reports the percentage of students in each type of school who have participated in community service. The results are similar to those reported in the first row, with the exception of private secular schools. While more of their students participate in community service than do students in assigned public schools (52 percent to 47 percent), the difference ceases to be statistically significant at even the .10 level (note, however, that there are few cases in this category).

Another valid criticism of both rows 1 and 2 of table 12-1 is that they do not account for systematic differences in students who attend these types of schools that might in turn affect whether they engage in community service. Owing to the extensive questionnaire for the NHES, a wide array of factors can be incorporated into a model predicting whether a student has performed community service. The third row of table 12-1 reports the percentage of students in each type of school who participated in community service, controlling for possibly confounding factors. Most important, these figures control for whether the student's parents engage in community service.[16]

As displayed in the third row of table 12-1, the basic picture does not change dramatically when statistical controls are introduced. Students in assigned public schools are still the least likely to participate in community service (48 percent), while Catholic school students are the most likely (59 percent). The introduction of controls, however, does wipe out the statistical significance of the differences between assigned public school students and students in every other type of school except Catholic schools.

The results of this model are consistent with the research of Anthony S. Bryk, Valerie Lee, and Peter B. Holland into the relationship between Catholic schools and their communities. They report that in all of the

Catholic schools they included in their study, community service work was available as an elective course. Furthermore, an ethic of service was frequently found among both the staff and students they interviewed.

> These service programs signify Catholic schools' commitment to a just social community. One board member of a field-site school remarked, "A school should not call itself Catholic if it doesn't have a volunteer service program." The director of the program at St. Edward's [one of their case-study schools] commented: "I'm a believer in service. It's important for students to realize that the things they do make a difference. We can heal people and make their lives better. We can raise the awareness of others. Physical contact is vital for Christianity. Some of our students are sheltered from poverty and from people of different races. This program is important because it makes them more aware."[17]

Because community service is integral to the mission of many Catholic schools, it perhaps is not surprising that their students are the most likely to participate in volunteer activity. But when compared with assigned public school students, do students in Catholic or other types of schools come out ahead on alternative measures of civic capacity?

Civic Skills

Students in Catholic schools are not only more likely to perform voluntary community service, but also more likely to learn "civic skills" in the classroom when compared with students in assigned public schools and to believe that they could use those skills to make their voices heard in the political arena. Students in all three types of private schools have greater confidence in their ability to use their civic skills. And it is civic skills that serve as an indispensable resource for civic, especially political, activity.

In their landmark book *Voice and Equality: Civic Voluntarism in American Politics*, Sidney Verba, Kay Lehman Schlozman, and Henry E. Brady demonstrate that people differ in their capacity to perform the mundane tasks that constitute virtually all political activity, skills such as giving speeches, holding meetings, and writing letters. Those who lack these skills are extremely unlikely to participate in politics. While Verba, Schlozman, and Brady focus on how adults learn civic skills on the job or through participation in voluntary organizations, people are most likely to learn them in school when young.

An index of civic skills was created to test for systematic differences across the school types. The NHES asked student respondents:

Table 12-2. *School Type and Civic Skills Index*

Civic skills index (0–3)	Type of school				
	Assigned public	Magnet public	Catholic	Religious, non-Catholic	Private secular
Without statistical controls	1.69	1.76	1.88**	1.86	1.81
With statistical controls	1.56	1.63	1.69**	1.68	1.59
N	6,111	1,108	424	187	198

**p < .05.

During this school year, have you done any of the following things in any class at (your current) school . . .

(1) written a letter to someone you did not know (Yes or No)

(2) given a speech or an oral report (Yes or No)

(3) taken part in a debate or discussion in which you had to persuade others about your point of view (Yes or No)

Each positive response was coded as 1, and for each student the cumulative number of skills was tallied. Table 12-2 displays the simple comparison across school types. While there are not large differences, students in Catholic schools do learn more civic skills in the classroom than students in assigned public schools, a difference that is statistically significant at the .05 level. However, the real test consists of a model controlling for confounding factors.[18]

Given the litany of control variables included in this analysis, the variable measuring whether a student attends a Catholic school has a big hurdle to clear to reach statistical significance. The difference between Catholic school and assigned public school students is perhaps not dramatic but, because it is completely consistent with the other findings reported here, adds to the evidence for the high quality of civic education in Catholic schools. This measure has a restrictive ceiling on its total range (3) and a relatively high mean value (1.67), both factors working against finding an effect for any variable.

Civic Confidence

Learning civic skills is one thing; being able to use them is another. In addition to questions about what civic skills students acquire in class, the NHES asked respondents whether they feel that they could use two of those skills outside of the classroom. Specifically, the questions ask:

Table 12-3. *School Type and Civic Confidence Index*

Civic confidence index (0–2)	Type of school				
	Assigned public	Magnet public	Catholic	Religious, non-Catholic	Private secular
Without statistical controls	1.73	1.78	1.83**	1.85**	1.88**
With statistical controls	1.57	1.62	1.69*	1.80**	1.76**
N	3,230	578	223	80	102

*p < .10; **p < .05.

(1) Suppose you wanted to write a letter to someone in the government about something that concerned you. Do you feel that you could write a letter that clearly gives your opinion? (Yes or No)

(2) Imagine you went to a community meeting and people were making comments and statements. Do you think that you could make a comment or a statement at a public meeting? (Yes or No)

Responses to these items were combined to create an additive index of civic confidence. This is an important complement to the questions regarding whether students had the opportunity to learn a set of civic skills. These questions test whether students feel that they could transfer those skills from the classroom to the real world.

Table 12-3 displays the mean score on the civic confidence scale across school types. While all four types of schools have higher means than assigned public schools, the differences are only statistically significant for the three types of private schools. However, the multivariate model makes the convincing case for a school effect independent of other confounding factors. The model used to generate the results for table 12-3 is identical to the one used in table 12-2, and the results for every set of variables other than the school-type variables are consistent with the preceding model of civic skill acquisition.

Even with statistical controls, students in all three types of private schools are more likely than students in assigned public schools to have confidence in their ability to exercise civic skills if called upon to do so. Of these three, the religious, non-Catholic school students display the greatest degree of civic confidence.

Political Knowledge

The second objective of a civic education is that future voters learn specific, factual information about American politics. While disagreement may arise over whether or not schools should require community service, presumably everyone agrees that schools should require the acquisition of knowledge. Knowledge about politics is an intuitively important factor in facilitating civic involvement. Witness the ritual of newspapers regularly lamenting how much—or how little—Americans, and American adolescents in particular, know about politics.[19] For the most part, political scientists concur with this intuition (although there is a debate over how much information voters need to be informed, I am aware of no serious argument that political knowledge is not an important component of political involvement). Without understanding the particulars of American politics, people are unable to engage fully in the political process. John Zaller, for example, provides extensive evidence that knowledge of factual information about politics is the best measure of political awareness.[20] Likewise, in their exhaustive analysis of the causes and consequences of political knowledge, Michael Delli Carpini and Scott Keeter conclude that political knowledge is not only an indicator of psychic engagement with politics (the sense in which Zaller uses it), but also the key to full participation in the political process:

> Informed citizens are demonstrably better citizens, as judged by the standards of democratic theory and practice underpinning the American system. They are more likely to participate in politics, more likely to have meaningful, stable attitudes on issues, better able to link their interests with their attitudes, more likely to choose candidates who are consistent with their own attitudes, and more likely to support democratic norms, such as extending basic civil liberties to members of unpopular groups. Differences between the best- and least-informed citizens on all of these dimensions are dramatic. In our analyses, the impact of political knowledge is independent of, and thus over and above, that of other factors as interest in politics and political efficacy.[21]

Even though common sense would lead to the expectation that civics instruction in school results in greater political knowledge among students, for decades scholars could find little evidence of the relationship. This was due to a combination of factors: poor methods of teaching civics in the classroom, the fact that students learn about politics outside of the classroom (in a way that they are unlikely to learn about other subjects such as chemistry or math), and poor measures of political knowledge. With the publication of Niemi and Junn's *Civic Education: What Makes Students Learn?* which employs the 1988 NAEP civics assessment, considerable evidence is available that common sense is correct after all: Taking civics classes does contribute to

Table 12-4. *School Type and Political Knowledge Index*

Political knowledge index (0–5)	Type of school				
	Assigned public	Magnet public	Catholic	Religious, non-Catholic	Private secular
Without statistical controls	2.4	2.3	3.2**	3.4**	3.2**
With statistical controls	1.0	.97	1.33***	.96	1.22
N	3,230	578	223	80	102

**p < .05; ***p < .01.

civics knowledge. However, even though the 1988 NAEP was administered to students in all types of schools, Niemi and Junn do little to examine differences in the political knowledge of students enrolled in public versus private schools.

The NHES includes an index of factual questions about American politics, allowing for comparisons to be made for political knowledge similar to the measures of civic engagement. Ten questions were included on the questionnaire, although each individual respondent was asked only five of them. This was done to ensure that a parent and child in the same household did not receive the same questions, thus contaminating the results of the test. The two political knowledge indices are very similar. Consequently, the average scores do not differ much.[22]

Table 12-4 displays the comparison of how students in each of the various types of schools score on the political knowledge index. With no statistical controls, students in all three types of private schools score higher on the political knowledge index. Each difference is statistically significant at the .05 level. The second row displays the results of ordered probit models with the full gamut of control variables employed in previous models.[23] With the controls, scores for each school category drop considerably. Only the difference between students in assigned public and Catholic schools survives as statistically significant.

This finding about the cognitive dimension of political engagement is perhaps expected, given the literature on the academic effects of attending a Catholic school. If a school teaches math and reading well, it likely will also teach civics well. However, the fact that the acquisition of political knowledge is a function of the same mechanism as the acquisition of knowledge about chemistry, math, and literature does not detract from its consequences for civic activity. As young people enter adulthood and thus the electorate, those who were educated in a Catholic school would seem to be better equipped for, as Zaller puts it, "intellectual engagement with politics."[24]

Political Tolerance

While all three objectives are equally important components of a civic education the third—respect for opinions different from one's own, or political tolerance—seems to be most relevant to the debate over the civic consequences of attending private schools. This is often expressed as a concern that private (particularly religious) schools exacerbate social tensions. In the words of American Federation of Teachers president Albert Shanker, by sending students to private schools, widespread voucher programs "would foster divisions in our society; they would be like setting a time bomb." Similarly, Gutmann stresses the need for students in religious schools to be taught democratic norms under direction from the state, presumably owing to the fear that these schools cannot be trusted to provide instruction in a "common democratic character" on their own.[25]

The concern for teaching a respect for universal civil liberties is well placed, as democracy is defined as much by respect for minority rights as simple majority rule. As explained by John L. Sullivan, James Pierson, and George E. Marcus, in their thorough examination of political tolerance:

> Though liberal societies may be divided by intense conflicts, they can remain stable if there is a general adherence to the rules of democratic or constitutional procedure. Tolerance in this sense implies a commitment to the "rules of the game" and a willingness to apply them equally. Therefore persons are tolerant to the extent they are prepared to extend such constitutional guarantees—the right to speak, to publish, to run for office—to those with whom they disagree. Similarly, a fully tolerant regime applies such norms equally to all.[26]

Studies of political tolerance have a long pedigree, dating back to Samuel A. Stouffer's classic 1955 book *Communism, Conformity, and Civil Liberties.*[27] Following Stouffer's lead, decades of research into factors that contribute to and detract from tolerance have consistently demonstrated that education and tolerance move in tandem.

The bulk of research into education and tolerance has centered on adults and the level of education they achieve. Virtually unexplored has been the question of adolescents' attitudes and how they are related to enrollment in different types of schools. Two alternative hypotheses, drawn from different perspectives of what fosters political tolerance, examine this relationship. The first hypothesis is derived from distinguishing between schools as public versus private institutions. By this reasoning, private schools may be thought to foster an exclusivity among their students that translates into a disregard for minority opinions. In particular, religious schools may foster civic divisiveness, a fear reinforced by survey data that show religiosity to be negatively related to political tolerance.[28] The second hypothesis follows from studies demonstrating the positive cognitive effects of attending a private school. Norman H. Nie, Jane Junn, and Kenneth Stehlik-Barry report that education increases tolerance by enhancing general cognitive proficiency.[29] It would follow, therefore, that tolerance is greatest in those schools where students display the strongest cognitive performance, generally private schools.

The NHES contains two questions that gauge political tolerance, drawn from the standard measures that are regularly included in the General Social Survey and similar surveys.

(1) If a person wanted to make a speech in your community against churches and religion, should he or she be allowed to speak? (Yes or No)

(2) Suppose a book that most people disapproved of was written, for example, saying that it was all right to take illegal drugs. Should a book like that be kept out of a public library? (Yes or No)

The question about churches and religion provides a particularly strong test of political tolerance among students in religious schools, because the hypothetical situation involves someone advocating a position that they will almost certainly reject. Responses to these questions were coded so that a "tolerant" response equals one [that is, yes to (1) and no to (2)] and the opposite responses equal zero. The responses were then added together to produce a two-point scale.

Table 12-5 displays the simple bivariate relationship between students in the different types of schools. Students in Catholic and secular private schools have higher tolerance scores than students in assigned public schools, differences in means that are statistically significant. Students in magnet public schools have slightly higher scores, although the difference does not approach statistical significance, while students in religious, non-Catholic schools have significantly lower scores. Results in table 12-5 are derived from an ordered probit model incorporating virtually all of the same control variables used throughout this analysis.[30] As with the other parental variables, this control variable is to account for civic influences in the home, in this case the possibility that students are inculcated with the norm of political tolerance by their parents.

Students in secular private schools score substantially higher on the tolerance index than students in assigned public schools, while students in reli-

Table 12-5. *School Type and Political Tolerance Index*

Political tolerance index (0–2)	Type of school				
	Assigned public	Magnet public	Catholic	Religious, non-Catholic	Private secular
Without statistical controls	1.43	1.48	1.60**	1.22**	1.76**
With statistical controls	1.34	1.38	1.44*	1.12**	1.64***
N	3,230	578	223	80	102

*p < .10; **p < .05; ***p < .01.

gious, non-Catholic schools score substantially lower. Students in Catholic schools score slightly higher, but the difference is only statistically significant at the .10 level. The conclusion to be drawn from this analysis, therefore, is that the verdict on private schools and tolerance is mixed. Students in secular private and Catholic schools appear to have higher levels of tolerance (the former more than the latter), while religious, non-Catholic school students display lower levels of tolerance.

The work of Sullivan, Piereson, and Marcus raises the issue of whether these results are not an artifact of the particular questions that were asked. They show that evaluating responses to survey questions about civil liberties must take the content of the question into account. Because one of the questions on the tolerance index deals specifically with the rights of a speaker who is opposed to religion, students in religious schools might be expected to be especially wary of granting full freedom of expression. This is not to diminish the importance of respect for religious differences as an important component of political tolerance, but only to suggest that other questions might provide more of a hard case for students in secular schools. To test whether these results are driven by the question that specifically mentions someone giving a speech opposing religion, the same models were run on each question separately. These results, as well as the bivariate comparisons, are reported in table 12-6.

The results for the political tolerance index are driven by the question about allowing a controversial book in the public library, not the one about a speech opposing religion. In the bivariate case, students in Catholic and private secular schools display a greater willingness to permit a controversial book to be placed in a public library and students in religious, non-Catholic schools display greater reluctance. By contrast, no statistically significant differences are evident on the question of permitting an antireligious speech. When statistical controls are introduced, students in religious, non-Catholic

Table 12-6. *School Type and Individual Political Tolerance Items*

	Type of school				
Tolerance item	Assigned public	Magnet public	Catholic	Religious, non-Catholic	Private secular
Allow unpopular book					
Without statistical controls	55	59	67**	39**	83**
With statistical controls	44	47	51	29***	71***
Speak against religion					
Without statistical controls	88	89	93	83	93
With statistical controls	87	87	90	81	89
N	3,230	578	223	80	102

**p < .05; ***p < .01.

schools are considerably less likely to approve of a controversial book, while students in private secular schools are considerably more likely to approve of it. Students in Catholic schools are also more likely to permit the book than students in assigned public schools, but the difference just misses the conventional threshold for statistical significance (p = .11).

In sum, the concern expressed by critics of private education that it has the potential to foster political intolerance has some credence. While students in Catholic schools (the most common form of private education) and secular private schools (perhaps the most vilified type of private education) are more politically tolerant than students in assigned public schools, the 2 percent of America's students in religious, non-Catholic schools—an amalgam of schools sponsored by many different faiths—score lower on the political tolerance index. Further, these results do not seem to be an artifact of asking religiously devout students about a hypothetical situation that involves criticism of religion.

Discussion

This analysis provides evidence to conclude that students in Catholic schools perform better than students in assigned public schools on all three objectives of a civic education—capacity for civic engagement, political knowledge, and political tolerance. For one component of civic capacity—confidence in one's civic skills—students in Catholic; religious, non-Catholic; and secular private schools all score higher than assigned public school students. Evidence further suggests that two other school types differ from assigned public schools on political tolerance, secular private and Catholic school students scoring

Table 12-7. *School Type and Five Facets of Civic Education*[a]

Facet of civil education	Magnet public	Catholic	Religious, non-Catholic	Secular private
Community service	...	↑	...	...
Civic skills	...	↑	...	...
Civic confidence	...	↑	↑	↑
Political knowledge	...	↑	...	...
Political tolerance	...	↑	↓	↑

a. Results are from probit and ordered probit analyses reported in tables 12-1–12-6. All comparisons are with students in assigned public schools. An arrow indicates a statistically significant difference at p < .10 (at least), and the direction indicates whether the effect is negative or positive.

higher on the tolerance index and religious, non-Catholic school students scoring lower. The results are summarized in table 12-7.

Does social capital, in Putnam's sense of facilitating a norm of reciprocity, explain all the civic effects reported here? It can explain the high rate of volunteering among Catholic school students, which is a form of collective action. Bryk, Lee, and Holland, writing after Coleman's work on social capital but before Putnam's, agree.[31] The conceptual connection is not so tight, however, between norms of reciprocity and the acquisition of civic skills and political knowledge. What seems more likely is that these civic objectives are analogous to the purely academic output measured in most studies comparing public and private schools. Accepting this explanation does not mean rejecting the causal role of social capital. It simply means that the effect is a function of the process Coleman, not Putnam, describes: Social capital produces good schools, and good schools provide a good education, of which civic skills and political knowledge are only two of many components.

The effects of political tolerance could be explained the same way. Secular private and Catholic schools could teach respect for civil liberties as part of a rigorous curriculum, while religious, non-Catholic schools could fall short because of their weaker academic environments. The story does not seem to be this simple, however. For neither civic skills nor political knowledge is a positive effect observed for secular private schools and a corresponding negative effect for religious, non-Catholic schools. If the explanation for the political tolerance findings is simply a variation on the same theme as for these other facets of civic education, consistent effects should be observed across all of them.

A plausible explanation for the positive impact of secular and Catholic schools and the negative impact of religious, non-Catholic schools centers on the content of their curricula. And it is probably not a matter of what is taught, but what is not. Given that religiosity generally correlates with low levels of political tolerance, religious schools not unexpectedly produce students with similarly low tolerance levels. This need not be because students are taught to disrespect the civil liberties of people who hold unpopular opinions, but because in these schools tolerance is not emphasized to the degree that it is in secular schools.[32]

Implications

Do private schools fray the civic bonds holding Americans together? For the most part, the answer is no. Students in Catholic schools display greater civic proficiency than students who attend assigned public schools. And this finding is the most relevant to the debate over school voucher programs, because Catholic schools are by far the most common type of private school in the United States and, consequently, the most common type of school that voucher recipients attend. For example, in Washington, D.C., 63 percent of recipients of a Washington Scholarship Fund voucher attend Catholic schools. This compares with only 18 percent who attend schools that would be included in the religious, non-Catholic category used in this analysis.

The results reported here are generally robust to different econometric specifications. They are also consistent with four similar studies. The 1973 High School Seniors Cohort Study, the National Educational Longitudinal Study, the Latino National Political Survey, and a study of college students in Texas each draw similar conclusions. Few findings in social science can be replicated with four independent sources of data. In short, strong evidence has accumulated that private—particularly Catholic—schools are a means to the public end of facilitating civic engagement.[33]

There is one cautionary note. Students in religious, non-Catholic schools demonstrate a lower level of political tolerance than any other group of students. They also display the highest level of civic confidence—an explosive combination. For these schools, it is legitimate to question whether the civic education that they offer conforms to the liberal democratic norm of simultaneously facilitating both civic engagement and political tolerance. However, do not make too much of this finding. Because of the consistently negative relationship between religiosity and standard measures of political tolerance, a better test of the effect of religious schools would include controls for the religiosity of both students and parents. Unfortunately, the NHES includes only a single question about religion, a relatively weak measure of how frequently parents attend religious services. Without better measures of religiosity, caution should be taken in attributing the negative relationship between attending a religious, non-Catholic school and political tolerance to a school effect alone.

The conclusion that any type of private school provides a civic education superior to that offered by public schools is admittedly provocative, if only because of the connotations the words *public* and *private* carry in contemporary discourse. In the United States, when the word *public* is used in referring to education, it refers only to the source of a school's funding and not to the population served by a school.[34] Yet when advocating on behalf of public schools, American critics of private education often implicitly extend the limited definition of *public* to mean the population the school serves, not how the school is funded. Critics speak of high-priced preparatory schools as though they are the only, or at least the most common, type of private education in the United States. Often, all private schools are grouped together and thus caricatured as exclusive and insular.[35] While nonpublicly funded schools have the prerogative to apply virtually any criteria they want for admissions, in practice Catholic schools, at least, are very inclusive.

> Catholic high schools are not highly selective in their admissions. The typical school reports accepting 88 percent of the students who apply, and only about a third of the schools maintain a waiting list. Indeed, the school does not operate as the principal selection mechanism; the real control rests with the students and their families through their decision to apply for admission.[36]

Bryk, Lee, and Holland also report that "religious affiliation is not a routine consideration" in admissions to Catholic schools.[37] And even though Catholic schools charge tuition, 87 percent offer financial aid.[38] Contrast this to public schools, which almost exclusively enroll students who live in the geographic area surrounding the school. How public is a school in an exclusive suburb with high housing costs, especially when compared with a Catholic school that offers financial aid to assist with its tuition (which for high school is on average about $4,000 per year; $2,000 for elementary school)?[39]

In conclusion, I must stress that this study is not an end but only a beginning for the study of the civic education offered by America's schools. Many questions remain about why the variation exists among students of different types of schools. However, this paper was written to consider the civic implications of vouchers, seeking to answer the narrow question of whether school voucher programs will sacrifice the civic education of their participants. The evidence presented here provides an answer to this relatively narrow question: Concern for the purportedly negative civic effects of voucher programs appears mostly—but not totally—unwarranted. For scholars interested in political socialization, I hope these results will encourage consideration of how different types of school environments vary in the civic education that they offer their students and why that is the case. Perhaps public schools could even learn from Catholic schools about what makes democratic education work.

Notes

1. *Brown* v. *Board of Education*, 347 U.S. 483 (1954).

2. Peter G. Arlos, letter to the editor, *Boston Globe*, November 13, 1998, p. A30; and Betty Phillips, letter to the editor, *New York Times*, November 13, 1998, p. A26.

3. Stanley M. Elam, Lowell C. Rose, and Alec M. Gallup, "The 28th Annual Phi Delta Kappa/Gallup Poll of the Public's Attitudes toward the Public Schools," *Phi Delta Kappan* (September 1996), p. 247.

4. Margaret Stimmann Branson, *The Role of Civic Education* (Calabasas, Calif.: Center for Civic Education, 1998), p. 24.

5. Amy Gutmann, *Democratic Education* (Princeton University Press, 1999), pp. 46, 33, and 316, respectively.

6. Lowell C. Rose and Alec M. Gallup, "The 31st Annual Phi Delta Kappa/Gallup Poll of the Public's Attitudes toward the Public Schools," *Phi Delta Kappan* (September 1999), p. 51.

7. James S. Coleman, Thomas Hoffer, and Sally Kilgore, *Public and Private High Schools* (U.S. Department of Education, National Center for Education Statistics, 1981); and Derek Neal, "The Effects of Catholic Secondary Schooling on Educational Achievement," *Journal of Labor Economics*, vol. 15 (1997), pp. 98–123.

8. James S. Coleman, Thomas Hoffer, and Sally Kilgore, *High School Achievement* (Basic Books, 1982); Robert Crain, *Private Schools and Black-White Integration: Evidence from Two Big Cities* (Stanford University, Institute for Research on Educational Finance and Government, 1984); Jay P. Greene and Nicole Mellow, *Integration Where It Counts: A Study of Racial Integration in Public and Private School Classrooms*, PEPG98–13 (Harvard University, Program on Education Policy and Governance, 1998); and Jay P. Greene, Joseph Giammo, and Nicole Mellow, *The Effect of Private Education on Political Participation, Social Capital, and Tolerance: An Examination of the Latino National Political Survey*, PEPG98–14 (Harvard University, Program on Education Policy and Governance, 1998).

9. Andrew M. Greeley and Peter H. Rossi, *The Education of Catholic Americans* (Chicago: Aldine Publishing, 1966); Richard G. Niemi and Jane Junn, *Civic Education: What Makes Students Learn?* (Yale University Press, 1998), p. 84; U.S. Department of Education, *The NAEP 1998 Civics Report Card for the Nation*, NCES

2000–457 (National Center for Education Statistics, Office of Educational Research and Improvement, 1999); and James S. Coleman and Thomas Hoffer, *Public and Private High Schools: The Impact of Communities* (Basic Books, 1987), p. 79.

10. Robert D. Putnam, *Making Democracy Work: Civic Traditions in Modern Italy* (Princeton University Press, 1993); Robert D. Putnam, "Bowling Alone: America's Declining Social Capital," *Journal of Democracy* (1995), pp. 65–78; Robert D. Putnam, *Bowling Alone: The Collapse and Revival of American Community* (Simon and Schuster, 2000); and Coleman and Hoffer, *Public and Private High Schools.*

11. Mark Schneider, Paul Teske, Melissa Marschall, Michael Mintrom, and Christine Roch, "Institutional Arrangements and the Creation of Social Capital: The Effects of School Choice," *American Political Science Review,* vol. 91 (1997), pp. 82–93.

12. Nancy Tatom Ammerman, *Bible Believers: Fundamentalists in the Modern World* (Rutgers University Press, 1987).

13. Note that these data only include youth respondents who were enrolled in school at the time of the survey and therefore cannot reveal anything about the civic education of young people who drop out of school.

14. Putnam, *Making Democracy Work;* and Putnam, "Bowling Alone."

15. Paul Allen Beck and M. Kent Jennings, "Pathways to Participation," *American Political Science Review,* vol. 76 (1982), pp. 94–108; and Sidney Verba, Kay Lehman Schlozman, and Henry E. Brady, *Voice and Equality: Civic Voluntarism in American Politics* (Harvard University Press, 1995).

16. These control variables can be broken into three categories: individual level, family level, and school level. Space limitations preclude a detailed discussion of each variable, but each one has been included because either past research or theory (most often both) suggests that it is a factor affecting civic participation. Because the dependent variable is dichotomous, probit analysis is used. The reported results are generated from the probit coefficients, with each control variable set to its mean value. Those interested can turn to the appendix for the full results.

Individual level: age, gender, native language, region of residence, race, ethnicity, academic performance, college expectations, frequency of reading the newspaper or watching television news, and hours spent working at a part-time job.

Family level: parents' education, family income, whether the child lives in a two-parent home, frequency of church attendance, parental community service, parental volunteer work in the child's school, and parental political participation.

School level: racial composition of the school, size of the school, whether the school arranges community service for students, students' perception of whether their opinions matter, whether the student has taken a course that required attention to politics, and whether the school has a student government.

17. Anthony S. Bryk, Valerie Lee, and Peter B. Holland, *Catholic Schools and the Common Good* (Harvard University Press, 1993).

18. Table 12-2 displays the results of ordered probit models (appropriate because the dependent variable is no longer dichotomous), which include all of the control

variables described above except for three factors that would be expected to affect participation in community service but not learning civic skills at school: a measure of hours spent working at a part-time job, whether the child has a parent who volunteers in his or her school, and whether the school arranges community service opportunities for students. In addition, one new variable has been included. To control for the possibility of students living in households where their parents provide an example of civic behavior and thus might lead them to seek opportunities to exercise civic skills, a parental civic skills index is included. This is an additive scale of whether the parent feels he or she could write a letter on behalf of a cause or give a speech at a meeting.

19. See, as only one example of many, Richard T. Cooper, "Old Enough to Vote But Ignorant of Why," *Los Angeles Times*, November 19, 1999, p. A18.

20. John Zaller, *The Nature and Origins of Mass Opinion* (New York: Cambridge University Press, 1992).

21. Michael Delli Carpini and Scott Keeter, *What Americans Know about Politics and Why It Matters* (Yale University Press, 1996), p. 272.

22. *Political knowledge index 1:* (1) What job or political office is now held by Al Gore? (2) Whose responsibility is it to determine if a law is constitutional or not . . . the president, Congress, or the Supreme Court? (3) Which party now has the most members in the House of Representatives in Washington? (4) How much of a majority is needed for the U.S. Senate and House to override a presidential veto? (5) Which of the two major parties is more conservative at the national level? Mean: 2.02

Political knowledge index 2: (1) What job or political office is now held by Newt Gingrich? (2) Whose responsibility is it to nominate judges to the federal courts . . . the president, Congress, or the Supreme Court? (3) Which party now has the most members in the U.S. Senate? (4) What are the first ten amendments of the U.S. Constitution called? (5) Which of the two major parties is in favor of the larger defense budget? Mean : 1.74

23. The only variation from the variables used to model civic skills and civic confidence is the substitution of a variable that gauges parental political knowledge for one measuring parental civic skills. Parental political knowledge is a potent control variable given the body of research that has long demonstrated the role of the family in providing political cues and information.

24. Zaller, *The Nature and Origins of Mass Opinion*.

25. Albert Shanker, "Keeping Public Education Together," *Where We Stand: A Regular Column by the President of the American Federation of Teachers*, March 3, 1997; and Gutmann, *Democratic Education*, pp. 117–18.

26. John L. Sullivan, James Piereson, and George E. Marcus, *Political Tolerance and American Democracy* (University of Chicago Press, 1982), p. 2.

27. Samuel A. Stouffer, *Communism, Conformity, and Civil Liberties: A Cross-Section of the Nation Speaks Its Mind* (Garden City, N.Y.: Doubleday, 1955).

28. Clyde Wilcox and Ted Jelen, "Evangelicals and Political Tolerance," *American Politics Quarterly*, vol. 18 (1990), pp. 25–46.

29. Norman H. Nie, Jane Junn, and Kenneth Stehlik-Barry, *Education and Democratic Citizenship in America* (University of Chicago Press, 1996).

30. The only variation from the array of control variables included in the previous models is that the parental political tolerance index score is used in lieu of the other parental measures. The parental political participation index has been dropped.

31. Bryk, Lee, and Holland, *Catholic Schools and the Common Good*.

32. Stephen Macedo, *Diversity of Distrust: Civic Education in a Multicultural Democracy* (Harvard University Press, 2000).

33. David E. Campbell, "Civic Education in Public, Private, and Parochial Schools," paper presented at the annual meeting of the Northeastern Political Science Association, 1998; Jay P. Greene, "Civic Values in Public and Private Schools," in Paul E. Peterson and Bryan Hassel, eds., *Learning from School Choice* (Brookings, 1998), pp. 83–106; and Greene, Giammo, and Mellow, "The Effect of Private Education on Political Participation."

34. The best example of why this usage of the term is "public" is somewhat arbitrary can be found in England, where what Americans would call "private" schools are instead known as "public" schools.

35. See, for example, Albert Shanker, "We'd Love to Help, But . . .," *Where We Stand: A Regular Column by the President of the American Federation of Teachers*, October 20.

36. Bryk, Lee, and Holland, *Catholic Schools and the Common Good*, p. 128.

37. Bryk, Lee, and Holland, *Catholic Schools and the Common Good*, p. 129.

38. Bryk, Lee, and Holland, *Catholic Schools and the Common Good*, p. 376.

39. U.S. Department of Education, *Digest of Education Statistics* (National Center for Education Statistics, 1999), table 62.

Table 12-A1. *Complete Results*[a]

Variable	Community service[b]	Civic skills index[c]	Civic confidence index[d]	Political knowledge index[e]	Political tolerance index[f]	Allow unpopular book in library?[g]	Allow speech against religion?[h]
Type of school							
Private, secular	.08 (.16)	.01 (.10)	.44 (.21)**	.20(.15)	.60 (.20)***	.72 (.20)***	.11 (.22)
Catholic	.28 (.12)**	.15 (.07)**	.25 (.13)*	.28 (.09)***	.18 (.11)*	.19 (.12)	.15 (.16)
Magnet public	.01 (.06)	.07 (.05)	.10 (.26)	–.04 (.07)	.07 (.07)	.08 (.08)	.02 (.10)
Religious, non-Catholic	.21 (.15)	.14 (.10)	.55 (.22)***	–.06 (.14)	–.37 (.16)**	–.40 (.19)**	–.25 (.20)
Individual-level variables							
Age	.02 (.01)	–.05 (.01)***	.09 (.03)***	.13 (.02)***	.10 (.02)***	.10 (.02)***	.07 (.03)***
Gender	.17 (.04)***	.15 (.03)***	.19 (.06)***	–.44 (.05)***	–.06 (.05)	–.08 (.05)	.02 (.07)
English-speaking	.25 (.10)***	.05 (.08)	–.02 (.15)	.18 (.10)**	.31 (.11)***	.15 (.13)	.47 (.13)
Live in the South	–.02 (.05)	–.02 (.03)	–.22 (.06)***	–.03 (.05)	–.18 (.05)***	–.22 (.06)	–.06 (.07)
Race	–.10 (.07)	–.08 (.05)	.09 (.10)	–.27 (.07)***	–.07 (.08)	–.13 (.09)	.05 (.11)
Hispanic	–.05 (.08)	–.12 (.07)*	–.02 (12)	–.23 (.08)***	.01 (.09)	–.01 (.11)	.06 (.12)
Academic performance	.17 (.03)***	.06 (.02)***	–.0004 (.04)	.31 (.03)***	.03 (.03)	.02 (.04)	.04 (.04)
College expectations	.15 (.08)**	.07 (.06)	.15 (.09)	.24 (.08)***	.09 (.08)	.14 (.09)	–.01 (.11)
Interest in news	.06 (.01)***	.09 (.01)***	.12 (.02)***	.11 (.01)***	.02 (.01)	.02 (.02)	.004 (.02)
Hours spent working at part-time job	.01 (.003)*						
Parent-level variables							
Parents' education	.07 (.02)***	.02 (.02)	.004 (.03)	.13 (.02)***	.07 (.02)***	.06 (.03)**	.06 (.03)*
Family income	–.01 (.01)	.01 (.01)	–.004 (.01)	.001 (.01)	.013 (.01)	.02 (.01)	.004 (.02)
Two-parent household	.07 (.06)	–.04 (.04)	.04 (.07)	.08 (.06)	–.02 (.06)	–.02 (.07)	–.02 (.09)

Frequency of church attendance	.04 (.02)***	−.01 (.01)	−.01 (.02)	.01 (.02)	−.07 (.02)***	−.06 (.02)***	−.07 (.03)***
Parental volunteer service	.28 (.05)***	.09 (.04)**	.13 (.06)	.004 (.05)	−.004 (.05)	.02 (.06)	−.05 (.08)
Parent volunteers in school	.10 (.05)**						
Parents' participation index	.01 (.02)	.02 (.01)*	.018 (.02)	.02 (.02)			
Parents' civic skill index		.11 (.04)***	.15 (.07)				
Parents' political knowledge index				.12 (.02)***			
Parents' tolerance index					.19 (.04)***	.17 (.04)***	.17 (.05)***
School-level variables							
Racial composition of school	.02 (.03)	−.04 (.02)**	.01 (.04)	−.02 (.03)	−.02 (.03)	−.01 (.04)	−.02 (.05)
Size of school	.004 (.002)**	−.001 (.001)	−.003 (.002)	.002 (.002)	−.001 (.002)	−.00004 (.002)	−.001 (.003)
Students' opinions matter	−.07 (.03)**	−.017 (.02)	−.03 (.04)	.12 (.03)***	.07 (.04)*	.10 (.04)***	−.02 (.05)
Course required attention to politics	.09 (.05)*	.26 (.04)	.05 (.06)	.38 (.05)***	.04 (.06)	.02 (.06)	.06 (.08)
School has student government	.15 (.06)***	.15 (.05)***	.20 (.09)**	.36 (.08)***	.19 (.08)**	.23 (.09)***	.07 (.11)
School arranges community service for students	.59 (.06)***						

*p < .10; **p < .05; ***p < .01.

a. All estimates are weighted to ensure results representative of the U.S. population. A blank cell indicates variable not included in the model.

b. Constant: −3.03 (.27)***; N = 5907; Wald χ^2 = 453.72***; pseudo R^2 = .09.

c. Cur 1: −.46 (.20); cur 2: −.52 (.20); cur 3: 1.66 (.20); N = 7101; Wald χ^2 = 342.54***; pseudo R^2 = .03.

d. Cur 1: .91 (.47); cur 2: 2.1 (.47); N = 3784; Wald χ^2 = 139.19***; pseudo R^2 = .05.

e. Cur 1: 4.2 (.35); cur 2: 5.0 (.35); cur 3: 5.6 (.35); cur 4: 6.2 (.36); cur 5: 6.9 (.36); N = 3784; Wald χ^2 = 215.17***; pseudo R^2 = .05.

f. Cur 1: 1.12 (.39); cur 2: 2.6 (.39); N = 3784; Wald χ^2 = 937.86***; pseudo R^2 = .11.

g. Constant: −2.4 (.44)***; N = 3784; Wald χ^2 = 174.85***; pseudo R^2 = .06.

h. Constant: −.68 (.50)***; N = 3784; Wald χ^2 = 69.35***; pseudo R^2 = .04.

13

Private Schooling and Political Tolerance

PATRICK J. WOLF, JAY P. GREENE,
BRETT KLEITZ, AND KRISTINA THALHAMMER

Political tolerance, defined as the willingness to extend constitutionally protected rights and legal protections to groups and individuals whom one personally dislikes, has been an important civic value in the United States since its founding.[1] Although the country has not always lived up to its aspiration to operate as a fully tolerant society, political tolerance has remained a central aspect of the American creed. Scholars in the fields of political ideology, public opinion, and political psychology have carefully studied the causes and consequences of political tolerance levels. Much is already understood about the factors that influence the levels of political tolerance in mature adults, yet little is known about the factors that affect political tolerance in the formative years of adolescence and young adulthood.

In particular, it has not been determined if students' tolerance levels vary based on the school sector in which they receive their elementary and secondary education. This gap in understanding of political tolerance is an oddity, because the effects of private education on educational outcomes have been thoroughly studied and the earliest public school systems in the United States were established for the express purpose of molding children into responsible citizens. Whether or not public schools do a better job than private schools of inculcating civic values such as political tolerance in their students is an important and unresolved question.

In this chapter we present the results of an empirical test of the commonly held assumption that public schools outperform private schools in promoting the civic values of their students.[2] Using data from a survey of 1,212 college students in Texas, most of whom were fresh from their various K–12 educational experiences, and standard regression analysis techniques, we demonstrate that the levels of political tolerance of students who were educated in private schools tend to be higher than the tolerance levels of comparable students who were educated in public schools.[3] Surprisingly, the positive effect of private schooling on political tolerance is roughly similar for both secular and religious private schools. Although more extensive research will be required to establish conclusively that private schooling has a positive effect on political tolerance, at a minimum these results call into question the assumption that public schools are necessarily more effective at instilling civic values in young Americans.

Political Tolerance as an Important Civic Value

What values need to be embraced by a broad swath of the citizenry for a democratic republic such as the United States to function properly? A complete treatment of that momentous and disputatious question cannot be undertaken here. However, political tolerance is clearly a civic value vital to an effective democracy. To ensure that patriotism or nationalism does not engender repressiveness toward other people and their political ideas, tolerance for diverse and even extreme opinions is an essential characteristic of democratic citizenship.[4] The importance of political tolerance is manifested by the prominence of the First Amendment freedoms of speech and demonstration in U.S. political, social, and judicial history. This crucial civic value is best captured by Voltaire's declaration: "I disapprove of what you say, but I'll defend to the death your right to say it."[5]

Political tolerance is not the only important civic value in a democratic republic. Patriotism, political participation, support for majority rule (within limits), due process protections, and voluntarism are also central civic values worthy of study. We are examining tolerance because it is a vital civic value that we can measure using a single survey research instrument with well-established reliability. The extent to which, and the conditions under which, students from different types of educational backgrounds support majority rule and due process and participate in both politics and community service are similarly important concerns. However, they are not the focus of this study.

The Importance of Schools for Inculcating Civic Values

While schools are not the only source of citizenship education—they compete with homes, churches, workplaces, and media outlets—they have long been a primary institution for shaping the values of future citizens.[6] Given the current obsession with using standardized test scores to evaluate how well America's schools are performing, it may seem surprising that, from the nation's founding through World War II, the most important function of elementary and secondary schools was to prepare students for their responsibilities as citizens. Many founders of the American republic recognized that their revolutionary experiment with representative government required a citizenry that was sufficiently educated and informed to make responsible decisions in elections. Shortly after authoring the Declaration of Independence, Thomas Jefferson directed his attention to creating a publicly financed education system that would help to ensure the development of individuals capable of protecting liberty and responsibly managing self-government.[7] Jefferson's contemporary, Benjamin Rush of Pennsylvania, undertook a similar project manifested in his "Plan for the Establishment of Public Schools."[8]

This drive to impart civic values to American youth continued and intensified throughout the nineteenth century. Although political disagreements arose regarding which civic values were most important, a strong consensus existed that schools bore the fundamental responsibilities for preparing their charges for citizenship. Rogers M. Smith writes that, during the early part of that century, "education came to be so identified with preparation for citizenship that noncitizens [sic] were often denied it."[9] Horace Mann, founder of the first truly public school system in the United States during the 1830s, justified his proposal that government establish and operate "common schools" by claiming that it would enhance civic values, particularly in the children of Catholic immigrants.[10]

The emphasis on teaching civic values and transforming immigrants into true "Americans" (and Catholics into Protestants) was disconcertingly dramatic and Anglo-centric during the first 150 years of the republic. Nevertheless, the importance placed on the role of elementary and secondary schools in producing responsible democratic citizens throughout U.S. history is undeniable. The dawn of the information age during the latter half of the twentieth century has led to a greater emphasis on the duty of schools to impart educational skills and scholastic knowledge to their students. Yet many contemporary education researchers maintain that the role of schools in imparting values, including civic values, should and does remain important.[11] However, the question is: What sort of schools—public, private secular, or private religious—best instill civic values in their students?

Civic Values and Public Versus Private Schools

At first blush it might seem obvious that public schools are better positioned than their private counterparts to instill civic values such as political tolerance in their students. After all, they are public—fully financed and operated by the government. As state-run institutions, insulated from the consumer mentality of markets, public schools should be particularly adept at inculcating civic values in their students.[12] The melting-pot function of mixing children from diverse economic, social, racial, and religious backgrounds, central to the common school vision in theory though not always in practice, should be particularly conducive to promoting the tolerance of diverse lifestyles and political ideas.[13] From the establishment of the first public school systems in America, "public education was to be republican civic education."[14] In theory and based on popular notions of the public school as the diverse melting pot for forging American citizens, public schools should outperform private schools in imparting civic values to their students.

To date few empirical studies have been published of the relative effectiveness of public versus private schools in promoting civic values.[15] Several champions of public schooling warn that an expansion of voucher programs to permit more public school students to attend private schools would precipitate a decline in racial integration and the civic values of students.[16] Yet their warnings are based on the unproven assumptions that public schools are more diverse than private schools and are more effective in imparting civic values to their students. Exactly which educational sector does a better job in promoting civic values remains an open question. Whatever hopes may be harbored for public schools, firm evidence is needed about the reality of how they compare with private schools in promoting civic values such as political tolerance. This study is an initial effort to provide an empirical description of the effect of private versus public schooling on political tolerance.

Methodology

To analyze the impact of private schooling on political tolerance, the tools of survey research and multivariate regression were employed. Such techniques possess certain shortcomings when applied to questions of educational impacts. Yet we think that they provide a solid initial glimpse at the general effect that private schools have on the willingness of students to tolerate distasteful political groups.

Data

A survey was administered to 1,212 students in the fall of 1997 at four universities in Texas. The survey was completed in required introductory courses on American government at the University of Texas—Austin, the University of North Texas, the University of Houston, and Texas Christian University.

While the institutions were not selected at random and while Texas college students do not constitute a representative sample of young people, good reasons exist to accept the reliability of this research approach. First, by using required introductory courses as the target population, we almost certainly obtained a representative sample of students at these colleges and universities who are little removed from the impact of their public or private elementary and secondary school experiences. Second, by restricting our analysis to Texas colleges, we have stacked the deck in favor of confirming a public school advantage in promoting political tolerance. Texas private schools, especially those affiliated with a particular religion, are reputed to be places of intolerance, whereas we would expect Texas public schools to fit closely the ideal of the common school as a melting pot of ethnically diverse children to be forged into responsible citizens. If the reputations of Texas private and public schools are to be believed, our focus on college students in the Lone Star State biases our study in favor of public schools.[17]

The anonymous survey (available from the authors by request) consisted of a series of questions regarding the students' tolerance of extremist political groups, educational experiences, and attitudinal and demographic characteristics that previous research has indicated predicts levels of political tolerance.[18] Following the approach pioneered by John L. Sullivan and his colleagues, our conceptualization of political tolerance requires that individuals be willing to extend "the full legal rights of citizenship to groups they themselves dislike" and convey "a willingness to permit the expression of ideas or interests" that they oppose.[19]

First, respondents selected the political group that they least liked from a list of groups from across the political ideology spectrum. The results of their choices appear in table 13-1. The Ku Klux Klan (KKK) was the most commonly selected least-liked group, chosen by nearly 60 percent of respondents. Almost 20 percent of the sample said that American Nazis were their least-liked group. The Religious Right was cited as the least-liked group of nearly 6 percent of respondents. None of the other nine political groups was selected as the least-liked group by more than 3 percent of the students in the sample.

Table 13-1. *Least-Liked Group Selections*

Group	Percentage
Ku Klux Klan	59.2
American Nazis	18.7
Religious Right	5.7
Gay activists	3.0
Pro-life on abortion	2.8
Pro-choice on abortion	2.7
Atheists	2.4
Feminists	1.3
Militia groups	1.2
Nation of Islam	1.2
American Communists	1.2
Environmentalists	0.3

The selections of least-liked groups by the respondents gave us confidence in the appropriateness of our sample. George E. Marcus and his colleagues' recent study of political tolerance in adults similarly found that a majority of respondents consider the KKK or "American racists" to be their least-liked political group, followed by American Nazis.[20] In addition, we expected few college students, ripe with social idealism, to select liberal political groups such as environmentalists, feminists, or gay activists as prime targets of their abhorrence. The choices of our respondents confirmed those expectations.

After they had selected their least-liked group, respondents then answered a series of questions regarding their willingness to permit legal or constitutionally guaranteed activities by their least-liked group (see table 13-2). The students were least likely to allow the government to tap the phones of their least-liked group (possibly because they would not want their parents to get any similar ideas), as over 60 percent of respondents agreed or strongly agreed that a prohibition against government wiretapping was proper. Clear majorities of students also were willing to permit members of their least-liked group to make a public speech or hold a public rally. Near majorities of respondents said that their least-liked group should not be outlawed and should be allowed to run for public office. The students were least tolerant of permitting members of their least-liked group to teach in the public schools, as only 17 percent of respondents agreed or strongly agreed with that proposition. The answers to all six hypothetical questions were averaged to produce a tolerance scale score for each respondent. The scale demonstrated a high level of reliability, with a Cronbach's α of .83. The distribution of tolerance

Table 13-2. *The Tolerance Scale*[a]

Percent

	Response (value assigned to each answer)				
Statement	Strongly disagree (1)	Disagree (2)	No opinion (3)	Agree (4)	Strongly agree (5)
1. The government should not be able to tap the phones of members of your least-liked group.	7.1	13.8	17.3	23.6	38.2
2. Members of your least-liked group should be allowed to teach in public schools.	56.1	17.5	9.4	9.0	8.0
3. The group you least like should not be outlawed.	27.7	13.2	11.0	21.2	26.9
4. Members of your least-liked group should be allowed to make a public speech.	13.5	12.5	12.8	29.3	31.9
5. Members of your least-liked group should be able to run for president or other elected office.	31.3	12.7	10.4	16.5	29.1
6. Members of the group you like least should be allowed to hold public demonstrations or rallies.	21.0	13.3	11.3	27.7	26.8

a. Figures reported represent the percentages of valid responses within each category. Cronbach's $\alpha = .83$; valid $N = 1,212$; mean = 3.09; standard deviation = 1.07; minimum = 1.00; and maximum = 5.00.

scale scores was approximately continuous and approximately normal, which allowed us to use ordinary least squares (OLS) estimation in the subsequent analysis.

The primary independent variable of interest in the analysis was the sector in which the student received his or her elementary and secondary school education. Respondents were asked what type of school they attended (public, private nonaffiliated, private religiously affiliated) most of the time during three distinct periods: kindergarten through fifth grade (elementary school), sixth through eighth grade (junior high school), and ninth through twelfth grade (high school). Based on those responses, the educational experiences of the students were categorized as described in the appendix. First, scale scores for extent of private education and extent of private secular and private religious education were calculated for each respondent. Second, to test whether or not the effect of the treatment of private education was smooth—that is, consistent across values on the scale—we disaggregated the scale scores into a series of distinct dummy variables to measure the relative effect of each amount of treatment on levels of political tolerance. Because subsequent analysis revealed similar effects for the treatments "all private" and "mostly private," and their secular and religious corollaries, those categories were combined to form the variables "majority private," "majority secular," and "majority religious."

Missing data among the variables were a minor problem. The deletion of observations lacking data for one or more variables in the regression estimations excluded about 20 percent of the data. A secondary analysis of the observations that contained missing data indicated that they were similar to the included data in all relevant respects. After excluding the observations with missing data, a representative sample of nearly 1,000 student responses remained—a sufficient sample to reach preliminary conclusions about the effects of schools on civic values such as political tolerance.

The Models

Our goal is to determine the independent effect that different amounts and types of private schooling have on the civic values of young adults. Thus we estimate the effects of the treatment variables on the political tolerance dependent variable while simultaneously controlling for the effects of demographic and attitudinal variables that otherwise might confound the analysis. The operational definition of the treatment variables was varied to measure the following effects on political tolerance: (1) the overall effect of private schooling, (2) the separate effects of different amounts of private schooling, (3) the effects of a majority of private schooling versus only some private schooling, (4) the effects of private secular schooling versus private religious schooling, (5) the effects of different amounts of private secular and private religious schooling, and (6) the effects of a majority and some private secular schooling compared with a majority and some private religious schooling. The control variables for the models consist of demographic and attitudinal variables that previous research and theory indicate are likely to influence the levels of political tolerance of young adults, including race, gender, age, citizenship, family income, parental education, geography, religion, and political ideology.[21] The models also control for the extent to which each respondent felt personally threatened by their least-liked group and the extent to which average tolerance levels differed among the various campuses.

We seek to determine if the effects of private schooling on civic values vary based on the extent of exposure to the treatment and the distinct form that the treatment takes—that is, secular versus religious private education. Based on the conventional view that public schools possess an advantage relative to private schools regarding the inculcation of civic values such as tolerance, our working hypotheses are:

HYPOTHESIS I. Exposure to the treatment of private education has a negative effect on tolerance.

HYPOTHESIS 2. More extensive exposure to the treatment of private education has a greater negative effect on tolerance than less extensive exposure.

HYPOTHESIS 3. Exposure to the treatment of private religious education has a greater negative effect on tolerance than exposure to private secular education.[22]

Results

The three hypotheses were tested by estimating statistical models using OLS regression. First, we consider the effects of various amounts of private schooling on levels of political tolerance. Hypothesis 1 predicts that private schooling will have a significant negative effect on the willingness of students to grant civil liberties to distasteful political groups. Model 1 in table 13-3 provides an initial test of that hypothesis. The results of the Model 1 estimation are not consistent with the hypothesis of a public school advantage regarding political tolerance. The treatment variable "extent of private education" has a positive coefficient of .096. Although this effect is substantively small, amounting to less than one-tenth of a standard deviation on the tolerance scale, it is statistically significant beyond even the highest commonly used threshold of $p < .01$. The data speak clearly here: Students with more private education are more politically tolerant, all else being equal. Hypothesis 1, that private education will be associated with lower levels of political tolerance, is disconfirmed.

Models 2 and 3 in table 13-3 test Hypothesis 2, that more extensive exposure to the treatment of private schooling will be associated with lower levels of tolerance. We find that the opposite is true: More extensive exposure to private education is associated with even higher levels of tolerance. Students who received all of their prior education in private schools, on average, exhibit tolerance levels nearly four-tenths of a point higher than comparable public school students. The positive effect of an all-private education on political tolerance amounts to an increase of more than one-third of a standard deviation on the tolerance scale and is statistically significant beyond the $p < .01$ confidence level. Students who received most but not all of their education in private schools exhibit a tolerance advantage of almost one-sixth of a standard deviation, although the effect is statistically indistinguishable from zero. The effect of some private education on tolerance also is not statistically significant. In Model 3, by combining the "all private" and "mostly private" categories into the "majority private" classification, we generate an estimate of the private school tolerance advantage of .278, which is statistically significant beyond the p < .01 level. The data indicate the opposite of Hypothesis 2: Higher amounts of private schooling are associated with higher levels of political tolerance, all else being equal.

Do private religious schools in particular foster intolerance, as is predicted by Hypothesis 3? The data in table 13-4 describe the results of the statistical tests of the assumption of religious school intolerance. The Model 1 estimation compares the effect of the extent of secular private education with the effect of the extent of religious education on levels of tolerance. Both types of schools tend to have a positive effect on tolerance, although the religious schooling effect is not statistically significant. The coefficient for the effect of the extent of private secular education on tolerance of .109 is larger and more precise than, but not statistically distinguishable from, the coefficient for the positive effect of private religious education on tolerance of .079. These results do not confirm the hypothesis that private religious schools promote greater intolerance than private secular schools. Exposure to either type of private schooling appears to produce greater tolerance than public schooling, although we can only be confident of the general positive effect of secular schooling on political tolerance.

Models 2 and 3 in table 13-4 provide a more fine-grained test of the hypothesis that religious schools are a source of political intolerance. With the exception of "some secular private education," all of the treatment variables indicate a positive association between the various types and extent of private schooling and political tolerance. However, only the coefficients measuring the positive effects of "all secular private," "majority secular private," and "all religious private" education on political tolerance are statistically significant. Students whose previous education took place exclusively in private secular schools exhibited levels of political tolerance nearly half a point higher than comparable students whose schooling took place exclusively in public schools. This positive effect of all private secular schooling amounts to an average gain of more than one-third of a standard deviation on the tolerance scale. The positive effect of experiencing a majority of one's education in private secular schools was only slightly smaller, amounting to one-third of a standard deviation on the tolerance scale. Education exclusively in private religious schools contributed one-third of a point to students' tolerance scores, an effect of nearly one-third of a standard deviation.

Table 13-3. *Effect of Private Schooling on Political Tolerance*[a]

Variable (range)	Model 1	Model 2	Model 3
Treatment			
Extent of private education (0–3)	.096***		
	(.01)		
All private education (0,1)		.372***	
		(.01)	
Mostly private education (0,1)		.164	
		(.25)	
Majority private education (0,1)			.278***
			(.01)
Some private education (0,1)		−.041	−.041
		(.65)	(.65)
Demographic controls			
Age (17–64)	.027***	.027***	.027***
	(.01)	(.01)	(.01)
Freshman (0,1)	−.260***	−.262***	−.258***
	(.00)	(.00)	(.00)
U.S. citizen (0,1)	.288	.272	.281
	(.17)	(.19)	(.18)
Female (0,1)	−.339***	−.339***	−.334***
	(.00)	(.00)	(.00)
African American (0,1)	−.514***	−.526***	−.520***
	(.00)	(.00)	(.00)
Asian (0,1)	−.419***	−.422***	−.428***
	(.00)	(.00)	(.00)
Hispanic (0,1)	−.149	−.148	−.149
	(.15)	(.16)	(.15)
Native American (0,1)	.411*	.399*	.414*
	(.07)	(.08)	(.06)
Father's education (1–6)	.146***	.149***	.147***
	(.00)	(.00)	(.00)
Mother's education (1–6)	.017	.016	.016
	(.61)	(.63)	(.62)
Income (1–8)	−.043**	−.043**	−.042**
	(.01)	(.01)	(.01)
Intact family (0,1)	.080	.075	.075
	(.29)	(.32)	(.32)
Siblings (0–10)	.039	.040	.040
	(.12)	(.11)	(.11)
Suburban high school (0,1)	.133**	.129**	.131**
	(.04)	(.05)	(.05)
Southern high school (0,1)	−.008	−.009	−.004
	(.91)	(.90)	(.96)

continued on next page

Table 13-3. *Effect of Private Schooling on Political Tolerance*[a] *(continued)*

Variable (range)	Model 1	Model 2	Model 3
Attitudinal and ideological controls			
Jewish (0,1)	−.739***	−.732***	−.723***
	(.00)	(.00)	(.01)
Catholic or Orthodox (0,1)	−.512***	−.524***	−.516***
	(.00)	(.00)	(.00)
Mainline Protestant (0,1)	−.438***	−.443***	−.442***
	(.00)	(.00)	(.00)
Evangelical or fundamentalist (0,1)	−.410***	−.416***	−.416***
	(.00)	(.00)	(.00)
Other religion (0,1)	.015	.007	.017
	(.94)	(.97)	(.93)
Religion unimportant (0,1)	−.040	−.043	−.039
	(.70)	(.67)	(.70)
Liberal political ideology (1–10)	.051***	.051***	.052***
	(.01)	(.01)	(.00)
Identify or lean Democratic (0,1)	.140*	.139*	.134*
	(.07)	(.07)	(.09)
Registered to vote (0,1)	.161*	.152*	.148
	(.08)	(.10)	(.11)
Seriousness of threat (1–7)	−.315***	−.313***	−.313***
	(.00)	(.00)	(.00)
Fixed effects and constant			
University of Texas (0,1)	.285**	.299**	.288**
	(.02)	(.01)	(.01)
University of Houston (0,1)	.228	.249*	.236*
	(.11)	(.08)	(.10)
University of North Texas (0,1)	.137	.153	.141
	(.25)	(.20)	(.23)
Constant	3.460***	3.478***	3.466***
	(.00)	(.00)	(.00)
R^2	.31	.31	.31
F-statistic	14.16***	13.36***	13.76***
	(.00)	(.00)	(.00)
N	962	962	962

*p < .1; **p < .05; ***p < .01.

a. Figures are unstandardized regression coefficients with p values (in parentheses) based on a two-tailed test. For the estimation of fixed effects due to college attended, Texas Christian University was the omitted reference category.

Table 13-4. *Effect of Secular and Religious Private Schooling on Political Tolerance*[a]

Variables (range)	Model 1	Model 2	Model 3
Extent of private secular education (0–3)	.109**		
	(.03)		
Extent of private religious education (0–3)	.079		
	(.13)		
All secular private education (0,1)		.452**	
		(.02)	
Mostly secular private education (0,1)		.269	
		(.13)	
Majority secular private education (0,1)			.351***
			(.01)
Some secular private education (0,1)		−.080	−.092
		(.47)	(.41)
All religious private education (0,1)		.333*	
		(.09)	
Mostly religious private education (0,1)		.051	
		(.80)	
Majority religious private education (0,1)			.196
			(.17)
Some religious private education (0,1)		.048	.044
		(.71)	(.73)
R^2	.31	.31	.31
F-statistic	13.59***	12.13***	12.85***
	(.00)	(.00)	(.00)
N	958	958	958

*p < .1; **p < .05; ***p < .01.
a. Control variables included were the same as in the table 13-3 models, with identical effects. Figures are unstandardized regression coefficients with p values (in parentheses) based on a two-tailed test.

All three of these effects are substantively large by the standards of education research.

Hypothesis 3 is largely disconfirmed by the data. The effect of religious schooling on political tolerance is positive and statistically significant at least at the modest threshold of p < .10 for the students who received all of their education in religious schools. And the size of the effect is not markedly different from the size of the effect for students who received all of their education in private secular schools. A significant amount of exposure to either private secular or private religious schools appears to increase the political tolerance of college students in Texas.

Discussion

How reliable are these surprising results regarding the effects of private schooling on political tolerance? When we examine the regression models in toto, we find reasons to suspect that these school sector effects are accurate. The control variables used in the model are drawn primarily from the richly developed empirical literature on political tolerance. As a result, the statistical models are well specified. About 30 percent of the variance in tolerance levels is explained by the models, and nearly all of the control variables are statistically significant with the expected signs. Those students who are older, non-freshmen, male, white, offspring of well-educated fathers, graduates of suburban high schools, not affiliated with one of the major religions in the United States, liberal in their political ideology, Democrats, registered to vote, and less threatened by their least-liked group tend to be more politically tolerant than students who are differently situated. These results are consistent with previous studies of tolerance in adults.[23]

The major surprises in the results are the negative effect of family income and the positive effect of private schooling, both secular and religious, on political tolerance. The small negative effect of family income on political tolerance may signal that young adults from more prosperous families are somewhat less likely to tolerate extremist groups and the social disruptions that such groups can cause. We uncover such an effect for the first time possibly because our eight-point income scale is more fine-grained than the three-point scale used by previous researchers.[24]

But why would college students who were educated in private schools be more politically tolerant than similarly situated undergraduates with public school backgrounds? First, we must rule out sample selection bias as the reason for the apparent private school tolerance advantage. There are at least three reasons to doubt that selection bias explains the private school advantage in promoting political tolerance identified by our analysis. First, our models control for elite background characteristics, such as income, parental education, and suburban schooling that might otherwise confound our analysis of the effect of private schooling itself on political tolerance. In building our statistical model, we found that the positive effect of private schooling on political tolerance grew in size and statistical significance as we controlled for more background factors. This development strongly suggests that the private schooling variables are capturing an actual positive effect of the private school experience on political tolerance, net of the background characteristics of the students.

Second, our respondents are all college students. Enrollment in college levels the playing field, at least somewhat, in the sense that it requires a certain amount of academic achievement and at least some financial sacrifice from all students and their families, whether their previous schooling was public or private. Unmeasured parental educational values, the most commonly cited source of selection bias in educational achievement studies, are likely to be more similar in the public and private school students in our college sample then they would be in a sample of current public and private elementary or secondary school students. Granted, students from families that do not view education as valuable are far less likely to attend private school. However, students from such families also are less likely to attend college and thus be in a position to drag down the numbers of the publicly schooled group in our sample. Because the overwhelming majority of privately schooled students go on to college, our sampling method most likely compares a group of more successful public school students with a group of average private school students, thus mitigating at least somewhat the problem of selection bias that might explain the private school advantage over public schools in elementary and high school academic achievement studies.

Third, surveys of parents in various school choice experiments indicate that civic values are not even a consideration, much less an important one, in parental decisions to enroll students in private schools. In surveys of choice parents in Cleveland, Ohio; New York City; Massachusetts; Dayton, Ohio; and Washington, D.C., academic concerns dominated the list of important factors in choosing a private or public school that was not the family's neighborhood school. Considerations of values such as political tolerance or civic responsibility were not among the thirteen most common reasons for school selection given by parents.[25] The evidence argues against the dubious claim that the private school advantage in producing tolerant young adults is merely because parents who strongly value political tolerance are more motivated to send their children to private schools than parents who only weakly value political tolerance. Moreover, scholars who criticize voucher programs by warning that private schools are magnates for intolerance cannot then argue that graduates of private schools are more politically tolerant because legions of civic minded students are drawn to such private schools.[26]

If the positive effect of private schooling on political tolerance is not an artifact of statistical bias, then what might explain such an unexpected result? In spite of the commonly held assumption that public schools are the ideal place to foster civic values, there are reasons to expect that private schools might be as good as or even better than public schools at inculcating values such as political tolerance. First, many public school systems have not lived up to their aspirations to be bastions of social and racial diversity. Efforts at mixing students of different races and social classes in public schools have been confounded by white and wealthier families migrating to suburban school districts.[27] Even within public school districts, the prevalence of assignment to schools based on segregated housing patterns and then the further segregating effect of academic tracking and race-based social cliques have hindered integration in public schools.[28] A recent Harvard study determined that 69 percent of black students and 75 percent of Hispanic students in public school systems attend schools that are "predominantly minority."[29] In New York City, supposedly the greatest melting pot in America, over two-thirds of the 235 public junior high schools are racially segregated, with racial minorities constituting over 90 percent of the student body. Twenty-seven percent of the junior high schools consist of greater than 98 percent racial minorities and nearly 5 percent do not have a single white student enrolled.[30] The empirical research that addresses the question of race and modern American schools suggests that privately operated schools, perhaps because their students freely choose to attend them and the schools are not bound by racially segregated housing patterns, are better able to promote positive race relations and integration than are publicly operated schools.[31] This environment of better racial integration and less racial tension may explain the private school advantage in producing tolerant citizens.

Second, private schools may exceed public schools in imparting civic values because of a greater overall emphasis on values. Studies of the effect of social science curricula on students' levels of political tolerance indicate that civic values are difficult to impart in the classroom.[32] A curriculum must be specifically tailored to address questions of intolerance toward particular disliked groups to generate an appreciable increase in political tolerance.[33] Quentin L. Quade argues that the legal and political restrictions commonly placed on public schools because of their publicness tend to diminish the extent to which values of any kind are discussed openly there.[34] Denis P. Doyle claims that the stress on character formation at private religious schools naturally brings with it an emphasis on civic values such as tolerance and respect for others.[35] With clear advantages over public schools in promoting moral and religious values, many—though certainly not all—private schools may also be particularly well suited to instill civic values in their students.

Third, characteristics of private schools that increase the academic performance of their students relative to comparable public school students might also enhance the civic values of their charges. Elements of the school environment including interactive teaching, the free exchange of student opinions, and student involvement in decisionmaking have been linked to higher levels of civic values.[36] The dearth of these practices in many public schools might explain the private school advantage in promoting civic values.[37] Our data provide some support for this explanation, as the tolerance scale question "Should members of your least-liked group be allowed to teach in the public schools?" provoked the least tolerant response, with more than 73 percent of the students surveyed opposing such a policy, 56 percent of them "strongly." An overwhelming majority of our respondents took the position that public schools are no place for teachers who might freely exchange their controversial political views.

Finally, the bureaucratic structure common to public schools—cited by researchers such as John E. Chubb and Terry M. Moe as the reason that private schools outperform public schools in imparting academic skills to their students—might explain the private school advantage in instilling political tolerance in its graduates.[38] Abraham K. Korman, in a review of workplace studies, found that adults who work in environments that stress hierarchical control tend to be less politically tolerant than adults who work in organizations that acknowledge ambiguity and encourage self-control.[39] Although we hesitate to infer that the effects of workplace characteristics on tolerance necessarily hold for students in educational environments, Korman's findings do offer a possible theoretical explanation for our unexpected empirical results.

While the finding that private schools promote tolerance is at odds with conventional wisdom, it is consistent with the limited amount of empirical work that has examined this issue. For example, Jay P. Greene and his colleagues examined a national survey of adult Latinos and found that, even after controlling for a variety of background characteristics, those Latinos who had received more private schooling were more tolerant of the political activities of their least-liked group.[40] Ken Godwin and his colleagues found a similar higher level of political tolerance among New York and Texas students currently enrolled in private junior high schools relative to their comparable peers currently enrolled in public junior high schools.[41] The finding that private education is associated with greater political tolerance may be surprising to many, but the few researchers who have examined this issue empirically have all identified this same result.

Our results reflect surprisingly well on the performance of private schools in promoting the essential civic value of political tolerance. College students in Texas who received a majority of their elementary and secondary education in secular or religious private schools produced an average tolerance score more than one-fourth of a standard deviation higher than comparable students of public schooling, an effect size that education researchers commonly describe as "considerable" or "large."[42] A stronger values component, less racial tension, a greater feeling of belonging, the more frequent use of interactive teaching methods, the freer exchange of ideas, and less hierarchy in private schools all are viable explanations for private schools' apparent tolerance advantage over public schools. A panel data study, preferably with random assignment of students to the various types of schools, would be required to identify the exact causal mechanism and definitively prove the tolerance advantage of private schools. Nevertheless, our results are highly suggestive that policymakers need not fear that private schooling—whether secular or religious—threatens civic values. Moreover, the assumption should not be made that public schooling necessarily promotes such values.

Conclusion

Much research has been conducted regarding the civic values of adults, especially their willingness to tolerate the legal activities of unpopular political groups. Even more scholarship has focused on whether or not private schools do a better job than public schools in preparing students to perform well academically. However, to date, few empirical studies have considered the effects of private versus public education on civic values such as political tolerance. A long tradition of educational and political thinkers, from Horace Mann to Benjamin Barber, has claimed that public schools ought to be a superior forum for preparing young people to assume their citizenship duties. Their assumptions about a public school advantage in inculcating civic values have been challenged, most recently by advocates of education vouchers, but have yet to be thoroughly tested empirically.

This initial study of the effects of schooling in different sectors on the political tolerance of Texas college students suggests that the assumption of a public school advantage in this area is undeserved. College students who received most of their prior education in private schools demonstrate higher levels of political tolerance than comparable publicly educated students exhibit. The precise source of the private school advantage regarding tolerance is uncertain. However, given the outcome under study (political tolerance) and the many study controls, the private school tolerance advantage is unlikely to be merely a selection effect. Apparently, something about the environment, curriculum, or pedagogy of private schools leads them to outperform public schools in promoting political tolerance in their graduates.

Our surprising results regarding the positive effect of private schooling on the political tolerance of college students may have been presaged by none other than Dr. Frank Macchiarola, former chancellor of New York City Public Schools. Macchiarola has been quoted as saying of private schools: "They promote tolerance in their curricula; they lead children to understand the importance of moral codes; and they contribute to the great diversity in this nation that has made it great."[43] As a result of our analysis, we agree with Macchiarola that, while more should be expected from public schools, society should be less fearful of private schools when it comes to instilling civic values in the next generation of American citizens.

Notes

1. The authors are especially grateful to Sandra Wood, who collaborated with us in the development of our research design and survey instrument and administered the survey at the University of North Texas. We thank Valerie Martinez for administering the survey at Texas Christian University and Kevin Hula for advising us regarding the coding of the religion variables. This paper was markedly improved based on comments on a previous draft made by Jeffrey Berry, John E. Brandl, Frederick Hess, Paul E. Peterson, and Kay Schlozman. We claim ownership of the remaining flaws.

2. Horace Mann, *The Republic and the School,* ed. Lawrence A. Cremin (New York: Teachers College Press, 1957 [1837]); John Dewey, *Democracy and Education* (Macmillan, 1963 [1916]); Amy Gutmann, *Democratic Education* (Princeton University Press, 1987); Benjamin Barber, *An Aristocracy for Everyone* (Ballantine Books, 1992); Peter W. Cookson, *School Choice* (Yale University Press, 1994); and Henry M. Levin, "Educational Vouchers: Effectiveness, Choice, and Costs," *Journal of Policy Analysis and Management,* vol. 17 (1998), pp. 373–92.

3. Our preliminary analysis indicated that when we limited the observations to just freshmen and sophomores, or just respondents under the age of twenty, the positive effects of private schooling on political tolerance are even stronger than the results that we report here. However, in the interest of scholarly conservatism and the desire to learn from as much evidence as possible, we decided not to restrict our analysis to the respondents for whom the treatment is most fresh in their minds.

4. Gutmann, *Democratic Education,* pp. 5, 14; Dewey, *Democracy and Education,* p. 93; and Levin, "Educational Vouchers," pp. 373–92.

5. As quoted in Evelyn Beatrice Hall, "The Friends of Voltaire," in Jay Antony, ed., *Oxford Dictionary of Political Quotations* (Oxford, England: Oxford University Press, 1996), p. 76.

6. Bernard Bailyn, *Education in the Forming of American Society: Needs and Opportunities for Study* (University of North Carolina Press, 1960); and Carl F. Kaestle, *Literacy in the United States: Readers and Reading since 1880* (Yale University Press, 1991).

7. Richard Hofstadter and Wilson Smith, *American Higher Education: A Documentary History* (University of Chicago Press, 1968).

8. Frederick Rudolph, ed., *Essays on Education in the Early Republic* (Harvard University Press, 1965).

9. Rogers M. Smith, *Civic Ideals: Conflicting Visions of Citizenship in U.S. History* (Yale University Press, 1997), p. 189.

10. Paul E. Peterson, *The Politics of School Reform, 1870–1940* (University of Chicago Press, 1985); Charles Leslie Glenn, *The Myth of the Common School* (University of Massachusetts Press, 1988), p. 83; and Smith, *Civil Ideals*, p. 217.

11. See, for example, John Meyer, "Citizenship Development and Education: An Imperative," *International Journal of Social Education*, vol. 11 (1996–97): p. 1; Denis P. Doyle, "School Vouchers Provide Justice for the Poor," *Center for Urban Policy Research Report*, vol. 8 (1997), pp. 3, 5; and Levin, "Educational Vouchers," p. 374.

12. Gutmann, *Democratic Education*, pp. 117–18; and Benjamin R. Barber, *A Place for Us* (New York: Hill and Wang, 1998), pp. 72–73.

13. Mann, *The Republic and the School*, p. 33; Dewey, *Democracy and Education*, p. 21; Cookson, *School Choice*; and Levin, "Educational Vouchers."

14. Smith, *Civil Ideals*, p. 217.

15. An exception is Jay P. Greene, Joseph Giammo, and Nicole Mellow, "The Effect of Private Education on Political Participation, Social Capital, and Tolerance: An Examination of the Latino National Political Survey," *Georgetown Public Policy Review*, vol. 5 (1999), pp. 53–71.

16. Cookson, *School Choice*; and Levin, "Educational Vouchers."

17. We administered mail surveys at two colleges outside of Texas, because their introductory courses were too small to serve as venues for administering the survey in the classroom. Given that the response rates for the mail surveys were unacceptably low, around 20 percent, and the different survey protocol correlated perfectly with the factor "student at a college outside of Texas," we decided to exclude those non-Texas observations from the analysis. However, their inclusion did not alter our results significantly, suggesting, though not demonstrating conclusively, that a nationally representative sample of college students would generate similar results to those that we uncover in Texas.

18. John L. Sullivan, James Piereson, and George Marcus, *Political Tolerance and American Democracy* (University of Chicago Press, 1982); and George E. Marcus, John L. Sullivan, Elizabeth Theiss-Morse, and Sandra L. Wood, *With Malice toward Some* (Cambridge, England: Cambridge University Press, 1995).

19. Sullivan, Piereson, and Marcus, *Political Tolerance and American Democracy*, pp. 2, 76.

20. Marcus and others, *With Malice toward Some*, p. 68.

21. Sullivan, Piereson, and Marcus, *Political Tolerance and American Democracy*; and Marcus and others, *With Malice toward Some*.

22. Barber, *An Aristocracy for Everyone*; Cookson, *School Choice*; and Levin, "Educational Vouchers."

23. Sullivan, Piereson, and Marcus, *Political Tolerance and American Democracy*; and Marcus and others, *With Malice toward Some*.

24. Sullivan, Piereson, and Marcus, *Political Tolerance and American Democracy*; and Marcus and others, *With Malice toward Some*.

25. See the chapters in this volume on the evaluations of private voucher programs in Washington, D.C., and Dayton, Ohio: Jay P. Greene, "The Hidden

Research Consensus for School Choice"; and William G. Howell, Patrick J. Wolf, Paul E. Peterson, and David E. Campbell, "Effects of School Vouchers on Student Test Scores."

26. Barber, *A Place for Us*; Levin, "Educational Vouchers"; and Gutmann, *Democratic Education.*

27. James S. Kunen, "The End of Integration," *Time*, April 29, 1996, pp. 39–45.

28. John E. Chubb and Terry M. Moe, "Politics, Markets, and Equality in Schools," in Michael R. Darby, ed., *Reducing Poverty in America* (Thousand Oaks, Calif.: Sage Publications, 1996), pp. 121–53; Kunen, "The End of Integration"; and Jay P. Greene and Nicole Mellow, "Integration Where It Counts: A Study of Racial Integration in Public and Private School Lunchrooms," paper presented at the annual meeting of the American Political Science Association, Boston, September 3–6, 1998.

29. "Resegregation of Schools Grows," *Washington Post*, June 12, 1999, p. A12.

30. New York City Board of Education, *Annual School Report Data Base* (1996).

31. James S. Coleman, Thomas Hoffer, and Sally Kilgore, *High School Achievement* (Basic Books, 1982); and Jay P. Greene, "Civic Values in Public and Private Schools," in Paul E. Peterson and Bryan C. Hassel, eds., *Learning from School Choice* (Brookings, 1998), pp. 83–106.

32. Kenneth P. Langton and M. Kent Jennings, "Political Socialization and the High School Civics Curriculum in the United States," *American Political Science Review*, vol. 62 (1968), pp. 852–67.

33. Karen Bird, John L. Sullivan, Patricia G. Avery, Kristina Thalhammer, and Sandra Wood, "Not Just Lip-Synching Any More: Education and Tolerance Revisited," *Review of Education/Pedagogy/Cultural Studies*, vol. 16 (1994), pp. 373–86.

34. Quentin L. Quade, *Financing Education: The Struggle between Governmental Monopoly and Parental Control* (New Brunswick, N.J.: Transaction Publishers, 1996).

35. Doyle, "School Vouchers Provide Justice for the Poor," p. 5.

36. Lee H. Ehman, "The American School in the Political Socialization Process," *Review of Educational Research*, vol. 50 (1980), pp. 99–119; and Patrick J. Wolf, Rebecca Blackmon, Christopher Caruso, John Craig, Laura Dupuis, Carlos Fernandez, Jesus Moa, Elizabeth Menendez, Bernard Moon, Ya Ya Mousa, Masane Odaka, Kazuhiko Shigetoku, Ron Sokolov, and Toshihiro Tamura, *Democratic Values in New York City Schools*, Report of the Workshop in Applied Policy Analysis (Columbia University, School of International and Public Affairs, 1998).

37. Gutmann, *Democratic Education*, p. 65.

38. John E. Chubb and Terry M. Moe, *Politics, Markets, and America's Schools* (Brookings, 1990).

39. Abraham K. Korman, *Industrial and Organizational Psychology* (Prentice-Hall, 1971).

40. Greene, Giammo, and Mellow, "The Effect of Private Education on Political Participation, Social Capital, and Tolerance."

41. Ken Godwin, Carrie Ausbrooks, and Valerie Martinez, "Teaching Tolerance in Public and Private Schools," *Phi Delta Kappan* 82 (2001), pp. 543–46. Patrick J.

Wolf participated in the design, data collection, and analysis that is the basis for this article, although he was not listed as a coauthor.

42. Frederick Mosteller, "The Tennessee Study of Class Size in the Early School Grades," *Future of Children,* vol. 5 (1995), pp. 113–27; and John R. Lott Jr., "Public Schooling, Indoctrination, and Totalitarianism," John M. Olin Law and Economics Working Paper Series, 2d, no. 64 (University of Chicago, December 1998).

43. Comments of Dr. Frank Macchiarola at the twenty-sixth annual conference of the New York Collaborative of Public and Nonprofit Schools, as reported in the newsletter of the Council for American Private Education, *CAPE Outlook,* no. 253 (March 2000), p. 2.

Table 13-A1. *Sector of Prior Education Variables*

Treatment scale or dummy variable	Operational definition	Measurement
Measured as scales		*Range*
Private education	Number of periods for which a majority of education was private	0–3
Secular education	Number of periods for which a majority of education was private secular	0–3
Religious education	Number of periods for which a majority of education was private religious	0–3
Measured as categorical dummy variables		*Percent*
All private	Private secular or religious schooling for all three periods	6
Mostly private	Private secular or religious schooling for exactly two of the three periods	5
Majority private	Private secular or religious schooling for two or three of the periods	12
Some private	Private secular or religious schooling for exactly one of the three periods	13
All private secular	Private secular schooling for all three periods	2
Mostly private secular	Private secular schooling for exactly two of the three periods	4
Majority private secular	Private secular schooling for two or three of the periods	6
Some private secular	Private secular schooling for exactly one of the three periods	9
All private religious	Private religious schooling for all three periods	3
Mostly private religious	Private religious schooling for exactly two of the three periods	3
Majority private religious	Private religious schooling for two or three of the periods	5
Some private religious	Private religious schooling for exactly one of the three periods	6
No private (reference)	Private secular or religious schooling for none of the three periods	75

PART 5

Reflections
on the Evidence

14

Reflections on the School Choice Debate

PAUL HILL

The research presented in this volume leads to four observations about what has been learned and what remains to be done.

First, the effort to assess the effects of choice on student learning is paying off. Though die-hard opponents of choice in education will continue to resist evidence that vouchers lead to improved student learning, the middle ground, occupied by fair-minded people who are more interested in results than in preserving the status quo, is won. In the future the burden of proof will be on those who claim that vouchers do not bring about gains for participating students.

Second, without abandoning continued quasi-experimental studies of voucher programs, researchers need to look beneath the averages to understand the sources of variability in student outcomes. What are the attributes of schools in which students are benefiting strongly, as compared with those in which student outcomes are mediocre? What are the attributes of students who benefit most and least? This information is indispensable to the design of future voucher programs and to focusing future supply-side efforts (charter schools, new private schools, and district new-schools initiatives).

Third, opposition will now shift to claims that vouchers and other forms of choice harm students who remain in public schools. Evidence for this assertion is weak, but opponents have found a line of argument that gives them a rhetorical (if not a substantive or moral) advantage. A balanced and rigorous look at the effects of choice programs on children in conventional public schools is needed.

Fourth, the next frontier is to define mechanisms of public oversight that are compatible with choice. Nobody wants the results of choice programs designed to help the poor to lead to public policies that do not accomplish the same ends. Rules governing the use of public funds matter, to ensure both that poor children have equitable access to educational opportunities and that children's time and the public's money are not wasted on ineffective schools. Proponents of choice have natural allies in this search—the supporters of standards-based reform.

The Promise of Vouchers Is Being Demonstrated

Though individual voucher programs (and thus the studies that document their effects) each have some imperfections, the newest results, as reported in this volume, all point in the same direction: Children are benefiting. The chapters by Jay P. Greene and William G. Howell, Patrick J. Wolf, Paul E. Peterson, and David E. Campbell show how the weight of evidence is accumulating. Learning gains, on average, are real, and students are showing the positive effects of the experience of being in schools their parents have chosen—the experience of a more orderly and studious environment, closer family-school ties, more consistent attendance, and (slightly) reduced mobility year to year.[1] Most large voucher programs are too new to demonstrate long-term effects on students' life prospects, but some evidence exists that children participating in the older private voucher programs have greatly enhanced long-term outcomes, including higher level employment and completion of college degrees.

The one exception to these positive findings, concerning middle school-age children in Washington, D.C., demonstrates the need for finer-grained research about what is working in schools. The fact that the study of school choice in Washington, D.C., reported in this volume was able to uncover this anomaly lends credibility to the whole enterprise, showing that the research designs are not just set to capture positive results.

The voucher experience clearly is having positive effects on average, but the results to date are not so spectacular as to convince skeptics. People who distrust the motives of choice advocates, or who staunchly believe that the public's children should be educated in government-run schools, will not change their minds in light of the available evidence. Perhaps they would remove their objections if voucher participation eliminated the correlation between race or income, on one hand, and student achievement, on the other. But this is unlikely to happen using existing schools and with the levels of expenditure possible under current voucher programs.

Neutral and more open-minded skeptics will be impressed with the evidence now available, but even they probably will not be completely convinced. According to recent polls, growing segments of the public, especially African Americans in the big cities, are now open-minded about vouchers and favor use of such ideas to increase educational options for children. But even the open-minded public stops short of endorsing educational choice as a proven or preferred instrument of public policy. The burden of proof still remains on those who believe, and have evidence that, choice benefits children.

A test of whether enough evidence has been gathered in favor of vouchers is if the burden of proof in public discourse shifts to those who claim choice harms children. That shift has not yet taken place. If vouchers are to become a more broadly acceptable way of providing educational opportunities for the public's children, researchers need to continue trying to get better evidence on their effects. There is every reason to continue studies using the high-quality randomization-based research designs such as those used by Paul E. Peterson and his colleagues in conducting studies in the volume have so rigorously followed.

However, other issues beyond documenting average effects on participating children need attention from researchers and policy analysts.

When Vouchers Lead to Student Learning and Why

Now is the time for finer-grained studies of voucher effects. Though a continuing need exists for more refined quasi-experimental studies of the kinds being conducted in Cleveland, Ohio; New York City; Dayton, Ohio; and San Antonio, Texas, more must be known about how vouchers lead to improved student learning. Private philanthropists and government leaders need to know what are the most promising circumstances for a voucher program, and parents need to know what kinds of choices are most likely to benefit their children. Voucher program sponsors need to know whether they should invest in creation of new schools and, if so, what the key attributes should be of the new schools.

Vouchers are a policy intervention, but they are not an instructional program. Children who use vouchers to enroll in schools other than their neighborhood public schools learn as a result of their experiences in the new school, not simply because they got a voucher. Whether a child who receives a voucher learns more depends on a number of conditional relationships: whether his or her parents consider options other than the neighborhood school, the quality of options available, the parents' choice of options, the appropriateness of the chosen school's program for the individual child, and the quality of instruction and other support the child experiences in the chosen school. The results available from the voucher experiments tell whether, on average, children, parents, and schools come together in positive ways. The available results do not answer questions such as: Do some groups of students regularly benefit more than others? Are there some groups of schools that, when chosen by families, lead to student gains much more regularly than others? Are there groups of students who seldom benefit from vouchers or groups of schools that seldom produce student gains?

The main value of answers to these questions would be to improve design and targeting of voucher programs. If vouchers and school selection were more sharply targeted, the results could be seen in future voucher research, in the form of more dramatic findings resulting from reduction of variance in student outcomes. This implies the need for studies that look at the differences in students' experience in various schools and at what underlies these schools' ability to provide effective instruction. This necessary approach would be by no means simple or quick. It would involve six steps:

1. Identify schools in the voucher experiments in which very high proportions of voucher students show gains. Determine whether the differences in gains are readily attributable to some nonschool factor, for example, gross demographic differences.

2. Assuming differences in student characteristics do not completely explain away variations in school performance, create a comparison group of schools, including voucher schools where low proportions of students show gains and possibly public schools that were used as controls in the voucher experiments.

3. Use surveys and in-school observation to identify consistent differences between what students experience in the high-gain schools and the others.

4. Create profiles of the high-gain schools and identify the processes whereby the high-gain schools were created and sustained.

5. Try to reproduce the high-gain schools, by creating new schools and transforming old ones.

6. Ultimately, use quasi-experimental methods to verify that the newly created schools are highly effective.

This line of inquiry would use some messy methods, including intensive school case studies in steps 3 and 4. But it is not unscientific; it is the essence of the scientific method in that it identifies an important regularity in the world (that some voucher schools produce better results than others), finds the essential process or ingredient, determines how to synthesize and reproduce it, and then subjects it to clinical trials. This fulfills the definition of science's goals—to explain, predict, and control (in this case, reproduce) naturally occurring processes.

Some might think this constitutes a step backward in research on vouchers. It goes from experiments using the "gold standard"of randomized student assignment to something much more messy and exploratory.[2] Some even claim that one cannot know anything about whether a given group of schools is working better than another without a whole new experiment, in which students are assigned randomly to specific schools. This might ultimately be necessary for step 6, though there is reason to doubt whether random assignment to schools is an appropriate test of a program in which choice (and its concomitant effects on relationships among parents, staff, and students) is an active ingredient. A draconian approach, in which some students would be randomly denied admission to schools that they had chosen (whether or not those schools had vacancies) might be possible. However, this approach could create major experimental artifacts, as control group children and their parents reacted to the apparently gratuitous thwarting of their aspirations.

A closer look at schools and their effects can resolve a major uncertainty about the utility of vouchers nationwide. Do the average results reported by the voucher studies blur the difference between large gains for students enrolled in certain schools and negligible gains from other schools? Is the effectiveness of vouchers contingent on the availability of schools with certain characteristics? Are schools with those characteristics common or rare?

Could the positive student learning results reported in this volume essentially be "Catholic school effects"? All of the voucher experiment cities have large numbers of Catholic schools, and many students use their vouchers to enroll in those schools. If students who enroll in Catholic schools experience the greatest gains, it would be difficult to anticipate the effects of a voucher program in a locality with few available slots in Catholic schools.

From the available evidence no one can tell how strong the Catholic schools effect is, or whether one exists. However, there is reason from other research to think that Catholic schools are unusually effective with poor and minority students. If a closer look at voucher results reveals a Catholic school effect, then the designers of future voucher initiatives will have to ask serious questions about the supply of schools in particular localities: Are there enough Catholic schools to serve high proportions of voucher recipients?

Can something be done to increase the capacity of Catholic schools or to create new schools that are likely to work as effectively?

The last question is vital to the entire education choice movement, including charter schools and school contracting as well as vouchers. As the early experience of charter schools demonstrates, it is not easy to create an effective school or to turn an ineffective school around.[3] Over-regulation might be responsible for the ineffectiveness of many existing public schools, but deregulation or independence alone does not create quality. Individuals who share an antipathy to the public school bureaucracy and certain general values (for example, diversity, optimism about human behavior, belief that all children can learn) nonetheless can have trouble sustaining an effective collaboration over time. Voucher proponents, investors, and analysts need to gain an understanding of the supply-side requirements of an effective voucher system.[4] The research agenda proposed above shows how this work can be undertaken.

Effects on Other Students and Schools

The clearer it is that vouchers lead to improvements in student learning, the more critics will say that the issue is whether vouchers are doing mischief elsewhere, by leaving behind the poorest of the poor and harming overall school quality by reducing the amounts of state funds public schools receive.

The accusations about "creaming the poor" reflect choice opponents' deeply ingrained belief that any movement favored by economists and business leaders must intend to exploit the neediest on behalf of the privileged. As the research presented in this volume has demonstrated—yet again— choice programs intended and designed to reach the poor do so. Constant assertion of the facts seems the only course available. But making the point that properly designed choice programs can reach the very poor is difficult, in light of a rhetorical strategy choice opponents have adapted from the ancient Greek philosopher Zeno.

Zeno claimed to demonstrate that a man could not walk from one place to another. His argument (which has become known as Zeno's dilemma) went thus: For a man to walk from point A to point B, he would need first to walk halfway. To walk to the halfway point, the man would need to go halfway to that point, halfway again, and so on. Because any distance could be divided into an infinite number of halfway points, in a finite period of time a man could never walk any distance.

Opponents of choice have created their own form of Zeno's dilemma. Whenever educational choices are offered to families, no matter how poor and disadvantaged, some families will accept the opportunity sooner than others. By being the quickest to accept an option the members of the first group reveal that they are advantaged over the others in some way, however subtle. Therefore it is impossible to offer choices to any group without benefiting the advantaged and leaving the most disadvantaged behind.

Zeno's philosophical opponents discredited his theory simply by walking. A similar course is the only one available to people who favor educational choice—that is, designing programs to favor the poor and continuing to publish the facts.

The other claims have bases in fact. Voucher and charter programs do draw children who would otherwise attend district-run schools, and they can, in states that fund schools on a per pupil basis, reduce funding. But that does not have to mean such initiatives in themselves damage existing district-run schools, or that other children suffer because some children use vouchers to depart their neighborhood schools, or that the children left behind lose as much as or more than the voucher-users gain.

There is not much evidence either way. To date, the numbers of children lost to any district-run school system, including those with large voucher programs such as Cleveland's and Milwaukee, Wisconsin's, have been far smaller than the numbers of children who leave district-run schools because of family moves and individual dropout decisions. During school year 1998–99, for example, 1,600 Milwaukee children used vouchers to enroll in private schools and more than 25,000 dropped out. Charter schools have similarly modest effects, except in a few cities (Mesa Arizona; Marblehead, Massachusetts), where more than 10 percent of students have left district-run schools.

Studies of the effects of competition on district-run schools in general show positive effects. As Carolyn Minter Hoxby has demonstrated, schools in localities with many private schools and with options provided by nearby district-run school systems have higher test scores and other indicators of quality.[5] This does not eliminate the possibility of harm to individual schools. Most of the children eligible for private or public vouchers cluster in particular low-income neighborhoods.

The little research that addresses effects on particular schools shows that everything depends on the actions of teachers and principals in the schools experiencing loss of pupils. Those schools where staff had habits of collaboration and joint problem solving adapt readily to marginal changes in enrollment and funding. Schools with noncooperative cultures (weak leadership, poor labor relations, little collaboration among teachers) adapt poorly.[6]

In this volume, Edward B. Fiske and Helen F. Ladd offer some observations about New Zealand, where schools that lost enrollment quickly declined due to parent and teacher flight. Whether these findings apply directly to the U.S. context is unclear, because New Zealand made it virtually impossible for declining schools to adapt to smaller size or compete more effectively for students. Declining schools were not allowed to reconfigure their administrative structures, recruit or choose teachers, or combine with other schools to share resources or programs.

What the New Zealand findings do demonstrate is that schools that are not free to change the ways they use staff, time, and money are in no position to improve or to cope with changes in financing or student needs. That is nothing new. In any competition, the contender who is most constrained by rules about programs and resources is the likely loser.

If neighborhood district-run schools are prevented from adapting to change, they will probably get worse as voucher students depart. If, however, district-run schools were able to adjust to their smaller size by reducing administrative expenses, intensifying teacher collaboration, and limiting the range of instructional offerings, they might become better. Charter and parochial schools typically operate with far less money per pupil than does the conventional public school system, and most can maintain a reasonable instructional program and adapt, albeit painfully, to changes in student enrollment.

Seen from a longer-term perspective, whether the departure of students for charters or voucher-redeeming schools harms the education of children left behind depends on the supply response of both district-run and alternative schools. Some district-run schools will probably get worse in the face of lost students and revenues. Schools that cannot marshal community support or teacher collaboration probably will get worse. So will schools that lose so many students that they can no longer afford to occupy their buildings. These results, however, put the finger on weak schools, possibly schools that no student should ever have been required to attend. Vouchers may bring these facts to the surface but probably will not create them. This reasoning can provide comfort for those who hope choice strengthens educational opportunities for all students in localities where charter and voucher programs operate. However, more concerted attention to the dynamics of schools left behind is necessary.

Public Oversight Is the Next Frontier

Choice advocates are not the only ones who think schools should be deregulated and held accountable for student performance. Supporters of standards-based reform, which is now official policy in all but two states, share the same aspirations. Until recently, however, standards-based reformers (which include both major political parties, the national Business Roundtable, and even some teachers union leaders) have thought that necessary changes could be made entirely within the conventional public school system.

Now, however, standards-based reform has matured to the point that some states are seriously trying to use student test scores to hold schools accountable. They are discovering this cannot be done without school freedom of action including control of funds and teacher hiring. Furthermore, schools cannot be held responsible for results unless they can make reasonable demands of parents, teachers, and students. This leads standards-based reform supporters away from involuntary assignments of families and teachers toward choice; that is, families and teachers choosing schools on the basis of what is promised and expected. Standards-based accountability also uncovers the need for an active supply side that creates new schools in place of failed ones.[7] These discoveries are moving some old-line educators to back away from standards-based reform.[8] But some sincere and committed supporters of standards, especially governors and business leaders, are waking up to the realization that choice is necessary.

Until recently, no state accepted responsibility for school performance. States generally operated on the theory that if everyone's rights are protected and the inputs were well regulated, school quality would be the inevitable result. Standards-based reform makes the inputs theory untenable.

Standards-based reform starts differently but ends up in the same place as initiatives such as charters and vouchers, which put schools in complete control of their budgets and staffing decisions and make them strictly accountable for performance. Thus, if choice initiatives had not already existed, states committed to standards-based reform would have had to invent them.

School performance accountability is an unsolved problem for all of public education. Some analysts have used the lack of government capacity as an argument against choice.[9] And studies of public agencies charged with authorizing and overseeing charters schools do show how far government has to go. However, some government agencies—usually new or special purpose organizations such as the Chicago city or Massachusetts state charter school office or the charter schools organization at Eastern Michigan University— are learning how to discharge these responsibilities.

My points here are simple. First, it is in the interests of people who believe in school choice to help figure out how public agencies can hold schools accountable for performance. Second, further research and development on public oversight mechanisms deserves support from philanthropies that want to advance the choice movement. Third, because standards-based reformers are being driven toward choice, choice supporters should be prepared to develop positive, not polarizing, relationships with these groups.

Conclusion

The movement for school choice via vouchers, charters, and school contracting is growing and entering the mainstream. But its progress will be slow and
perilous unless its supporters create a more self-conscious strategy.

To date, the plan for introducing choice into American public education
has had two elements. First, show that choice can help children. Second,
press for changes in public policy that allow parents to choose and permit
creation of new schooling options. These two strategy elements are working,
as demonstrated by the research reported in this volume and by the growth
of state charter school laws and policies that allow school boards to contract
out for instructional services and school management. Despite these suc-
cesses, however, the pro-school choice movement remains relatively small.
Though publicly funded schools of choice are common in a few localities,
vouchers, charters, and other choice initiatives remain rare and marginal in
most places. The legal and policy frameworks on which these programs
depend are also shaky and vulnerable to capping, watering down, or outright
repeal in legislatures and courts.

A third strategy element is necessary to complement ongoing research and
public policy activism. The educational choice movement needs deliberate
supply-side initiatives. Choice in education needs more than money and laws
that allow families to pursue options. It also needs options for families to
pursue. Shortages of empty slots in high-quality private and independent
schools are already constraining private voucher efforts in some cities, and
many charter schools have long waiting lists. Some public officials oppose
implementing charter school laws in big cities on grounds that so few choices
will be available that only the most aggressive parents will get them.

Some might argue that the supply side will take care of itself, which might
be the case in the long run. However, shortages of school options in the long
run can inhibit growth of the movement and possibly even kill it. Shortages
create competition for limited numbers of slots, which means that the most
committed and aggressive of the eligible families will get most of the available
places. This can give life to Zeno's dilemma-based attacks by choice opponents. Shortages can also add to the cynicism of poor and minority families
that have for years been promised much about their children's education but
delivered little. The choice movement cannot afford to lose the trust of
minority parents who find themselves all dressed up but with no place to go.

People in the choice movement also need to recognize the possibility that
supply could strengthen demand. If there were enough schools of choice that
few had waiting lists, schools would need to seek out families, create clear

images for themselves, promote informal links with other schools that educate older and younger students, and advertise. All these actions might increase demand and thereby strengthen the whole choice movement.

In the short term, the most important supply-side initiative would be to greatly increase business and philanthropic financial support for struggling urban Catholic schools. For the foreseeable future these will be the most reliable destination for voucher recipients. In some cities other religious and independent schools, with mixtures of financial and expert support, could also serve voucher students effectively.[10]

For the long run, great increases in the supply must come from new schools, most of which will probably be secular. Analysts and other supporters of choice need to encourage philanthropists to invest in groups capable of starting many schools and also in institutions that can help groups with good ideas for schools by pulling them together into actionable business plans. New private institutions that prepare potential principals of charter and independent schools would also enhance the supply capacity, both by increasing the numbers of people who want to start schools of choice and by limiting the numbers of school failures.

Examples of such supply-side innovations include school incubators being created in Washington, D.C., Dayton, Milwaukee, and Seattle, Washington; a new high-volume nonprofit school provider being created by Reid Hastings and Don Shalvey in Northern California; and a new principals training institute planned by the Fisher Foundation.[11] However, these organizations are small, underfunded, and disproportionately concentrated on the West Coast. A more concerted supply-side strategy, with efforts to create new schools of choice in and around all major cities, would greatly strengthen the choice movement.

In conclusion, the choice movement is alive, intellectually, politically, and financially. Its future, however, will depend on gaining support from people who are now skeptical, indifferent, or uninvolved. The things I have suggested—finer-grained analysis of schools of choice that work for students, greater attention to the effects of vouchers on those remaining in conventional public schools, a careful alliance with standards-based reformers, and a more explicit supply-side strategy—will ensure continued rapid growth.

Notes

1. To see how consistent these results are with earlier research on schools of choice, see Paul Hill, "Educational Consequences of Choice," in Terry M. Moe, ed., *Private Vouchers* (Stanford, Calif.: Hoover Institution Press, 1995), pp. 120–35.

2. The "gold standard" label is derived from medical sciences, in which much of the most important work is done via randomized clinical trials. However, the science of medicine does not progress by randomized clinical trials alone. Clinical observation, of the kind suggested in steps 1–4, typically both precedes and follows clinical trials. An example based on the discovery and use of aspirin makes the point. Someone observed that people who chewed a particular kind of tree bark felt relief from pain. The components of the tree bark were analyzed, and acetylsalicylic acid (aspirin) was identified as the key ingredient. Doctors learned how to isolate and concentrate this key ingredient. Aspirin passed into common medical use before modern clinical trials were invented, but today clinical trials would have been conducted sometime after the active ingredient was isolated. Aspirin is still the focus of some clinical trials, as practicing physicians discover previously unknown beneficial effects, and these are subsequently tested via controlled trials.

3. For a discussion of the start-up problems of many charter schools, see Paul Hill, Robin J. Lake, and Mary Beth Celio, *Charter School Accountability: A Report to the U.S. Department of Education* (Seattle, Wash.: Center on Reinventing Public Education, September 1999), available at crpe.org.

4. For much more on these points, see Paul T. Hill, "The Supply Side of Choice," in Stephen Sugarman and Frank Kemerer, eds., *School Choice and Social Controversy* (Brookings, 2000), pp. 140–73.

5. Carolyn Minter Hoxby, "Do Private Schools Provide Competition for Public Schools?" National Bureau of Economic Research Working Paper 4978 (Cambridge, Mass., December 1994).

6. See, in this volume, Frederick M. Hess, Robert Maranto, and Scott Milliman, "Responding to Competition: School Leaders and School Culture"; Paul Teske, Mark Schneider, Jack Buckley, and Sara Clark, "Can Charter Schools Change Traditional Public Schools?"; and Frederick M. Hess, "Hints of the Pick-Axe: Competition and Public Schooling in Milwaukee."

7. See Paul T. Hill and Robin J. Lake, *State Standards and School Accountability* (Brookings, 2000).

8. See, for example, John Mintz, "Education Experts Question Bush's 'Texas Miracle,'" *Washington Post*, April 21, 2000, p. A1.

9. See, for example, Amy Stuart Wells, Alejandra Lopez, Janelle Scott, and Jennifer Holme, "Charter Schools as Postmodern Paradox: Rethinking Social Stratification in an Age of Deregulated School Choice, *Harvard Educational Review*, vol. 69, no. 2 (Summer 1999), pp. 172–204.

10. For several rich analyses of existing schools that might become part of the supply side of the choice movement, see Diane Ravitch and Joseph Viteritti, eds., *City Schools: Lessons from New York* (Johns Hopkins University Press, 2000).

11. For more on possible supply-side investments, see Hill, "The Supply Side of Choice."

15

What Is to Be Done?

DIANE RAVITCH

I had not thought much about the question of choice in education until I served on a Twentieth Century Fund task force in the early 1980s. The task force, which was pondering the federal role in education, made several recommendations, including that the federal government should provide "special federal fellowships" that districts could offer to children who were failing in their regular public school setting, "to encourage the creation of small, individualized programs staffed by certified teachers and run as small-scale academies."[1] Even when I worked in the Bush administration as assistant secretary of educational research and improvement at the Department of Education, I was uncertain about choice and tended to steer clear of the issue. I let others take the lead because I could not say things that I did not believe to be true.

After my brief stint in the federal government, I went to the Brookings Institution for a little more than a year to write a book about standards. While I was there, I received a call from Jennifer Hochschild at Princeton University, asking me to participate in a conference on social policies for children. She asked me to write about a single policy intervention in education that might help the children with the most meager life prospects. As I spoke to her, my eye lit upon my first book, about the New York City public schools, whose subtitle was "A History of the Public Schools as Battlefield of Social Change." For some undefinable reason, I decided at that moment that schools should not be battlefields of social change. Instead, they should be wholly focused on helping children learn and grow to responsible maturity. In other words, schools should teach children, not use them for grand social and political purposes. And from that insight came an essay called "Somebody's Children," which advocated means-tested choice for the children who were poorest and neediest and most at risk of failing in school.[2]

I mention this background to suggest that I am not a fanatical supporter of choice programs and that I am predisposed to think that families should choose the school to which they send their children. However, I am open to being persuaded by evidence that my sympathetic disposition toward choice may be misplaced.

What is especially interesting about the papers collectively presented in this volume is that a genuine effort has been made to gather empirical evidence about the way that choice programs work. This is a significant step beyond the debates of the past, when opposing voices exchanged theories, hypotheses, hopes, and fears. That was necessary because there was no evidence.

To be sure, the evidence for the academic effects of choice is far from conclusive. It is often ambiguous, and it is almost always disputed. For some who oppose choice, data will never be enough to change their minds. For some who support choice, data are equally irrelevant, and they will not wait for the verdict of social scientists before moving their children out of what they perceive as an inadequate school. I know that I, as a parent, would be unwilling to defer to a social scientist who told me to keep my child in a poorly functioning school or that he was doing as well as could be expected for a child of his race, class, or gender.

On one level, the battle over choice is a political struggle. It will be resolved in the political arena by elected officials and by those whom they appoint. Nonetheless, there is a role for research, and this volume has demonstrated the potential as well as the current limits of that role. The scholarship presented here demonstrates that the range of disagreement remains large between friends and foes of choice strategies.

Vouchers improve achievement for some children in some circumstances, but it is too soon to say whether their gains are lasting or even why they occur.

Vouchers satisfy many parents, but not everyone is impressed with parental satisfaction as a measure of quality. Most parents are satisfied with their public schools, regardless of objective indicators of their performance.

Vouchers do not skim off the most motivated parents, said advocates, if programs are designed to target low-income children. Critics, not surprisingly, are unpersuaded.

Vouchers and charters may or may not drain away funds from public schools, depending on how the particular program is designed. In some states, public schools are held harmless, thus insulating them from the adverse effects of competition. In some urban districts, rising enrollments have protected the public schools from the effects of competition. The children who left regular public schools to use vouchers or to enroll in charter schools were quickly replaced by others.

Insulating the public schools from competition has mixed results. On the one hand, it possibly defuses anger against choice experiments because it protects the public schools' budgets. On the other hand, this protection makes it unnecessary for regular public schools to compete for students, thus vitiating one of the premises for starting charter schools. When regular public schools do compete with charter schools, they may become innovative in altering their curriculum and program, creating a net gain for both those who leave and those who remain.

However, some of the evidence suggests that regular public schools do not compete for students with charter schools. In some cases, they simply ignore their competitors, whose numbers and enrollments are usually sharply restricted by legislation. When the public schools are protected by hold harmless clauses, they can safely ignore the competition altogether.

A number of scholars say that charter schools are disappointing because they fail to be models of innovation. This may be an expectation that is unrealistic. It seems wiser to ask whether charter schools are "effective," rather than to ask whether they are "innovative." American education always seems to be chasing a chimera called "innovation" but regularly comes up short in effectiveness. Large numbers of parents, especially in big urban districts, may be more interested in finding schools that are safe, orderly, and well run than schools that are experimenting with new kinds of pedagogy.

In reality, charter schools are too busy surviving the rigors of their new institutional existence to take on the daunting task of reforming the system of public education or even of disseminating their methods. In most cases, their methods are still too new to deserve dissemination. One can only imagine how school superintendents and principals would react if a charter school of 300 students in their district were to offer to share their discoveries about curriculum or assessment, based on two or three years of experience. School systems have trouble learning from their own experiments, let alone allowing themselves to be "reformed" by those who have defected to become charters.

One point that seems to emerge with some consistency in this volume, at least to me, is that vouchers and charters will not destroy American public education. This fear, which is often expressed by both the fiercest opponents and defenders of the current education system, seems fantastic. There are about 48 million youngsters in American public schools; a few thousand children in voucher schools in Milwaukee, Wisconsin, and Cleveland, Ohio; and about 350,000 children in public charter schools. Less than 1 percent of American children are in voucher schools or charter schools. Various measures of parental satisfaction do show that parents are on the whole pleased with their local public school and are not looking for alternatives.[3] This being the case, the hysteria generated by fear of choice is difficult to understand.

Ironically, private schools may be most at risk because of charter schools. Vouchers might help sectarian schools by enabling more poor children to attend them with a public subsidy. But religious schools may be adversely affected by the spread of charter schools, which are proving politically safer than voucher programs and less vulnerable to judicial intervention. If children can go to a free charter school that is small, safe, and effective, they may abandon parochial schools because of their cost. Some have referred to charter schools as "free private schools," and religious schools would be hard pressed to survive in the face of free competitors. One conspiracy theorist of my acquaintance has darkly warned (in private conversation) that the growth in the availability of charter schools will lead to the closing of Catholic schools, which will be followed by reregulation of charter schools, thus restoring the status quo ante.

Another aspect of this debate concerns the problem of oversubscribed schools. In many cities, especially good public schools and especially popular charter schools have been deluged with more applicants than they can admit. The typical bureaucratic response is to hold a lottery to select those lucky enough to gain admission. It would make even more sense, I suggest, to permit those who run the best schools to open additional schools, thus increasing the supply of good schools instead of limiting access to eager, lucky students. Unfortunately, this seldom happens, and the lottery has become the preferred method of responding to high demand.

A fundamental issue raised in much of the charter school debate has to do with the nature of a good school. Little agreement exists about what constitutes a good school or how to assess school quality. Is a good school one with constructivist pedagogy, whole language, and portfolio assessment? Is it the result of whole school reform? Is it a school that stresses "direct instruction" and "core knowledge"? Is it a school with high test scores?

The lack of consensus is itself a strong argument for parental choice and public accountability. It is hard to argue that a parent who wants a back-to-basics school or a progressive school should be compelled to accept the opposite. It is equally hard to see how any state can dole out public funds to organizations that are unwilling to demonstrate that they have used the funds wisely and well. On the issue of assessment, public accountability must accompany public funds. One can argue about which is the appropriate tool to assess school quality, but sooner or later, every school must be able to show that students are learning to read, write, and compute and that they know and can do those things necessary to prepare for higher education, citizenship, and technical jobs.

Schools clearly should be able to demonstrate two kinds of progress: (1) that students have made gains during a marked period of time (that is, the school has "added value" to the students' knowledge and skills); and (2) that students are progressing on the basis of agreed-upon standards of performance. A school can show large "value-added" gains without coming close to appropriate standards, which is why schools must be able to show progress on both counts.

Choice may promote greater accountability in education, because both regular public schools and choice schools will be expected to meet the same standards. Surely those in the regular system will not permit the choice schools to evade even minimal standards, and this competitive spirit is likely to encourage all schools to meet the same public standards.

As the debate about choice evolves, it seems clear that two obligations must be met in the future—to keep an open mind about whether choice is beneficial, which children it helps or hinders, and under which circumstances; and to keep an active research program going.

You cannot study what does not exist. Data cannot be gathered unless choice programs are in operation. It would be valuable, for example, if a five-year moratorium were placed on all legal efforts to close down voucher programs so that research might proceed.

Those who admire public education should not fear its imminent demise. Public education is not threatened. Ninety percent of American students attend a public school; less than 1 percent are in a voucher or charter school. Friends of public education should stop acting as though everyone wants to flee them if the door is opened only a tiny bit. They do not.

Even if vouchers and charters were to proliferate, even if they were to dodge somehow the political and legal efforts to restrict or close them down, my guess is that regular public schools would still enroll about 80 percent of children, just as public universities enroll 80 percent of students in that sector.

The role of researchers and policymakers in education in this evolution—if evolution should occur—is to go beyond sterile arguments about whether choice is "good" or "bad"; to recognize that it is already available for many families in many forms; and to deal with problems of implementation and the specifics of program design.

To help public education break free of its current bureaucratic organizational patterns, forged a century ago in the great days of the factory system, may be the most valuable contribution that its friends can make to the nation's public education system.

Notes

1. *Making the Grade: Report of the Twentieth Century Fund Task Force on Federal Elementary and Secondary Education Policy* (New York: Twentieth Century Fund, 1983), pp. 19–21. Perhaps the most curious and little-noticed aspect of the task force report was the chasm between the task force and its executive director, Paul E. Peterson. The task force began its 22-page report with the assertion that "the nation's public schools are in trouble." Peterson appended a 150-page essay concluding that "the crisis in American education is greatly exaggerated" (p. 157).

2. Diane Ravitch, "Somebody's Children: Educational Opportunity for *All* American Children," in Irwin Garfinkel, Jennifer L. Hochschild, and Sara S. McLanahan, eds., *Social Policies for Children* (Brookings, 1996), pp. 83–111.

3. Anthony P. Carnevale and Donna M. Desrochers, *School Satisfaction: A Statistical Profile of Cities and Suburbs* (Princeton, N.J.: Educational Testing Service, 1999).

Contributors

Jack Buckley
SUNY at Stony Brook

David E. Campbell
Harvard University

Sara Clark
SUNY at Stony Brook

Chester E. Finn Jr.
Manhattan Institute for Policy Research

Edward B. Fiske
Education consultant; former correspondent for the New York Times

Jay P. Greene
Manhattan Institute for Policy Research

Frederick M. Hess
University of Virginia

Paul Hill
Center on Reinventing Public Education, University of Washington

William G. Howell
University of Wisconsin

Brett Kleitz
University of Houston

Helen F. Ladd
Duke University

Bruno V. Manno
Annie E. Casey Foundation

Robert Maranto
Villanova University

Scott Milliman
James Madison University

Michael Mintrom
Michigan State University

Terry M. Moe
Hoover Institute, Stanford University

Paul E. Peterson
Harvard University

David N. Plank
Michigan State University

Diane Ravitch
New York University

Mark Schneider
SUNY at Stony Brook

Paul Teske
SUNY at Stony Brook

Kristina Thalhammer
St. Olaf College

Gregg Vanourek
Charter School Division, K12, McLean, Va.

Joseph P. Viteritti
New York University

Patrick J. Wolf
Georgetown University

Index